AL QAEDA

Recent Titles in
PSI Guides to Terrorists, Insurgents, and Armed Groups

The ETIM: China's Islamic Militants and the Global Terrorist Threat
J. Todd Reed and Diana Raschke

The Phinehas Priesthood: Violent Vanguard of the Christian Identity
Movement
Danny W. Davis

The Militant Kurds: A Dual Strategy for Freedom
Vera Eccarius-Kelly

The Palestine Liberation Organization: Terrorism and Prospects for Peace
in the Holy Land
Daniel Baracskay

Armed for Life: The Army of God and Anti-Abortion Terror in the United
States
Jennifer Jefferis

The IRA: The Irish Republican Army
James Dingley

The Khmer Rouge: Ideology, Militarism, and the Revolution That Consumed a Generation
Boraden Nhem

The Lord's Resistance Army
Lawrence E. Cline

17N's Philosophy of Terror: An Analysis of the 17 November Revolutionary
Organization
Ioanna K. Lekea

The Taliban: Afghanistan's Most Lethal Insurgents
Mark Silinsky

Chechnya's Terrorist Network: The Evolution of Terrorism in Russia's North
Caucasus
Elena Pokalova

AL QAEDA

The Transformation of Terrorism in the Middle East and North Africa

Denise N. Baken and Ioannis Mantzikos

PSI Guides to Terrorists, Insurgents, and Armed Groups
James J. F. Forest, Series Editor

PRAEGER™

An Imprint of ABC-CLIO, LLC
Santa Barbara, California • Denver, Colorado

Library of Congress Cataloging-in-Publication Data

Baken, Denise N., author.
  Al Qaeda : the transformation of terrorism in the Middle East and North Africa / Denise N. Baken and Ioannis Mantzikos.
    pages cm. — (PSI guides to terrorists, insurgents, and armed groups)
  Includes bibliographical references and index.
    ISBN 978–1–4408–2870–6 (hard copy : alk. paper) — ISBN 978–1–4408–2871–3 (ebook) 1. Qaida (Organization) 2. Terrorism—Middle East. 3. Terrorism—Africa, North. I. Mantzikos, Ioannis, author. II. Title.
  HV6432.5.Q2B35   2015
  363.3250956—dc23   2015013237

ISBN: 978–1–4408–2870–6
EISBN: 978–1–4408–2871–3

19 18 17 16 15   1 2 3 4 5

This book is also available on the World Wide Web as an eBook.
Visit www.abc-clio.com for details.

Praeger
An Imprint of ABC-CLIO, LLC

ABC-CLIO, LLC
130 Cremona Drive, P.O. Box 1911
Santa Barbara, California 93116-1911

This book is printed on acid-free paper ∞

Manufactured in the United States of America

Contents

Introduction

As a young captain assigned to the National Guard Comptroller Office, I had to attend a budget analyst class. One day the course director came for the perfunctory "we are glad you are here" speech. During his presentation he made an off-hand remark that has stayed with me for almost 25 years. He was trying to make us understand how we fit into the whole scheme of national security when he very simply said, "You are in the business of controlled violence."

It was the first time I had had that truth clearly defined for me. I, as an individual, came face-to-face with the recognition that I was part of our nation-state's calculated use of explosive devices and materials. That line came back to me when I read Stephen Chan's *Fanon: The Octogenarian of International Revenge and the Suicide Bomber of Today*. Very early in this assessment of Frantz Fanon and the psychology of terrorism's violence, Chan states: "No one throws a bomb without first wrestling his or her own soul."[1] Each bomber must at some point believe he controls the violence that will result. It demonstrates both control and power.

Chan acknowledges the complication of and tenseness surrounding insurgency. Focusing on Algeria, he reflects on the compulsion within each individual to arrive at the decision to execute violence and contribute to the history of violence. The driving forces that come into conflict may only be a postscript in the grand scheme of things, but for the period in which the conflict plays, real people lose their lives because young men and women make a conscious decision to participate in these transformative events.

Between 1989 and 2013 terrorism transitioned from the use of top-down identification of attack targets, centralized training camps, and specialists in attack types to the current diffused hybrid of "self-immersers," satellites (AQIM [al Qaeda in the Islamic Maghreb] and AQAP [al Qaeda in the Arabian Peninsula]), and al Qaeda central. We also have to ask where and what is al Qaeda central today? As the international community tries to assess the status of al Qaeda, al Qaeda leadership seeks to hold onto the throne of chief terrorist media darling and fear monger.

Has the loss of well over 20 critical leaders left the organization critically injured? Yes and no. This book is an outgrowth of ongoing study to explain the yes and the no of that answer. What dramatically started with a declaration of war against the United States and its allies and a not-so-successful attack on American soldiers in two still relatively unknown Yemeni hotels—the Movenpick and the Gold Mohur—is not remembered in the popular media, not like the coldly calculated yet controlled violence of attacks executed against the embassies in Nigeria and Tanzania. Current attacks have morphed into the self-initiated savagery demonstrated in the execution of Private Lee Rigby.[2]

The questions that guided this investigation include:

How official is the tie between the "self-immersers" and al Qaeda central?
Is the Internet the new skeleton/framework, replacing al Qaeda central?
What is the cost to the international community as they continue to battle al Qaeda (central and otherwise)?
What measures are available to the international community to determine success as it counters al Qaeda central and al Qaeda diffused?
What rising terrorist trends are signals of the next al Qaeda?

The data presented within this book come from an ongoing study of al Qaeda's seeming "expansion" into Yemen and Northern Africa's Sahel region. It looks at the role the Internet plays in that expansion and the implications that new territory presents. The data used for conflict analysis come from the Uppsala Conflict Data Program and START datasets. These data capture violent conflict events dating back to the 1970s. Annual conflict data reports developed from these data incorporate variables identifying interstate, intrastate, and extra-state influencers on the ongoing conflicts. The nonstate conflict dataset covers the 1989–2011 time period, using variables such as start and end dates, death estimates, and locations. The footprints this dataset tracks reflect al Qaeda's pattern of violence and movement throughout the Middle East crossing into Africa. This does not preclude the movement al Qaeda made into Asia and the Americas. But it does offer a look at al Qaeda's change as it expands into the areas projected to have the most growth and workforce population by 2050. It gives the international community strategy background as it reengages a post-Osama bin Laden/Anwar al Awlaki al Qaeda. With all of these data available, it is important to focus on each individual who participated in the violence and the change each individual act brought to the total political force exerted to allow al Qaeda to leverage these acts as a whole to further its agenda. This book asserts that this cumulative individual contribution occurs because al Qaeda and its affiliates trade on the "good will"/reputation they have accumulated over the last 25 years as "doers" who value individual contribution and offer a variety of ways to express that contribution. Uppermost in the list of ways to contribute is violence. Trading on their known brand status, all of the associated groups are especially set for the task of rallying followers who want to express this individual contribution as a violent act. Some may be "radical followers," some may be "angry" (not always radical), and others may be participants for personal reasons.[3] However they have found their way to these violent acts, these participants may or may not agree that the term *radical* should be applied. As victims of the violence, Western nations have focused on the act because, until recently, it was felt the end result is the same: death and carnage. But as Westerners increasingly become the parents of young people who are becoming "those radicals," they are facing the realization that a new understanding of what is going on is imperative.

One way to that new understanding is through the individuals who are the very targets of al Qaeda-ISIS-et al.'s marketing and recruiting. Western nation-states could reach out to and enlist the help of this same target audience through the Internet. This book and its accompanying website, www.findingtheanswer.org, seek to do just that. The book presents some basic history of al Qaeda, one of the terrorism industry's better known participants; suggests a different look at available data on the group and its affiliates; and then invites readers or anyone else to contribute to "finding the answer." On the website are data on terrorism industry "corporations," ideas for new approaches to research on the industry, and research tools for do-it-yourself study of the groups for new ideas and approaches. The fact that there will not be total agreement that this is a productive approach to the problem is a given, but there will be agreement we have not reached out to this critical asset, and that fact may be the one major flaw in the approaches that have been employed thus far.

THE STRUCTURE OF OUR BOOK

The chapters in this book are designed to frame al Qaeda within the boundaries of its constituencies, and position the impact al Qaeda achieved when it leveraged the fear generated by its acts.

Chapter 1 offers background on ideology, key tenets, and significant figures from a pre-al Qaeda period to Ayman al-Zawahiri assuming leadership. Al Qaeda's Afghanistan origin is usually touted as one based in the freedom fight against the external Soviet Union "colonial" power trying to dominate an indigenous people. However, prior to the Soviet battles there was outcry about the dissolution of the Ottoman Empire by the colonial powers who divided what remained of the Ottoman Empire after World War I. While there had been dissatisfaction with the Caliph, there was no great desire to fall under rule by the West either. Discontent grew and Hassan al-Banna created organizations like the Muslim Brotherhood to provide reminders of the distinctions between the French and English "protectors" and the standards of Islam. This chapter discusses the movements that developed and the individuals who became established influencers, such as al-Banna and Sayyid Qutb. Qutb, in particular, was a monumental influence through his writings and his brother's continued efforts for his message. Later jihadists like Osama bin Laden, Ayman al-Zawahiri, and Anwar Awlaki cited Qutb's works as a major influence on their jihad position framing. The political framing that resulted from Qutb's impressions of the West can be seen in the resistance of people like Zawahiri to the early postcolonial period in Egypt. These series of actions offer argument for the position that political Islam and radical activism of the religion by al Qaeda are an alternative to the rising Arab nationalism that began in the 1930s.

This chapter looks at the al Qaeda ideology and its pan-Arabic, conspiratorial and neo-fundamental labels. No one label seems to capture all aspects needed to describe the group, but one consistency appears throughout the discussions: al Qaeda's efforts to harness a "nationalism energy" under the cloak of religion. Defining its market as all who profess Islam as their religion, al Qaeda has exploited the political and historical factors that contribute to its own definition of jihad. Here we explore the so-called Islamic revival and its purportedly subsequent increase in radicalized followers of Islam. But is this really an increase or just a greater awareness of the radicalized fragment that has continued to call for a return to the caliphate at the fall of the Ottoman Empire? The chapter looks at other historical influencers besides Qutb and Maulana Maududi, and their role in the lives of critical decision makers like Abdullah Azzam and the transformation and transitions that grew from the Afghanistan-Russia struggle period. It also looks at the post struggle period when fighters were deciding what to do next. Al Qaeda emerged during this decision-making period as did the disagreements on how to proceed with the struggle. A central point of disagreement was how to use the violence tools they now mastered. Azzam opposed attacking civilians and employing Afghanistan fighters against the Egyptian and Algerian regimes. His sudden death created a vacuum later filled by Ayman al-Zawahiri. Zawahiri's influence ensured a move away from Azzam's position on the future direction of violence perpetrated on victims.

After Azzam's death, al Qaeda emerged with a formal corporate structure, a structure that, over the years, has moved and morphed to accommodate external influences and pressures (like anti-money-laundering laws, sanctions on organizations and/or individuals providing material support, and pressure on Middle East governments) that prevented or modified established business operations and interactions.

Al Qaeda successfully mitigated the effect of these external influences and pressures by establishing associations that have been termed "franchises" and "affiliates." At the same time, al Qaeda leveraged the negative impact generated when U.S. policies and actions unleashed the United States' entire political and military arsenal on a nonstate entity and did not seem to be winning. The world's only remaining superpower could not even capture one lone man (Osama bin Laden). Moving through these stages, al Qaeda's strength emerged as an entity prepared to set in motion major satellites in the Maghreb and Arabian Peninsula. This made it a formidable opponent with whom the international community must contend, while trying to prepare for future attacks from lone wolves and cyber warriors. Current events, though, question whether al Qaeda was prepared for the total mutiny the Islamic State of Iraq and Syria (ISIS) presented. This shortcoming may offer opportunity for further investigation.

Chapter 2 provides a look at the evolution the group has experienced. Some aspects of this evolution were in response to external pressures but others were not. Those that were not were often the result of al Qaeda leveraging an opportunity. This leveraged opportunity ranged from talented personnel, international situation, and technology.

Al Qaeda's complicated story has phases. The press often looked at the early phase through the lens of Osama bin Laden's movements as he was forced to move from one place to another. In truth, al Qaeda's transition involved more than that. Yes, when forced, the bin Laden support system traveled to Sudan in 1995, and yes, the Osama bin Laden-Taliban connection was deemed the reason the United States waged war on a nation-state. But al Qaeda was more than Osama bin Laden. In Chapter 2 we look at the freedom fighter alumni who established connections in Somalia, Algeria, Yemen, Uzbekistan, and Sudan. These early established links served the organization well in the long run: starting with the Sudanese military coup in 1989, the UN/U.S. involvement in Somalia between 1992 and 1995, the rise of the Taliban in Afghanistan, the 1998 bombings in U.S. embassies in Kenya and Tanzania, and the *USS Cole*-Yemen connection.

These fighters deployed to all of the countries with the intent of pursuing al Qaeda goals. They were not always willingly received, but over time there was acceptance. Links have impact on the cultural, political, and economic conditions that helped establish al Qaeda in each of the locales. These are contrasted with the conditions that initially greeted the fighters when they first came to Somalia. There was no real acceptance. Once the fighters in Somalia and other locations secured their al Qaeda foothold, the resultant network began to bear fruit. They executed events ranging from the bungled 1992 Aden, Yemen attempts on U.S. marines, to the highly successful *USS Cole* and September 11, 2001, bombings. At the time we did not know the vastness of the al Qaeda network. Interrogations later identified al Qaeda ties in places as far flung as Bangkok, Malaysia (Quso),[4] and the Philippines. These connections are discussed along with their social, cultural, and political impacts. As the historical transitions occurred, it must be remembered that the group and its satellites, affiliates, and spin-offs are continuing the transition process. AQAP apparently orchestrated an attack on the offices of the Parisian magazine Charlie Hebdo.[5] The very same day, attacks were executed against shoppers in a Kosher supermarket.[6] The actions again offer a hint at the transition to localized "al Qaeda-ISIS-et al." controlled violence. This move indicates well-structured logistics, distributed locals for attack execution, and exit strategy considerations (one perpetrator's wife escaped to Syria). This, along with Boko Haram's surge on strategic towns like Maiduguri and Monguno in Nigeria, shows growing terrorism industry strength worldwide.[7]

Chapter 3 examines the violence perpetrated by al Qaeda-ISIS-et al. from the perspective of the specificity of the act and the individuality of each perpetrator. The chapter starts with the attack on Private Lee Rigby and transitions to the viciousness of the broad daylight assassination. It moves to discussions of attacks and attackers who, over the last 20 years, have bombed the Word Trade Center twice, devastated the two U.S. embassy buildings in Tanzania and Kenya, and video broadcast beheadings long before ISIS. Each transition of the violence is considered from the perspective of individuals who make the decision to participate in the act. An individual makes a decision, on an individual basis, to participate in the group act, an act that is portrayed from the group's perspective, even when the individual executes the attack. The violence is also examined from the backdrop of its use in early al Qaeda history. The differences between Abdullah Azzam's and Osama bin Laden's idea on the use of "violence" caused tension within the nascent organization. Patterns in casualty count are identified and considerations for examining the violence from a business perspective are presented. The chapter looks at violence discussions by ideologues such as Naji and the impact on terrorist organizations' industry relationships.

Chapter 4 gets to the heart of al Qaeda financing and the transitions that have occurred during the 1989–2012 time period. Gone are the days when it was necessary to travel to far-flung venues to petition for donations; now there is simply reliance on the profits from illicit activities such as kidnapping, drugs, or security for those involved in kidnapping and drug trafficking. This chapter discusses the controversy that ensued when all available information pointed to the bin Laden family (and its enterprises) as the source for al Qaeda funding. This early-on purported funding was reportedly in the millions. But the avenues needed to maintain a worldwide organization are large, and raising money from witting and unwitting donors, as well as mosques, and sympathetic imams is not sufficient if a steady stream of more-than-adequate funding is the end goal. We outline the avenues of fund-raising al Qaeda's "financial facilitators" have taken to ensure funding is available in order to achieve their desired results. One of the keen points is the role Islamic Banking had in the beginning and the benefits al Qaeda garnered from the one-to-one campaigns. We identify the benefits from involvement in the Liberian and Democratic Republic of Congo's commodities trade, along with a look at the relationship reported between al Qaeda and Charles Taylor. This relationship transitioned to becoming part of a global organized crime network. This network threads from Hezbollah to Israeli diamond brokers to Russian mafia and finally to Colombian drug lords. It is these shadow networks that have ensured a consistent cash flow and revenue stream. Al Qaeda recognizes that a variety of these illicit revenue access points permit them to weather the fluctuations in profits when law enforcement pressures impede activities—this often with the piracy revenues in Somalia. Al Qaeda has become one of the most dangerous criminal organizations in the world. Much like FARC (Fuerzas Armadas Revolucionarias de Colombia) did as it transitioned from a revolutionary organization to organized crime.

Chapter 5 delves into the critical areas of eternal communications for marketing the al Qaeda message. These tools have included the Internet but that instrument of message distribution will be handled in Chapter 6. Here we look at the marketing conducted, media used, and final recruiting results. The marketing and media tools were shrewdly mingled so that al Qaeda stakeholders received a seamless message, one that was, at times, inadvertently buttressed by U.S. foreign policy missteps. Al Qaeda has long been media savvy as demonstrated by very early instruments to communicate with its members, even during the days of the Afghanistan-Soviet conflict. This chapter looks at the entities used to communicate the message and the value the carefully orchestrated propaganda derived from that message. Al Qaeda's media team leveraged CNN and its internal communication organs like *Voice of Jihad* and *Inspire* magazines.

This chapter also addresses the marketing needed to encourage participation while maintaining control of the message through instruments not always close at hand. This control was enhanced with the creation of As-Sahab, and the importance of disseminating that message is never lost on even the most remotely deployed of their units. Ansar al Sharia units established a media office capable of creating very sophisticated propaganda materials in locations like Ja'ar. This chapter also addresses attempts to have both AQAP and AQIM work together.[8] Central to this chapter are the transitions that did not occur in the al Qaeda message. Even as the instruments of the message kept up with the pace of expectations of its young audience, the basic thrust behind that message did not change.

The United States and its allies remained the colonial power that must be stopped and subjugated the way, al Qaeda insisted, the United States had done to the Middle East. When Anwar al Awlaki began to recruit via the Internet video, Western potential recruits were often without a working knowledge of Arabic. This opened the door for them, and all of a sudden a new segment of the potential recruit pool was added into the mix. Central to the marketing and recruiting activities is the almost innate ease with which the young potential recruits use the Internet. This helped control recruiting costs and increase opportunity for one-to-one contact.

Chapter 6 looks at the critical role the Internet has played in all of these endeavors. This tool has moved from simply maintaining Osama bin Laden's names and personal information on all Afghanistan-Soviet conflict fighters. As the technology changed, so did al Qaeda's use of the capabilities available. This is not unexpected given the target audience and its proclivity to these capabilities. The target market has grown up with the technology always available, and their assumption it would move with them to their zealot activities with al Qaeda is logical.

Over the years the Internet has become a critical communication and collaboration tool. Communication was once lively on forums but now social media is the avenue to monitor if we want to know the latest discussion trends. Al Qaeda has benefitted from this boon because its infrastructure costs are minimal. Interested individuals connect using their own equipment and social media applications. They suggest ways to ensure privacy to exclude the peering eyes of the intelligence community.

This chapter looks at the boon that technology brought to the terrorism community. We then address how that boon brought the marketers, recruiters, and scheme makers within al Qaeda right to the homes of the inquiring. We show how those inquiring minds were presented with not only the teachings of Shaykh Ibn Taymiyyah and Anwar al Awlaki but also the videos of Zarqawi and the illegal commercial ventures and illegal venture management suggested by Irabi 007—someone who was young and (in some observers minds) making an impact on the world. The chapter concludes with identifying the steps the international community can take to mitigate al Qaeda's virtually unfettered access to all youth willing to venture into the supposed excitement of jihad. Emphasis is made to understand that in the past focus has been on the benefits failed state markets present for general functioning and attack potential, and while the young in the failed states have the example of governments (authority) unable to cope, all young are at risk. Young who are living day to day in "failed" or "fragile" nation-states have the daily comparison to al Qaeda and its seemingly excellent structure. The comparison may not result with action from the observing young that the world would want, but it is a comparison from which al Qaeda could benefit, as a whole, if we do not eliminate its attractiveness. Western young, too, are at risk, as many recent attacks have proven. They may be the ones who are disenchanted with their countries' policies, race relations, or perceived attitude toward issues of concern to them. Whatever the reason, they also see the same seemingly excellent al Qaeda structure and want to respond. They go for reasons not easily identified in a succinct quick-disposal "how to" list.

Chapter 7 focuses on Yemen, al Qaeda's relationship with the country, and its familial ties that cement the connections between the country, its people, and the organization. The ties are strong, but there is a question about their ability to weather the negative impact of the strong-arm tactics used by AQAP's enforcing arm Ansar al Sharia (Yemen). Yemen is also hampered by the insurgency of its Huthi rebels in the northern part of the country. Named for the charismatic leader Badral-Din al-Huthi, this Shia tribal resistance group had local tribal and religious support at its 2004 clash with the Yemeni government and continues to oppose Yemen government nearly 10 years later. This resistance is an additional irritant to the government as it contends with Huthi fighters in the north, al Qaeda/Ansar al Sharia in the south, and the unrest from the local populations that have lost lives because of U.S. drone strikes. This chapter looks at the relationships Yemen's leaders have had to establish, maintain, and delicately play in with al Qaeda. The government recognizes that AQAP is a U.S. government target. This has worked to the government's advantage and caused the United States to wind its way carefully as it pursues and targets AQAP members for drone strikes.

Chapter 8 covers Iraq and Syria, examining the vulnerabilities that al Qaeda faced and managed as it sought to expand to new opportunities like controlling towns and regions. It must contend with infrastructure requirements and economic demands to remain a viable force. If it is too much of a problem, potential investors can go elsewhere, residents can revolt, and members can defect. In Yemen, for instance, tribal leaders and towns people themselves have taken up arms against the formidable force. Iraq and Syria have rebels who have done the same. But they are less well resourced than ISIS and are finding the international community very slow to provide substantive support. However, as al Qaeda demonstrated against the United States, it is not always the one with the most technology who can win. In addition, the Arab League has become more vocal in its opposition to al Qaeda. This opposition is in part from weariness and in part from stakeholder revolt. This weariness comes from Islamic governments becoming tired of outright criticism heaped upon them from all sides with respect to al Qaeda and similar groups. The stakeholder revolt is the result of al Qaeda followers who realize they have outgrown the organization and can apply their tactics just as ISIS did during the Arab Spring. That period of chaos permitted terrorist groups in general and al Qaeda and ISIS the opportunity to leverage the dissatisfaction displayed with the Arab Spring. Terror groups infiltrated (come to the party uninvited) the movement and offered tangible support when resources and training were critically needed. Al Qaeda was able to bring both resources and training and thus usurp the movement, all at the same time. Here we discuss the time this infiltration provides for retooling and tailoring response to meet the specific needs of that time and place. The demonstrators are caught between giving up the fight and accepting help from al Qaeda, a source they would rather avoid. Thus far the help of al Qaeda has been the choice.

There are revolutions that al Qaeda did not engage: the Darfur and Kenyan uprisings in the late 2000s are just two examples. We look at this avoidance and suggest reasons why it may have occurred. Finally we analyze al Qaeda's support for the Syrian rebels as they battle the Assad regime. We address al Qaeda's call for the rebels to seek help in locations other than the West and the benefit al Qaeda reaped from the West's response to the rebels' calls for help.

Chapter 9 looks at another significant market that has seen an increase in al Qaeda presence. The African countries of sub-Sahara and the Sahel have been targeted by al Qaeda central's subsidiary, AQIM. Drug trafficking, security for traffickers, and even human trafficking are career paths for members of AQIM, and the revenues fund the execution of bigger events.[9] While not as cash-rich as ISIS, al Qaeda is now free to plan events as resource intensive as they feel they can execute. There is no longer a need to seek financial support from individuals or for business owners to risk being discovered for having donated to the cause. Stakeholders have accepted this monetary stream and do not appear to object. The ties are diverse. They run the gamut from Sicilian mafia to the Nigerian Kaduna mafia. Al Qaeda is adept at using the cover of legitimate businesses to conceal its efforts in illicit business ventures, but it is usually only a start in a region where law enforcement might diligently monitor activities. However, in locations liked Northern and Western Africa, where government officials either cannot or would not enforce local constraints on these actions, al Qaeda has successfully entered the worlds where money laundering and credit card fraud are rampant.

The people, while afraid of al Qaeda's tactics—especially with the death toll mounting in the thousands since 2009, are angry at the tactics against stolen girls and many killings.[10,11] There are open demonstrations against Boko Haram's tactics. The people continue to resist. For a long time, Western terrorism experts resisted the idea that Boko Haram was associated with al Qaeda. This offered time for the relationship to solidify. Osama bin Laden never acknowledged the tie, but he sent money and offered training. Boko Haram has benefitted from AQIM training and resource support. There was even a pledge of allegiance in 2010. But Boko Haram seems driven toward its own agenda. The relationship may have had more tentative aspects to it that was apparent because the group changed allegiance to ISIS and has incorporated the even more brutal tactics along with expansion of land claims for its caliphate.

Chapter 10 closes the book with an assessment of al Qaeda now and its projected future. It identifies the current threat to ensure we understand on what to focus resources in response. The ISIS and al Qaeda and its affiliates stand to expand their influence, the Taliban is expected to return, and the instability of the region will continue to increase. That increased instability is quite likely, as ISIS and al Qaeda will most assuredly continue to execute attacks and suicide bombings to ensure the regional governments' resources are appropriately stretched. The recent unrest and government chaos in Yemen with the Huthis and the death of Saudi Arabia's long-time monarch, Abdullah bin Abdulaziz Al Saud. The Houthis will exacerbate the distrust felt in southern Yemen and the Heraq separatists. The Heraq have not forgotten that until 1990, South Yemen was a country unto itself.[12] The Houthi actions also remind observers that Yemen's capital was under Houthi control in September 2014, and its advancement and taking control again in January 2015 only reinforced concerns for the fragility of the country's government and the opportunity available to AQAP.

International implications follow as we look at the way al Qaeda has long exploited the asymmetric balance its nonstate actor status affords it. Al Qaeda has the advantage of being able to target specific land locations and citizens of its target nation-states. However, retaliation was/is very difficult, as the United States realized after fighting this amoeboid opponent in Afghanistan and Iraq. The world's only superpower must also face the fact that it still has not eliminated the al Qaeda menace. Fighting an abstract concept called *terrorism* has given stature to bin Laden and offered frustrated youths an outlet for anger and hostility. The chapter closes with a discussion of the international implications of al Qaeda resurrecting itself to its former formidable opponent within the confines of the Sahel region of Africa and ISIS' expanded march through the Iraq-Syria-Lebanon region.

Al Qaeda has, over its 25-year history, continued to mine violence for the simple reason that exploiting fear works. It is logical, therefore, to assume this practice will continue, and be encouraged, with the Northern and Western Africa groups such as Boko Haram and Ansar al Sharia as well as al Shabaab. These groups already seem to be on the road to increased violent, savage attacks, if the numbers of dead tallied by Boko Haram are any indication.

But this tested and proven approach to attacks has evoked an international outrage that may offer a window of opportunity for opponents to the violence. Once considered an "asymmetric" conflict that is the problem of someone else, there are now the beginnings of discontent with the carnage and its consequences that might bear real response. It is critical, though, that any response pursued not be stovepiped.[13] Al Qaeda-ISIS-et al.'s is a concerted worldwide attack effort that must be met with a concerted worldwide response. This will be a challenge for the "al Qaeda-ISIS-et al." (i.e., terrorist industry's) opponents because al Qaeda-ISIS-et al. continues to taunt the United States and its allies and the response to that taunt has been disjointed and ineffective. Al Qaeda-ISIS-et al. has implemented a concerted effort that it believes limits options available to its targets/opponents, options the groups appear to feel are easily circumvented. But that concerted effort may be the only stance that results in repaired alliances and a secured unified response against an increasingly vicious violence. So, until that happens, all are invited to www.finding theanswer.org for a bottom-up approach.

1

Origins and Ideology of al Qaeda

Al Qaeda, and its associated groups, no longer garner the same fear-laden headlines they did in the past. ISIS, the Islamic State of Iraq and Syria, now commands that grand spot. It achieved this new position after devouring whole swaths of Iraq before moving on to Syria. Each military victory increased ISIS's mystique. That mystique has also been enhanced when each Western effort to stop ISIS has proven ineffective. ISIS's attractiveness to the many Western youth enthusiastically streaming to its violence and chaos has only frustrated Western authorities and increased the media coverage the group receives.

All of this attention on ISIS has pushed al Qaeda central farther and farther into the background. The Charlie Hebdo attack by al Qaeda of the Arabian Peninsula (AQAP) put al Qaeda back in the news for a bit, but the once powerfully frightening al Qaeda appears to have fizzled. ISIS has ceased being the al Qaeda breakaway group. It has instead supplanted every other Middle East and African group in the race to become terrorism media darling. Even Boko Haram, with its escalating attacks and mounting death tolls, is a distant contender for some of that media attention.

How can we effectively respond to this shift from al Qaeda to ISIS? How do we prepare for the next ISIS? How do we contend with the interest Western youth appear to have developed for this violent group. We need to understand the transitions that occurred between the time our major fear was an attack from al Qaeda to the present major fear of being put through the same anguish as the parents of the three Colorado high school girls who took a flight to Turkey to join ISIS. Parents now fear they may be faced with the same hard decision to report their sons or daughters to the police and FBI, hoping they have acted in time to stop their most precious asset from being swept away to ISIS.[1]

Even the use of foreign fighters is vastly different from recent history. As late as 2007, Abu Umar al-Baghdadi, then leader of the Islamic State of Iraq, proudly claimed that he had only 200 foreign fighters in his whole organization.[2] Al Qaeda's Ayman al-Zawahiri encouraged Iraqi Sunnis to join al-Baghdadi.[3] There was no general call for ummah across the globe to join the fight, and the relationship between the Islamic State of Iraq and al Qaeda was strong.

How do groups like al Qaeda and ISIS transition from boasting almost no foreign fighters to electronically reaching into homes in France, Germany, and the United States, to lure their target audiences from the known to war, beheadings, destruction, and vicious violence? Neither group has deep traditional roots in Muslim societies like the Muslim Brotherhood. Ideology and history may contribute to the acceptance. But there must be more. It is that more that demands a different critical review of these groups and their Svengali effect. However, this review should be accomplished not only by perceived terrorism subject matter experts but also by those who are the target of their attacks and extreme violence and those whose young are solicited to execute the attacks. These two groups may bring a perspective that offers a new approach to what appears to be a continually growing and constantly expanding problem.

This introduction charts the intellectual transitions that occurred in the groups between the often-cited Sykes-Picot Agreement and the current chaos and crises. Different groups declared they were fighting "imperialism" and "colonialism." Several Islamic scholars and ideologues participated in the intellectual transition from caliphate to battle-hardened fighters against nation-states created by World War I Allied forces. It is these scholars and ideologues who have had the most profound influence on current tenets of jihadi activism.

THE BEGINNING

It is generally agreed that al Qaeda emerged from the 1979–1989 Afghanistan-Soviet conflict.[4] At the time, most information on the group was limited, so very little was known about its ideology. This continued into the 1990s when Islamist groups such as Hamas, Hizbullah, and al Qaeda were grouped together, with no important differences identified.[5]

But as Strindberg and Warn suggest, to do so offers no opportunity to delineate the subtleties al Qaeda introduced as it began its journey to dominate the terrorism industry. One of the most striking of these subtleties was its use of ideology.

Al Qaeda, or actually Osama bin Laden, based the organization's ideology on the thirteenth-century scholar Shaykh Ibn Taymiyyah. Ibn Taymiyyah defined guidelines for waging jihad. He also devised metrics; metrics he insisted offered a means to exact adherence to the Qur'an and its guidance. No deviation was permitted. This lead to judgments from Ibn Taymiyyah, which pitted one Muslim against another.[6] Bin Laden was no different when he used Ibn Taymiyyah's interpretations of the Qur'an to determine Arab regimes he deemed true adherents of the Qur'an and those that were not. For those regimes that did not qualify as true adherents, war could be declared against them and their rule. Al Qaeda has made no secret of its intent to destabilize the Arab regimes in the Middle East and derail reform processes in the "Muslim" world.[7] It is therefore imperative that discussions of al Qaeda or any other terrorist organization include a backdrop of contemporary "Muslim" politics to frame the ideology espoused.[8] ISIS's and al Qaeda's rise to power had to tout a reliance on sacred text to create a foothold. This also permitted a distraction from the fact that each is a by-product of clashes within militant Islam and neither has traditional roots like Muslim Brotherhood. Bin Laden understood these facts only too well and developed an ideology that has been described as Salafi-Jihadist. Bin Laden, and more prominently Zawahiri, combined elements of religion with the fight in such a way that the result offered "respect for the sacred texts in their most literal form and an absolute commitment to jihad."[9,10] Zawahiri exploited the respect for sacred text the young sought as they fought their own personal struggle to self. Zawahiri simply crafted an ideology that co-opted each individual personal struggle and tied it to a "war sanctioned by Islamic tradition."[11] This ideology resulted in a personal struggle that melded with the organization's collective goal of removing political regimes it felt were not Islamic enough.[12] Removal of these regimes is almost certainly more political than religious and owes a great deal to the radicalization that occurred because of emotional response to the remaining European influence.[13,14]

Finding the Failures and Explanations

Prior to the events of September 11, 2001, the vestiges of colonialism were considered less a problem than other aspects. One culprit often cited as a source of terrorism was socioeconomic factors as terrorism was linked to underdevelopment.[15] Analysts like Tinka Veldhuis and Jørgen Staun concluded that poverty could breed resentment and desperation and support for political extremism. In addition, as well as providing grounds for grievance, poverty often means underdevelopment and poor or weak governance. That is to say, societies with the highest levels of social and economic inequality do not necessarily experience the highest frequency of terrorism or failed states, something that has been referred to as "back holes" within which fanaticism can emerge.[16] However, in the case of al Qaeda, the terrorists of 9/11 attacks were mainly from middle-class families.[17] These same al Qaeda members did not experience problems in finding employment even in foreign cities.[18]

As the number of Westerners joining al Qaeda or ISIS increase, and as the struggle for Syria and Iraq expands, questions on the triggers of radicalization have taken on a different hue.[19] Richard Barrett addresses this difference and the influences of social media in his June 2014 report *Foreign Fighters in Syria*.[20]

The use of the Internet, for example, and the fast diffusion of information around the globe have helped the group in organizational terms. Ideology is piped directly to the targeted audience.

Historical

Prior to the 1970s, nationalist ideologies predominated in most Islamist countries. The most dominant was the Muslim Brotherhood, founded in 1928 by Hassan al-Banna shortly after the abolition of the Ottoman Caliphate in 1924. The demise of the Ottoman Empire was more symbolic than essential in religious terms. However, it represented an ideal of spiritual unity for the Muslim world.[21] The Muslim Brotherhood was a major inspiration for what has been called the *politico* faction of Salafism.[22,23]

Once they were free of the Ottoman Empire's caliphate, Muslim states faced the dilemma of managing political Islam. The most profound examples in the Middle East were Egypt and Saudi Arabia.[24] In Egypt, Gamal Abdel Nasser leaned upon brotherhoods that emphasized devotion and were led by spiritual leaders. Saudi Arabia relied on an official Islam that insisted on strict interpretation of the Qur'an. Each approached its governance based on local needs. This approach seemed more appropriate, given the complexities faced across the Islamic world, but it later proved to be a problem when Nasser drove the Muslim Brotherhood from Egypt and the Brothers found refuge in Saudi Arabia.

Until then, though, the Arab world recognized the need for its governing bodies to cooperate if they were to hold its own against the West. Pan-Arabism evolved, with Egypt and Saudi Arabia as the two biggest players. Pan-Arabism represented a reaction against neocolonialism through the assertion of a nationalism founded on the notion that, through cooperation across state borders, the Arab world could mobilize indigenous resources in such a way as to challenge Western dominance of the international economic, political, and strategic milieu. But problems arose within this "Pan Arabism," the first was the reliance on these same two major players: Egypt and Saudi Arabia. The second was the lack of a "Pan-Arab" economy. Over 90 percent of Arab foreign investments were taking place outside the Arab world. Third, it was evident after the 1967 defeat that most Arab states leaders had to consider what was more advantageous for their own constituency, hence Egypt's pursuit of a separate peace with Israel.[25] As pan-Arabism devolved, Nasser began a violent crackdown on the opposition forces, particularly members of the Muslim Brotherhood. Egypt was not the only leader employing repression as a tool of control. Over the decades following independence, the rulers of Algeria, Egypt, Libya, Morocco, and Tunisia have repressed opposition forces (including potential ones), clamping down on groupings with very diverse origins, such as communists, socialists, Islamists, and Berbers.[26]

One of Nasser's most vocal opponents was Sayyid Qutb. Sayyid Qutb introduced the concept of *jahiliyyah*, "ignorance of Islam." To Qutb, modern Egypt and the Western world in general lived lives that reflected that ignorance. They had no moral compass, just as societies before the Qur'an reportedly did not.[27] Qutb influenced writers like Maulana Maududi and antigovernment protestors like Zawahiri. Qutb's writings also influenced the response of the government to protest. As the protests grew, pan-Arabism began to falter.

Chief among the casualties was the breakdown of the union of Egypt and Syria in the United Arab Republic. This short-lived attempt at solidarity lasted only from 1958 to 1961. The early 1960s also saw clashes in Yemen and the Six-Day War of June 1967. The effects of the July 1967 war were particularly devastating due to the magnitude of the Arab defeat and the loss of Arab Jerusalem, a factor that concerned the whole Islamic community. Aside from their human and economic costs, these defeats produced shock waves affecting both Arabs and non-Arabs. The manifest inability of the Arab states to remove the Israeli occupation of Arab territory sapped the legitimacy of Arab ruling elites and their military regimes. It was a defining moment since elites among the Arab leadership had to accept the harsh realities of the impact from those defeats.

Toward the end of the 1960s and into the early 1970s, it was Sayyid Qutb's writings, Maududi's influence, and the Wahhabi sect in Saudi Arabia that paved the way for the rise of Islamist politics in the following decades. Sayyid Qutb's writings offered a clean break with the past in the Islamic world.[28,29] Qutb-ism and Wahhabism filled the vacuum created by the demise of Arab nationalism. The then Islamist intelligentsia mobilized the social ingredients of Islamism. By social ingredients we mean the social fabric that faced rising unemployment, rapid urbanization, and housing needs. These were the problems of the post–World War II generation, which along with a devout middle class of merchant families associated with the bazaars contributed to the heart and the rise of contemporary Islamism, as Gilles Kepel has written.[30,31]

Two militant Islamist organizations emerged in the late 1970s that would become Egypt's primary security concern for the next two decades. Both coalesced around former radical members of the Muslim Brotherhood.

Al-Jihad, or al-Jihad al-Islami (Egyptian Islamic Jihad, EIJ), and al-Jama'a al-Islamiyya (Islamic Group, IG) began as an alliance of various groups and leaders that had been affiliated with the Brotherhood. Both sought to replace the secular Egyptian regime with Islamic rule.[32,33]

While the Iranian Revolution is often cited as the turning point (which partially was) for the Islamist politics, the milestone was actually six years earlier in 1973, after the second Arab-Israeli War and the Saudi Arabian oil embargo. At this point the potential strengths that Wahhabism could entail in Saudi politics were being reflected in a wider and in a sense more influential project. Indeed, the Saudis had embarked on a deeper reorganization of their religious landscape than Iran did. From the late 1970s onward, a more pan-Islamic view emerged in the Muslim world, with emphasis on the *ummah* and the idea that Umma were being systematically attacked by the Western world. The concept of all Muslims having a responsibility to help all other Muslims in need began to emerge.[34] Since the late 1970s, the Salafiyya movement has been closely identified with very stringent sacred text interpretations that define a more pure Islam than that which has modern influences.[35] But this strict interpretation differs significantly from the late-nineteenth and early-twentieth-century "open and flexible religious approach" used by political philosophers Jamal al-Din al-Afghani, Muhammed Abduh, and Rashid Rida.[36]

Using the more strict interpretation as a metric, the Muslim states began to take on two connotations: countries aligned with the West (such as Tunisia and Turkey) and those less comfortable with Western alignment (such as Libya, Egypt, and Iraq). The latter group viewed Islamic politics with caution and tried to contain its influence. In Egypt, Nasser's containment efforts employed such repressive tactics that Saudi Arabia "invited" a large number of Egypt's Islamic scholars and activists to seek refuge within its territories.[37,38] Among the scholars were Muslim Brotherhood activists like Mohammed Qutb, Sayyid Qutb's brother. When it became clear Nasser's pan-Arabism would not work, more politically active Arabs turned to Islamic militancy, Salafism, and related ideologies to pursue their goals.[39,40] As they did, the dynamic shifted within many Muslim-controlled governments.

One example of that shift occurred when students in the 1970s Saudi educational system began to adopt the beliefs of the Muslim Brothers who had emigrated in Saudi Arabia. These students followed political Salafist doctrines strictly, with many influencing the future of the Salafist movement.[41,42] In addition, the transitioning of these young educated Islamists into Salafists may have been helped by the lack of credible pan-Arabism alternatives when it failed and the Saudi government's encouragement of Islamism as counterweight to student groups who were leaning toward Marxist organizations.[43,44,45] By the early 1980s Egyptian jihadi ideology crystalized, leading to the 1990s dramatic intensification of Islamic insurgency. This insurgency had been fueled by the development of jihadi activism that resulted from veterans of the Soviet-Afghanistan war returning to their homelands.[46] The Soviet invasion of Afghanistan was a watershed event, as it revived the concept of participation in jihad to evict an "infidel" occupier from a Muslim country as a "personal duty" for every capable Muslim. The basis of this duty derives from the "irreversibility" of Islamic identity both for individual Muslims and for Muslim territories.[47] The Soviet war in Afghanistan, along with the Saudi policy of inviting Egyptian radicals and dissidents, proved central to the radicalization and emergence of later core al Qaeda. It is important to note that core members of what would later become al Qaeda started as Egyptian volunteers to this fight to save Afghanistan. Many were from the urbanized middle class. They fought alongside others from Tunisia and Algeria. They left their homelands, to go to Afghanistan in order to fight the Soviets. The few urbanized and traveled Afghans who participated in the war drew their experiences from Egyptian universities and radical thinkers as well as Pakistani Jamaat Islami. The Soviet-Afghanistan war not only influenced the first generation of al Qaeda members spiritually but also gave them the opportunity to meet key figures of Islamist organizations from around the world who traveled to Afghanistan.

Another seismic shift was the Iranian Revolution. The Saudi government viewed the Shia Iranian Revolution as potentially threatening to its own Sunni majority.[48] The Afghan experience was the first-hand opportunity for radical jihadis to meet as we noted, and it was the first time that Egyptian Qutb-ism and radical Islamism melded with Saudi jihadi elements.

The Afghan experience contributed to the deterritorialization of Islam. Jihad defined the territory not the political boundaries. Muslims who embraced jihad while living in countries that purported to follow Islam accepted the alienation of their own governments. It became a badge of courage. It also made the younger radicals aware that they had to search for unity on their own terms.

Key Tenets

As it has been shown very briefly, the failure of secular pan-Arabism, during the 1950s–1980s, to usher in a new political order and unite the Middle East encouraged Islamic revivalists to forge a new Arab-Islamic identity using religion as a legitimizing agent.

Al Qaeda, with one such Arab-Islamic identity, offered an ideology that provided legitimacy and philosophical foundations for those who wished to pursue the Islamic imperial dream of creating the new golden age in the form of a contemporary caliphate, as well as any number of local objectives directly or indirectly linked to this overarching concept. Al Qaeda's historical leadership belongs to the post-1970s more narrow interpretation of post 1970's Salafi movement. This movement became associated with the concept of restoring an Islamic Caliphate, using violence to establish Islamic states in this new Salafi definition and ignoring the tenets of Jamal al-Din al-Afghani (1838–1897), the concept's modern originator.

Al-Afghani was an Iranian-born political thinker and Islamic nationalist who worked for pan-Islamism.[49,50] The term *Salafism* derives from the Arabic word *Salaf,* referring to righteous predecessors, specifically the immediate successors to the Prophet. Al-Afghani used the Salaf as "role models for religious, social, and political reform."[51] There is no certainty he considered himself a "Salafist."[52] The term *Salafiyya* was popularized by the Egyptians Muhammed Abduh and Rashid Rida as a response to then Muslim leaders ideological stagnation.[53,54] The term *Salafi* or *Salafi-Jihad* is often described as if it is a cornerstone of al Qaeda's ideology and that of other jihadi groups, often implying that it is a defined doctrine current within Islam that al Qaeda adopted and adapted to advance its agenda.[55] Doing so relies on assumptions that do not permit us to function from the stronger position that evidence would offer.

The al Qaeda ideology is, according to Osama bin Laden and Ayman al-Zawahiri based in the historical process of Islamic thinking that led to its creation and its implications for international relations as an ideology in and of itself. It is also important to stress here that bin Laden and Zawahiri were adamant that they were following the steps of al-Wahhab and Ibn Taymiyyah.[56,57] They believed they were searching for answers to their problems as these thinkers did in the centuries before them.

Islam, it is argued by Salafists, was perfect at the time of the Prophet, and since that time there has been a consistent straying from the original.[58] Wiktorowicz says that Salafis are united by a common religious creed, which provides principles and a method for applying religious beliefs to contemporary issues and problems.[59,60] Salafi Islamist activism is based on that organization's interpretation of the Qur'an, and the Sunnahs of the Prophet Muhammad outline numerous rules about politics, economics, society, and individual behaviour.[61,62] To function within the modern period, Salafism (and other Muslims) filter actions through the lens of what they think the Prophet would do if he were alive today.[63] Bin Laden and Zawahiri advocated challenging any perceived threat to ummah only following the laws of the Qur'an, as interpreted by them.[64,65,66] No human-made law could prevail over the law of the Qur'an. Moreover, as Olivier Roy argues, one of the primary objectives is "de-culturation"—to jettison folk customs and delink Islam from any cultural context.[67]

For bin Laden and Zawahiri the fundamental Islamic doctrine of tawhid had a deep political importance. It could eradicate divisions among the Muslim countries.[68] For Salafis, tawhid is essential for the purity of their defined Prophet Muhammad governance model.[69,70]

Salafis rejected human-made laws because they were deemed an interference with the word of the God. This word offers religious guidance that is central to the Salafi creed. As noted, the Qur'an is considered the first source of guidance, and Salafis often refer to "clear-cut" verses within that guidance to support their religious rulings.[71,72] The translation of Qur'an into contemporary practice and world is one of the most important concepts for Salafi doctrine. It is for this reason that some Salafis refer to themselves as Ahl al-Hadith.[73,74] Hence, interpretations of the Qur'an that incorporate philosophy or history are rejected. The Qur'an and Sunna are the sources of Islam; only they offer the correct form of worship and the propagation of Islam.

IMPORTANT TERMS

When discussing Salafism, it is necessary to go back to Qutb and three important definitions.

The first is tawhid, the second is hakimiyyah, and the third is jahiliyyah.[75,76] According to Qutb, tawhid, or oneness of God and unity in God, is more than just theological; it is "political" as well. Political in that no human government can have sovereignty over the Umma, only God can.[77] Therefore, only God's laws should be followed. In fact, not following other laws is strongly advised. According to Qutb, following only God's law acknowledges his divinity. Tawhid is the cornerstone of Qutb's argument.

This leads to the other two terms: hakimiyyah and jahiliyyah. Hakimiyyah is defined as the judgment and legislation of God alone over all in this creation.[78] Jahiliyyah is a "state of ignorance" similar to the period before Islam. The pre-Islamic period is characterized as a period when unbridled human desires ruled with unfettered brutality. For Salafists the return to *jahiliyyah* began shortly after the period of the Prophet and what was deemed rightly guided caliphs (622–661 CE).[79,80,81]

To Qutb this state of ignorance applies to Islamic and non-Islamic societies.[82] Qutb best articulates the significance of the concept of *hakimiyyah*, in relation to the concept of *jahiliyyah*, as follows: the jahiliyyah is a condition and not a period in time. The significance of the term *hakimiyyah* rests in its political meaning, which is closely bound to the concept of tawhid. These two ideas are derived from the comprehensive and integrated Islamic concept concerning the nature of the relationship between the Creator, the creation, the universe, life, and humankind. The first idea is the unity of humanity in race, nature, and origin. The second is the general world order accepted by God.[83] Under bin Laden and Zawahiri, al Qaeda conceives of itself as outside of a corrupt *jahiliyyah*, changing it from the outside.[84]

OTHER TERMS

Maududi was the first contemporary Islamist writer who applied the term against modern Muslim societies.[85,86] For Maududi the Prophet

Muhammad offered the path for eternal divine justice through the Qur'an and his example. It is conceptualized as a condition of ignorance that the Arab peoples lived prior to God's revelation to Muhammad.

Jihad is the action that will bring an end to *jahiliyyah* and bring about the solution, which is subjugation to God through the establishment of a new caliphate encompassing the territory acquired at the height of the Islamic conquests. The followers of al-Wahhab believed that fighting a holy war would give them entry to heaven as martyrs of God.[87] The word *jihad* comes from an Arabic root that means "to make an effort" or "to strive towards a goal." English translations usually refer to it as a "holy war" or a "crusade," and it was given various meanings throughout Islamic history, such as a "struggle against one's evil inclinations or an exertion for the sake of Islam."[88] Here an important point that differentiates Salafis from Salafi-Jihadists is the issue of jihad. The more moderate Salafis advocate jihad through da'wa (education and preaching), whereas radical jihadists consider jihad a priority. However, the Qutbist approach of jihad advocates that it is wrong to expect an immediate result from jihad.

In Islam, there are two types of external jihad: offensive and defensive. In Islamic jurisprudence, the offensive jihad promotes the spread of Islam, enlightenment. The defensive jihad (jihad al-dafa'a), however, is a widely accepted concept that is analogous to international norms of self-defense and Judeo-Christian just war theory.[89] Defending the faith-based community against external aggression is considered a just cause.

For Sayyid Qutb, jihad is a sacred task, both "mystical and physical," that every Muslim nation has to perform. It would be wrong, he states, to follow the Muslim apologists and to conclude that such a war is only defensive.[90] Rather, the goal of jihad is to restore the lost unity between people and God, namely to eliminate the various Jahili regimes and social systems that disturb the tawhid and thus prevent humankind from seeing the light of Islam.[91]

Another important tenet for the Salafi-Jihadist is the preparation that must be made for jihad. Take Muhammad's Hijra as an example; Muhammad's preparation for his trip was both physical and spiritual. His migration to Medina established an independent state and a secure power base. Muhammad then conducted a successful war against the Meccans, eventually converting them to Islam. During this process the believers moved from their preexisting tribal identities and replaced them with an Islamic identity, one that tied everyone to the concept of the "Umma."[92] According to Esposito, this formed a model for modern jihadists. They moved into an area, and established a base within the community to spread Islam.[93] Hijra, although a practical component of the al Qaeda operational model, contains an important historical and spiritual context that also makes it a defining element of the al Qaeda ideology.[94]

Takfir has also defined the al Qaeda model. The term is usually used when there are issues of contention within the Salafi movement. It is one of three internal issues of debate. The other two are the targeting of civilians and suicide attacks. The debate over whether Muslims can declare incumbent rulers apostates (a process known as *takfir*) represents one of the most prominent sources of fissure within the Salafi community.[95] Wiktorowicz cites three reasons to which most jihadis adhere: the person could be ignorant or coerced or the incident inadvertent. For example, a ruler may receive erroneous advice about what is and is not Islamic. He could then follow with rulings based on that advice. The second reason, coercion, may occur because the individual was under significant pressure. An individual who acts un-Islamically at knifepoint is not responsible for his actions. The third reason, the intention of the individual may have nothing to do with disbelieving Islam, is the most controversial.[96] However, if the charge is initiated, that is, if a Muslim leader is labeled *takfir*, he or she is considered an infidel and therefore, according to the logic of takfir, permitted to be killed.[97]

KEY IDEOLOGUES OF SALAFI-JIHAD

When referring to Salafi-Jihad, most analysts cite the deep impact of Ibn Taymiyyah. A professor of law, Taymiyyah was a scholar of Hanbali law who worked in the thirteenth and fourteenth centuries, a time of intense external pressure on the Islamic world. He was the first to apply the terms *jahiliyyah, apostasy, jihad*, and *legitimate rule* that reemerged in the twentieth and twenty-first centuries. Ibn Taymiyyah fled his native Iraq for Syria in 1268 in order to escape the Mongols, who had destroyed the Abbasid caliphate. The Mongols established a center of power in northeastern Iran, near Tabriz. From this stronghold they threatened Syria, Palestine, and Egypt. In 1300, the reigning Mongol Ilkhan, Ghazan, a direct descendant of Genghis Khan, invaded Syria. Ghazan had converted to Islam in 1295; he projected himself as a legitimate Muslim ruler.[98] But Ibn Taymiyyah pronounced him an apostate for having failed to raise up Islamic law in his realm. Ibn Taymiyyah cited Ghazan's use of the Yasa code instead of Sharia law for the law of the land. He ignored Ghazan's claims of being a Muslim and jihad was permissible against them.[99]

His work was profoundly influential on contemporary Islamic political thinkers such as Salam Faraj, Sayyid Qutb, Maulana Maududi, and Ayman al-Zawahiri. He is considered a foundational contributor to what became known as the al Qaeda ideology.

Another thinker who was influenced by Ibn Taymiyyah's works is Muhammad ibn Abd al-Wahhab. Al-Wahhab was a Saudi theologician who wrote a book called *Ten Voiders of Islam*, which served as the justification for al Qaeda leadership's opposition against the Saudi regime that allowed the stationing of American troops in the 1990s.[100]

Another influential figure among al Qaeda's leadership was Jamal al-Din al-Afghani. His philosophy reopens the door for ijtihad considered closed by the Ulema, and introduces the concept of Salafism.[101] Afghani adopted pan-Islamism in the 1880s, when this idea was becoming increasingly popular in the Muslim world. However, he was unique in that he reconciled nationalism with pan-Islamism. He argued that "ijtihad" is necessary to respond to the contemporary crisis of the decline in prosperity and power of imperial Islam.[102] Afghani tried to bridge the gap between the outright secular modernists and the traditionalists to save the Islamic world from its relegated position as a civilization that was no longer influential in the way it had previously been.

But most influential, besides Ibn Taymiyyah, was Pakistani thinker Maulana Maududi. He was the founder of Jamaat-i-Islami; he provided the link between Hassan al-Banna's vague methodological approach to establishing an Islamic state and the sophisticated ideology of Sayyid Qutb.[103] Maududi is argued to be a direct "product" of the Deobandi tradition of Islam in India. He regarded all kinds of nationalism as dangerous to religion. Drawing upon Ibn Taymiyyah's work, he built the concept of a new jahiliyyah. In his observations of the new jahiliyyah, Maududi noted that Muslims had essentially removed God's sovereignty and replaced them with secular legal structures.[104] Concerned about the corruption in modern society and living, he believed that the split between secular Muslim leaders and Islamist leaders in contemporary Muslim society must end.[105] Maududi believed the Muslim community's decline resulted from practicing a corrupted form of Islam, one that was contaminated by non-Islamic ideas and culture. He therefore supported the jihad's aim of establishing an Islamic state. He felt this could be achieved only through political action. An overall influence, Maududi's importance is especially significant when viewed through his impact on Sayyid Qutb, often considered the godfather of revolutionary Sunni Islam.

Sayid Qutb, as discussed earlier, is both the key link to and the point of divergence from the mainstream Muslim Brotherhood and its more radical cousins. Qutb read Maududi's most influential works, including *Jihad in Islam*, *Islam and Jahiliyyah*, and *Principles of Islamic Government*, which were translated into Arabic beginning in the 1950s. These led to Qutb merging Maududi's "modern jahiliyyah" and Ibn Taymiyyah's argument that the unity of God requires that Muslims follow divine law, creating a synthesis that reinforced the stark distinction between the Party of God and the Party.[106] A more direct connection existed through one of Maududi's most important protégés, Abdul Hasan Ali Nadvi, who was a central figure in transmitting his mentor's theories to the Arab world.[107] Qutb's enormous influence on al Qaeda and the radical Islamist movements has been acknowledged in the memoirs of Ayman al-Zawahiri. It is especially seen in the intellectual justification for extreme anti-Western sentiment on a cultural as well as political level. Qutb adopted Hassan al-Banna's idea that Islam is an "integral" or "total" system that controls all aspects of life and responds to all human needs. He provided justification for establishing an Islamic society based on Sharia, Islamic law.[108] Qutb, who was highly interested in social justice and social reforms, had traveled extensively gathering data and ideas. During that period, he was more secular than religious. However, as he traveled through the United States, he realized every country had problems. If he needed to address the critical problems facing his people, he did not have to leave his home to do it.[109] Qutb transitioned from secular modernism to radical Islam around 1947, when he was writing his first Islamist work, *Social Justice in Islam* (al-'Adalah al-ijtima'iya fi al-Islam). By the 1952 revolution that removed King Faruq from power, Qutb was calling for a cleansing of those advocating constitutional activity.

To Qutb, political systems that were not Islamic were in a state of jahiliyyah. He wanted an Islamic society based on Sharia; he was sure this would be superior to the corrupt societies of the West. He bound his argument to the concept of tawhid and supported his view with a considerable number of Qur'anic verses. Qutb's jihad was in the nature of a revolutionary movement, where the masses from below would be under the leadership of an elite disciplined vanguard—a classical communist revolutionary modus operandi. He never mentioned the need to call the Caliph or any higher earthly authority for the jihad.[110]

These same concepts are later seen in Muhammad abd-al-Salam Faraj's *The Neglected Duty*.[111] Faraj was a member of Islamic Jihad and used the book as a kind of internal discussion paper to explain and defend the group's ideology, an ideology that sought Sharia law for Egypt.[112] Faraj believed violent jihad was the only answer and demonstrated that with the assassination of Egyptian President Anwar Sadat and his criticism of the Muslim Brotherhood. Faraj objected to the Brotherhood's working within the Egyptian political process, its acceptance of gradual change, and its lack of emphasis on forcing change through the sword of jihad.[113]

Faraj believed that jihadis had an obligation to defeat Muslim leaders who were not implementing Sharia law within their countries. He recognized there was a segment of Muslims who were reluctant to be governed by purely Islamic laws. These Muslims were categorized in dar al-kufr (an abode of unbelief), and as such, were targets of the jihad. For Faraj there could be no compromise.[114]

Faraj believed killing "the Pharaoh," as he referred to Sadat, would spark an Islamic revolution in Egypt. To his disappointment, the revolution did not occur. Instead the ensuing crackdown on Islamist organizations hindered operations in the region and forced jihadists like Abdullah Azzam to look abroad for sanctuary. It was at this moment that the jihad began to evolve into a global rather than a regional phenomenon.[115] The assassination of Anwar Sadat by Faraj's organization changed the nature of the Islamist struggle.

After the assassination of Sadat, many jihadists sought refuge in Afghanistan. It is there that Abdullah Azzam met Osama bin Laden. Azzam was neither a theorist nor a theologian. His goal was not to establish an Islamic state in Afghanistan but rather to leverage the opportunity the Soviet occupation provided. Like Qutb, Azzam favored the idea of building an Islamic vanguard, one that could potentially build an ideal Qu'ranic society. Unlike Qutb, however, Azzam opposed the taking of arms against fellow Muslims. He stated this when objecting to employing Afghan Arabs against the Egyptian and Algerian regimes.[116] Moreover, Azzam opposed attacking civilians. He was strongly against using terrorism against non-combatants. Azzam established the Jihad Training University in 1984, as well as a service movement to provide logistics and religious instruction to the mujahideen fighters. The operation came to be known as al Qaeda al-Sulbah (also known as al Qaeda, or "the solid base"). His murder left a mentoring vacuum that al-Zawahiri filled.[117]

Ayman al-Zawahiri was an Egyptian jihadist who came from a distinguished family that seems to have never faced social or economic hardships; many of its members would be considered part of the elite in any society.[118]

Zawahiri adopted both Qutb's Manichean view of the world and his unwavering desire to establish an Islamic state at any cost, using violence if necessary. This dichotomous struggle for God's sovereignty on earth eliminates the middle ground and sets the stage for a millennial, eschatological battle between good and evil. Qutb dramatically impacted Zawahiri's *Knights Under the Prophet's Banner*. Zawahiri called Qutb "the most prominent theoretician of the fundamentalist movements."[119] He also noted that Qutb's words acquired greater dimensions after he was executed.

Zawahiri's jihad journey started when he was 15, as a member of Jam'iyat Ansar al-Sunnah al-Muhammadiyya (the Association of the Followers of Muhammad's Path), a "Salafi" movement. As he matured, Zawahiri drew a strict distinction between his movement, the Islamic Jihad, and others like al-Jama'a al-Islamiyya and the Muslim Brotherhood movement.[120] He condemned the Brotherhood for renouncing jihad as a means to establish the Islamic state. He was also equally opposed to al-Jama'a al-Islamiyya for renouncing violence and upholding the concept of constitutional authority.

SUMMARY

It is apparent that each of these past ideologues contributed to the current state of violent attacks executed under the banner of jihad. More important, though, is the need to identify the newer influencers and their impact on current and future fighters waging war. ISIS introduced vicious attacks and beheadings. The response was fighters flocking to its ranks. The focus on youth remains. But the distinct move toward ISIS-styled violence may indicate a drifting away from the spiritual path advocated by Zawahiri. If so, is Zawahiri still relevant? Just as the old ideologues empha-sized the guidance of previous thought generators, does the guidance of Ibrahim al-Rubaish or Harith bin Ghazi al-Nadhari of al Qaeda in the Arabian Peninsula demand more of our attention? Will the influence of Abu Qatada continue? He is said to have influenced both Richard Reid and Zacarias Moussaoui.[121]

Zawahiri tried to draw Islamist struggles away from their local dimension and move them into a united front against a common Qutb-type Western enemy.[122] He wanted to remove any confusion Muslim youth might feel if there was mixed message pitting local needs against that of the jihad.[123,124] This is perhaps where a fundamental difference lies between Qutb and Zawahiri. Qutb never advocated for internationalizing jihad or attacking the West. Fawaz Gerges supports the premise that Zawahiri actually dis-torted Qutb's ideas in order to fit his purposes.[125] In his 2001 book *Knights Under the Prophet's Banner*, Zawahiri identified and prioritized the goals of what he calls the "the revolutionary fundamentalist movement": first, achievement of ideological coherence and organization, then struggle against the existing regimes of the Muslim world, followed by the establish-ment of a "genuinely" Muslim state at the heart of Arab world.[126]

It is incumbent upon terror analysts to move beyond the focal point of "9/11," that is, looking at events from the perspective of "the aftermath of 9/11." It is true the period after 9/11 brought a new al Qaeda generation, as well as another generation of radical Islamic ideologues came to the sur-face. But as with any evolution, the new generation of militants challenged the old. At the core of the new thinkers are several ideological perspectives. The Salafi-Jihadi writers and ideologues are not a homogeneous group. There are religious scholars like Abu Muhammad al-Maqdisi who issue fatwas and write books. There are also strategic thinkers like Abu Musab al-Suri.[127,128] Maqdisi refers to the loyalty or allegiance that every Muslim should have toward God, Islam, and other Muslims, and he is applying it to both social and political aspects. Suri reiterates the goal of establishing an Islamic state. Suri framed "a call to all followers of Islam to participate in a global resistance whereas al-Maqdisi was pointed in his call for jihad that concentrates its efforts against the Muslim world's own regimes. Maqdisi distanced himself from Suri, who al-Maqdisi thought advocated "reckless fighting" and the unlimited use of suicide bombings.[129] Al-Maqdisi openly criticized methods such as kidnappings in Iraq. To him they are counterproductive.

There is also a need to recognize and monitor the influence of local forum members whose words have impact. For instance, the member of the al-Shumoukh forum known as "Galvanize the Believers" advocated lone wolf attack on Christian shopping centers, churches, and cafes.[130] Then, of course, there is also Abu Bakr Naji. His "Management of Savagery" almost acts as a blueprint for ISIS actions thus far.[131]

The bottom line is we have to find the centers of gravity that cause the shifts. There was one in 2003, when al Qaeda shifted from Iraq and Afghanistan to the Arabian Peninsula. There was another in 2014, when the shift moved most activity from the Arabian Peninsula and Sahel to Iraq and Syria. Erasing the Sykes-Picot lines appears to be the 2015 target in the bulls eye.[132,133] The task at hand now is to identify the newest critical thinkers as early as possible to pinpoint the vital processes they may influence and the steps needed to mitigate.

2

---◦◦◦◦---

Al Qaeda: The Evolution Process

Al Qaeda's complicated rise to prominence occurred outside of international view until September 11, 2001. Even the 1998 U.S. Embassy bombings in Tanzania and Kenya did not propel the group into the household name it enjoys now and until recently it was one of the most feared groups in the world.[1] Before that infamous day, al Qaeda was unknown to many in the Western world; it was just one of many terrorist groups and organizations. However, the merging of Osama bin Laden's charisma with the Ayman al-Zawahiri jihad experience, guidance, and jihad commitment set the groundwork for al Qaeda becoming a new standard for terrorist groups, a standard that ISIS once embraced but discarded when it was no longer advantageous, and Boko Haram pursued and exploited until a better terrorism partner was available.

These two men had very different backgrounds and different lifestyles, but through a circuitous route, they came together to lead a new multinational band of terrorist event executors.[2] Al Qaeda evolved from a 1988 post-Afghanistan embryonic group of rebel fighters that had its heyday of world attention after September 11, 2001, to the current discord period within the terrorism industry. During those 25 years the group has survived several transitions. Here we will examine the international framework that has supported al Qaeda's survival and the jihadi relations that proved important during five critical periods: formation, the period from 1989 to early 1991; bin Laden's return to Pakistan, the period from early 1991 to early 1992; the Sudan period, from 1992 to 1996; the formation of the

World Islamic Front, from 1998 to 2001; and finally the post-9/11 land-scape, until roughly 2005/2006.

THE EARLY FORMATION YEARS

Al Qaeda was formally founded in August 1988, just as the *jihad* against the Soviets was ending.[3] During the Afghanistan-Soviet conflict the United States was a major benefactor of insurgent groups acting against the Soviet threat in Afghanistan.[4] While resistance groups fighting against the Soviets benefitted from that U.S. help, several used their own networks to garner support for the fight.[5] Abdullah Azzam was one such individual. Azzam, the spiritual mentor and ideologist of the Global Jihad movement, used his extensive network to recruit and seek funding and then he established the "Maktab Al-Khadamat (MaK)" (the service bureau) to provide guest-houses and support accommodattions for the new arrivals in Peshawar. Osama bin Laden supplemented MAK support with a record of information on fighters so that families inquiring about their fighter's status could receive the most accurate information available. Bin Laden and Azzam's efforts in Afghanistan mainly supported Arab fighters, but fighters from several countries including Egypt, Yemen, and Iraq fought in the conflict.[6] The conflict provided the experience many fighters would take back to their homelands to fight in conflicts there.

While in Afghanistan, Azzam and bin Laden's fighters were focused on ousting the Soviets from Afghanistan. During this period bin Laden had that same intent as he established ties to Islamic Jihadi groups that were critical to al Qaeda's existence. Some of those relationships lasted until bin Laden's death in 2011.[7,8] One of the most crucial of those ties was with Jala-luddin Haqqani and his Haqqani Network. The Haqqani Network had insurgency roots that dated back to 1973 when it targeted King Zahir Shah's cousin Muhammad Daoud Khan.[9] Khan was assassinated in 1978, but Haq-qani's efforts against him began in 1973 when Khan, who had overthrown his cousin, espoused closer ties with Moscow.[10] Haqqani and other Kabul Islamists opposed this position and worked to stop Daoud.[11,12]

Bin Laden and Azzam began their jihad careers as "volunteer fighters at Haqqani network fronts," and its core of followers remained with the Haqqani Network from then to the present.[13] An Afghani and Pakistani insurgent group, the Haqqani Network is a familial organization with a hierarchical senior leadership structure. As a matter of fact, Jalaluddin's Haqqaniyya madrassa classmates became his field commanders.[14] The Haqqanis provided bin Laden's supplies for his training camps in Paktia and connections to people like Mustafa Hamid (Abu'l-Walid al-Masri) and Abu Hafs al-Masri.[15] Jalaluddin Haqqani's 1980 declaration of able-bodied Muslim individuals' obligation to support the Afghanistan fight against the Soviets came at least four years before Azzam declared to his individual responsibility fatwa.

The Haqqani connection was essential to al Qaeda successfully emerging from its first stages of the evolutionary process. But Haqqani is not known for its large-scale or news headline–grabbing attacks. According to a 2011 Harmony Project report: "Most of the operations conducted by the group over its three decade long history have been carried out by small, local, and semi-autonomous fighting units organized along tribal and sub-tribal lines, with Haqqani commanders often coordinating activity and providing logistics."[16,17]

The Haqqani Network's evolution from a collection of like-minded tribal fighters in the mid-1970s into a most-sought-after structured network offering a high-quality violence product line. Its low profile belies the sophisticated command and control and media operation created by Jalaluddin Haqqani. In fact the Haqqani Network has consciously portrayed itself as a local actor preoccupied with local concerns as a way to stay out of the limelight and continue its current business growth trajectory. The group has been able to do so through a deceptive and segmented strategic communications campaign that masks the variety and depth of its relations with other actors. This has allowed the Haqqani Network to tailor its messages to different audiences.[18,19] Haqqani and his network seem to manage two important training camps, which also served embryonic al Qaeda's training purposes. These were the camps in Paktia in the Paktika province of Afghanistan, which was controlled by Haqqani. According to both Harmony Project releases: "In 1988, al-Qaeda officially established itself as a clandestine, hierarchical organization and organized its first training camps. Until the late 1990s, these camps would remain the core elements of al Qaeda's infrastructure, and agents of all of al Qaeda's major attacks during the 1990s would be trained in these facilities."[20] It seems though that the answer to the scholarly debate on whether or not bin Laden established a solid organization is not clear. Fawaz Gerges points to the fact that some Arab Afghans complained about Azzam, and he was pushed to set a separate training facility.[21]

This same Afghan alumni and their jihadi connections have received wide scholarly attention, with most of that scholarly attention focused on the jihadi violent actions since the end of the Afghanistan-Soviet conflict. The multiethnic assembly of volunteers had one mission: expel the Russians from Muslim lands but not through the doctrinaire jihadi activism. Indeed, most of the foreigners adhered to an ultra-conservative and contextualized Wahhabi-Salafi version of Islam while the Afghans were mostly of the Deobandi school. The consolidation and unification under the banner against the Russians made the idea of the action under the concept of defensive jihadism plausible. What the Afghan war did to its participants was what Bruce Riedel called infusing the jihadist movement with global sensibilities and ambitions.[22] The Afghan war paved the way for globalism by challenging the operational hegemony of localism.[23]

Al Qaeda's founding moments were documented during the jihad against the Soviets in August 1988.[24] The participants at the meeting included bin Laden, Abu Ubaidah al-Banshiri—al Qaeda's military commander—and Abu Hajir al-Iraqi—al Qaeda's religious advisor (real name: Mamdouh Salim). They formally established an advisory council, a list of membership requirements, and an oath of allegiance for new members of al Qaeda.[25,26] In the group's consolidation, the most important component of its structure was the Military Committee,[27] as one of the most recent documents of Harmony Project supports.[28,29,30]

There were two important problems, though, for militant Islamists to overcome: inter-Arab and Muslim differences and the split within the jihadi movement. The conflicts between the factions in countries such as Yemen or Syria kept the jihad-battling Muslim and Western enemies. There was also the problem of defining the future direction of the jihad movement after the Afghanistan-Soviet conflict. Abdullah Azzam envisioned an Islamic pioneer vanguard that could establish the ideal Quranic society in the Muslim world. The main preoccupation of the radical Islamist movement was dislodging the near enemy and removing the rulers in the Muslim world who had been subservient to the far enemy (the United States or the Soviet Union). Sayyid Qutb's influence seemed to encourage the goal of a Quranic society, removing these rulers and establishing Islamic polities that would reignite the caliphate and bring Sharia law back to Muslim lands, Azzam agreed with Shariah law, he opposed taking up arms against fellow Muslims, that is, against Mubarak.[31] Bin Laden appears to have had the same focus. Most captured documents have no significant mention of taking jihad into the global stage or instigating a world front of crusader jihad.[32] Bin Laden did not want his new organization to develop into a force against Israel and the West.[33] He did not even finance Egyptian and Algerian terrorist activities, and became preoccupied with internal politics of Afghanistan. A "global terrorist force" was not part of the initial plan.[34] This did not become an issue until after the Zawahiri-bin Laden merger of powers.

Between 1988 and 1991 when bin Laden returned to Saudi Arabia, the group kept its sights on Muslim countries it felt were not Sharia law compliant.[35] But bin Laden began to separate his vision from that of Azzam. Here it is important to stress some parts of the debate that has been going on in the scholarly journalist community: Peter Bergen stressed the importance of bin Laden's differentiation from Azzam's view of establishing a separate military wing.[36] According to Bergen, "Abdullah Azzam was opposed to the idea of a separate Arab-Islamist military force because he saw the presence of Arabs scattered throughout all of the Afghan factions and regions functioning as morale boosters who could simultaneously teach the

Afghans about true Islam, aid them with education and medicine, and bring news of the Afghan *jihad* to wealthy donors in the Middle East."[37] Nevertheless, we should keep in mind that Azzam's role in al Qaeda's creation has been widely and greatly exaggerated in the sense that the roots of the movement's creation do not lie in the Islamic tradition but within the contemporary divisions in the Islamist world.[38] Sayyid Qutb's manuscripts did not mention anything about waging a long-term far enemy struggle. Since neither hakimiyyah nor jahiliyyah at home were the founding and guiding principles of the bin Laden-Zawahiri group, both men adopted Qutb's writings to fit their purpose.[39] By all means, it seems that the transnational jihad transition was an outgrowth of al Qaeda's local jihad. The international approach was taken when focusing on local did not secure the desired results. First hints of America as a target was the purported call for a boycott of American products in Saudi Arabia. According to Peter Bergin, bin Laden urged the boycott during the 1980s to boycott American products in Saudi Arabia.[40]

Now it has been reported that during the war against the Soviets, bin Laden served as a contact between Saudi and Pakistani intelligence while also acting as a point of contact with Prince Turki al-Faisal.[41] The possibility that bin laden had been a CIA liaison has also been raised. If he had contacts with the agency during the 1980s, it was probably not extensive as recent documents and analysis indicate that U.S. officials and CIA agents had limited dealings with Afghan Arabs. What is perhaps most close to truth is that most connections and contacts were being conducted through the ISI (Pakistani secret intelligence).[42]

After the withdrawal of Soviet forces from Afghanistan in 1989 and between the Iraqi invasion of Kuwait and the first Gulf War in August 1990, Abdullah Azzam had been assassinated, but the cause of his death and its implications are not a matter to be discussed here.[43] As noted above, predominantly Egyptian militants at the end of the 1980s advocated something more radical: the violent overthrow of governments across the Muslim world they deemed "apostate," a concept of *jihad* that Azzam and many of his followers rejected, as they did not want conflicts between Muslims. Therefore, the Egyptians around al-Zawahiri had a very specific concept about how to attract bin Laden's funds and how to use recruits. Al-Zawahiri was still determined in this period to overthrow Mubarak's regime in Egypt.[44] This is also a disputed concept since some argue that Zawahiri believed that he could finally outsmart bin Laden and squash his financial resources for his own purposes,[45] but at least the fact that Zawahiri switched and turned his back to dislodging the near enemy and 30 years of struggle was seen as curious.

In Peshawar, al-Zawahiri entered a period of contention with his former movement, the Islamic Jihad, and other Islamist movements, like al-Jama'a al-Islamiyya and, to a lesser extent, the Muslim Brotherhood movement. Thus, there was serious contention with Gama'a al-Islamiyya, whose leaders called for its members to refrain from joining Zawahiri. What Zawahiri achieved finally was to persuade some middle rank members of al-Jihad to join al Qaeda. These middle and lower rank members are critical to the continuance of the movement.

When bin Laden returned to Saudi Arabia in 1989, he did not express any resentment against the United States, and his main goal was ousting the South Yemeni regime. At that point bin Laden did not seem to share Zawahiri's aim for toppling Mubarak in Egypt. It rather seemed more convenient and logical for Laden to continue assisting pro-Soviet yet Communist regimes that occupied Muslim lands, yet the concept remained: the unholy alliance with the United States (despite bin Laden's calls for boycotting American and Israeli products) and a far enemy (the Soviet Union). Thus, it seemed that at that point Laden was reluctant to fight against any Muslim ruler, secular or not.

However, radical Islam was active in Egypt and Algeria. Initially radical jihadis attacked these as domestic struggles and civil wars. There was no international agenda despite the fight against a foreign intruder in Afghanistan.[46] In the *Rise and Fall of Jihad*, Fawaz Gerges supports the suggestion that these jihadis chose to surrender to the demands of their individual country domestic problems. According to Gerges, it was a minority (a minority that included bin Laden and Zawahiri) that chose to fight the world's lone superpower. Moreover, it should be noted that the turn against the United States could have been a consequence rather than the cause of the failure of the Islamist movement with the near enemy. The failure of religious nationalists and their inner factionalism made an international cohesive Islamic army impossible. Thus, the top-down approach instead of a grassroots approach marked the end of the fight against the near enemy. After some years, intelligence in these countries assisted by Western governments responded with force and crushed the local jihadists. The Islamists in Egypt and Algeria became preoccupied with toppling the regimes and gaining political power rather than building a society from the start.

Evolution of al Qaeda's aims in the November 1989 to early 1991 period halted for the simple reason that bin Laden was physically absent from the organization's training camp system in Afghanistan/Pakistan during that entire period. He took part in the struggle against Najibullah, and some of his cadres were present in the siege of Jalalabad. One essential perspective is that of the radicals close to bin Laden and Zawahiri. This group voiced opposition to not to join the Jalalabad siege; mainly Abu'l-Walid and Abu Mus'ab al-Suri were trying to sound the alarm and convince the Arab fighters not to join such an ill-prepared and foolhardy mission.[47] It seems that at that point he became disenchanted with the Najibullah regime in Afghanistan, the communists, and the differences between local warlords and jihadists. A significant part of the Afghan mujahedeen were led by

Jalaluddin Haqqani, who was a close associate of Gulbuddin Hekmatyar's Hezb-e Islami until 1995, at which time he switched his loyalties to the Taliban.[48] According to the much helpful study by the Harmony Project on the Haqqani Network: "Some of the so-called 'Arab Afghans', or mujahidin volunteers from Arab countries, fought around Khost under Haqqani's leadership during this period, while many of them formed their own groups, the largest of which was led by Abu'l-Harith al-Urduni."[49] Haqqani was widely recognized as one of the most effective mujahidin commanders in Afghanistan and was heavily supported with money and arms from the Saudi and Pakistani intelligence agencies; CIA officers stationed in Islamabad at the time viewed Haqqani "as perhaps the most impressive Pashtun field commander in the war." Haqqani was also very close to Osama bin Laden.[50]

Bin Laden's interest in South Yemen in the early 1990s has been relatively understudied, but it must be understood because it helps to put bin Laden's later actions and movements into context.[51] The roots lie deeply in his ultra-nationalistic agenda and his desire to prove to the Saudis that he could carry out successful "special" missions. In Yemen, bin Laden waged a war against the same Communist Soviet Union enemy that he had faced in Afghanistan. This was to counter the rejection bin Laden experienced when, according to Bruce Riedel, he approached the Saudi intelligence and Prince Turki al-Faisal offering his assistance in repelling the Iraqi invasion. However, Faisal turned down bin Laden's offer. Bin Laden turned his focus toward the overthrow of the South Yemeni regime.[52] The Yemeni Afghans returned triumphant after 1989; they immediately directed their jihad skills against the crumbling of the People's Democratic Republic of Yemen, hoping to establish the unification of Yemen in May 1990. But unified Yemen was still unstable. The Saudi militants were shocked when their government invited 500,000 American troops into the country in 1990, following Saddam's invasion of Kuwait. This happened at a time when the Sahwa movement had grown particularly strong, and it soon began confronting the regime by adopting pan-Islamist rhetoric, thus contesting the government's monopoly on pan-Islamism as a source of political legitimacy. Thomas Hegghamer supports the idea that Sahwist clerics such as Salman al-Awdah and Safar al-Hawali accused the regime of hypocrisy by saying that it could not claim to be protecting the Muslim nation while it allowed American soldiers to roam the land of the Prophet Muhammad.[53] This moment marks the break between bin Laden and his native Saudi Arabia. But it was again not a cultural resentment against the Western values but something deeper: a partly personal resentment on Laden's account against the Saudi monarchy but in a true nationalistic tone. As it has been noted elsewhere,[54] bin Laden's Yemeni family background often was not considered a truly Saudi match with his family's connection with the Saudi government, which according to his worldview should serve another cause. Despite trumpeting that the Gulf War was an American conspiracy to strip off oil revenues and dominate Muslim lands through their military,[55] it was partly a personal public outcry against a government that bin Laden thought served its people. His disaffection with the kingdom grew stronger as he offered Prince Sultan the Minister of Defense to organize an Islamic army in order to defend his country, but the offer for al Qaeda forces to defend the Saudi was turned down. It is important to note at the point that bin Laden did not mobilize al Qaeda as an independent military wing against either Saddam or the United States. The most growing challenges for the Saudis came when the Iran and Sudan Islamic Revolution(s) somewhat challenged the Saudis. Sudan and the Revolutionary Command Council (RCC) offered to assist Iraq's Saddam Hussein's invasion of Kuwait. It is still unclear who was behind this decision, Turabi or President Bashir. But the official explanation was that while Sudan opposed the invasion, the condemnation of Iraq could help toward an Arab solution. Nevertheless, that decision caused a rift within the regimes right from the first months of Bashir and Turabi in power. That does not mean the decision was unanimous. There was some discord between the RCC, which openly supported Iraq, and the National Islamic Front (NIF) allies, who were for a more conciliatory position.[56]

THE SUDANESE CONNECTION (1992–1996)

It is important to explain several issues that were pressing for Bashir and Turabi's Sudan regime shortly before bin Laden's arrival in late 1991. Most academic and scholarly analyses on bin Laden's arrival support the terrorism-safe haven status that Khartoum had in the early 1990s and try to prove if he was involved in active operations within or outside Sudan, which has merit, but it is not the most important issue; the important issue perhaps is his collaboration and meddling with Hassan al-Turabi.[57] Of course, Sudan served as kind of new headquarters for disaffected Afghan Arab fighters and offered them shelter.[58]

On the other hand, we don't wish to exaggerate the role of Hassan al-Turabi and Khartoum in the consolidation of al Qaeda or at least in bin Laden's Islamic thought. In 1992 Sudan was trying to establish its regional and interregional power meddling and quickly involved with actors stretching from Iran to Libya and from Bosnia to Tanzania. On June 30, 1989, a military coup in Sudan, lead by Lt. General Omar Hassan Ahmad al-Bashir, overthrew the democratic parliamentary civilian regime of Sadiq al-Mahdi. The RCC, which took over the reign of the country under the leadership of Bashir, took an approach to government very close to what had been advocated by Turabi for many years based on consultation and consensus (*shura and ijmaa*).[59] Nevertheless, before the Islamic revolution in Sudan and soon after, an essential actor from Saudi Arabia was the main banker of the NIF and Turabi, the Faisal Islamic Bank, which had opened charters in Khartoum since 1983. Saudi investors had close relationship with Turabi. Soon after the consolidation of the revolution, President Bashir sent delegations to Iraq, Iran, Libya, Saudi Arabia, and Egypt. A meeting with an Egyptian delegation was made in Alexandria to confirm the Egyptian support for the new regime. But while Sudan rose on the international Islamic scene, its regional meddling soon complicated things and reflected the old saying "my enemy's enemy is my friend." As the relationship between Egypt and Sudan was unveiled, we found out bin Laden's and al Qaeda's role as well.[60] Hosni Mubarak, the Egyptian president, did not at all want an Iraqi connection in Khartoum, because he despised Saddam Hussein and his aspirations.[61] The first to send military assistance to the new regime was Baghdad. In addition, NIF's opening to Islamic actors from across the spectrum continued and it was surprising when Sudanese emissaries were sent to Tehran. Indeed, Ayatollah Khamenei and Hashemi Rafasnjani were suspicious and partly furious because Sudan was not declared an Islamic republic, but furthermore the emissaries were Sunni, the historic rivals of the Shi'a Iranians. In addition, Sudan had supported Iraq in the bitter rival war of 1980–1988, but the delegates lead by Ali Osman Taha tried to persuade the Iranians that they were trying to open a new chapter in the bilateral relations. Suffice it to say that Mubarak, Hussein, and Qaddafi were alarmed. However, Bashir maintained the position that competition for aiding Sudan would only benefit his country at that time.

In addition, Mubarak also had two important reasons to get further alarmed. First it was Sudan, which dropped its visa requirement for the so-called Afghan Arabs and provided Sudanese passports to some of them in 1993. Second, Sudan became host to thousands of Egyptian militants ranging from Sheikh Omar Abd al-Rahman to close affiliates of Zawahiri. Sheikh Omar had been an Afghan Arab alumnus, and soon in his years in Peshawar, he met with bin Laden as well as Azzam. Burr and Collins notice that Sheikh Omar symbolized the continuous alienation of Egyptian radicals against the secular Egyptian state.[62] In addition, Sudan also welcomed several dissidents from neighboring countries, including Algeria.

It is clear when Turabi met Laden exactly; some analysts place the meeting between both men in the mid-1980s in Afghanistan,[63] but we cannot be sure when the two men introduced themselves to each other. The important issue is when their mutual relationship was consolidated; it was around 1988 when the two men started to have more personal contacts, and in early 1990, soon after the NIF took over, Turabi contacted bin Laden to discuss some investment projects and the possibility of relocating to Sudan. He also had to contact him soon in order to ask for funds for his Popular Arab Islamic Congress project. In 1988, according to Max Taylor and Mohammed El Bushira's time line, "Bin laden established an initial holding company in

Khartoum (wadi al-aqiq). Wadi al-aqiq used as its bank the Al Shamal Islamic Bank in Khartoum that had ties with al-Turabi and the Ikhwan through one of the bank's founders, Mutasim Abd Al-Rahim."[64] In 1989 bin Laden reportedly began to buy property in Sudan,[65] while in late 1990 bin Laden's family construction company (The bin Laden International Overseas Company) gained contracts to build a new airport at Port Sudan. Osama bin Laden does not appear to have been directly involved in the construction of the airport, but he was subsequently awarded contracts to operate and maintain it.[66] Soon after Laden's arrival in Khartoum, Turabi provided him administrational assistance, security guards, and a house next to his.[67]

During that period the Haqqani Network remained intertwined with al Qaeda. The network, except for his training, assistance, and ideological support, had also been involved in Africa, following bin Laden's footsteps. Jalaluddin had assisted the Eritrean Islamic Jihad Movement (EIJM),[68] while leaders of the EIJM were also enjoying Sudan's hospitality during this period, and al Qaeda reportedly extended financial aid and training to the group at this time.[69]

There was a tendency among the international community to attribute most bombings and terrorism attacks anywhere in the world to him during his period in Sudan; indeed as the records show, the reality is more complicated and even more distorted.[70] The first incident to support that argument was his reluctance to finance terrorist attacks inside Egypt in that period.[71] As noted above, his initial activities in Sudan focused on military training and business ventures in the Horn of Africa. Indeed, he was infuriated with the continuing presence of U.S. military forces in the "holy land" of Saudi Arabia and could not remain for a long time a simple businessman in Khartoum. However, bin Laden provided funding for one of Turabi's most inspired projects, the Popular Arab and Islamic Congress (PAIC), in 1991. The government of Sudan could not support such a project, and the Iranian government failed to fulfill its promise; thus, bin Laden according to reports donated $1 million.[72] The PAIC despite not receiving much publicity had a very unique message from Turabi to the Islamic world, which partially influenced bin Laden: Khartoum and he would always welcome the community of Islam, Sunni and Shia, Arabs and non-Arabs. This first conference, as it is already known,[73] brought together such unlikely bedfellows as Rachid Ghannouchi, the exiled Tunisian Islamist; Georges Habash, Christian Palestinian leader of the Popular Front for the Liberation of Palestine; Shia jihadists of Lebanon; the infamous Carlos the jackal; and representatives of the Iranian Revolutionary Guard.

Much has been written about al Qaeda's connection and involvement in Somalia in 1991–1993.[74] The most compelling study in a Harmony Project issue reports that "by the end of 1992, he began openly discussing the issue of U.S. troops in Somalia. Together with his religious advisor, Mamdouh Salim (aka Abu Hajer al-Iraqi), bin Laden began a campaign to recast the far enemy of Islam as the United States."[75] To begin with, despite the fact that Somalis have participated in the Afghan war against the Soviets and were among the first who were in the forefront of Al-Ittihad al-Islami (AIAI) in the Somali civil war, they seem to have acted independently of al Qaeda's commands and support at least in the early beginnings. A first initial problem within AIAI, which al Qaeda soon confronted, was the nature of Islam in Somalia, which was alien to the strict Wahhabi doctrines. In addition, Somali culture as it has been stressed elsewhere[76] was split into clan lines and xeer. These are the primary sources of law in Somalia, instead of Sharia. Furthermore, AIAI faced internal problems mostly related with field commanders whose approach was more radical and top leaders who were interested in the more moderate approach that Somalia was not ready for being an Islamic caliphate. Indeed, al Qaeda's operatives, as the Harmony document suggests, failed to manage the gap between the AIAI leadership and the poor Islamic education of Somali people.[77] We should always keep in mind that perhaps as in Afghanistan, Somalis were mostly preoccupied with resolving their own internal problems and fighting against the U.S. operations in terms of defending their own country; al Qaeda's objectives at the time were shortsighted and related only to striking the United States to leave the country.

If we would like to summarize al Qaeda's operatives in the Horn in the period of bin Laden's presence in Sudan, we could argue that as he had Khartoum as the base of his operations, he had contacts mainly through Turabi with the Somali leader Mohammed Farah Aideed and AIAI leadership. However, Turabi and Sudanese intelligence worked in a parallel level with Iranian Revolutionary Guards. While the United States was the common enemy, official documentation does not show an established working relationship between these actors, that is, Iran, al Qaeda, Turabi, and Aideed. bin Laden provided Aideed funding and some fighters from Yemen and from the camps he managed in Somalia and Sudan, while Muhammad Atef (aka Abu Hafs al-Masri) made multiple trips to Somalia from al Qaeda's base in Khartoum and met with militant leaders, accessed capabilities, and made connections to provide training and arms to fighters there. The aim of these visits, according to the indictment against him by the U.S. Department of Justice, was to support local forces in attacking U.S. and UN forces in Somalia. It also coincided with a fatwa from bin Laden in 1993 calling for attacks on Western interests in Somalia. This culminated in the deaths of 18 U.S. military personnel on October 3–4, 1993, when three helicopters were downed by al Qaeda-trained Somali militants.[78] However, the early al Qaeda during the period of Somali involvement was somewhat divided as some leaders such as Abdu Walid believed that despite the success of the "Black Hawk Down" operation, the organization should have made strategic rather than tactical actions, thus focusing on their ultimate goal *of Umma*.[79]

Yet, while in Sudan, bin Laden broke his ties with the Saudis. During that period the Saudi government stripped Laden's passport and placed pressure on his family in order to ease his criticism against the kingdom. It was in Sudan that his beliefs crystallized that he fought for a fair cause as he had defended Islam and Muslim lands in Afghanistan, Yemen, and Somalia, and he could accept American presence in his native land and the support of the Saudis in the Palestine peace process.[80] This has been stressed in his letter to the most respected Islamic cleric Abdul Bin Baz in which he pledges for "right of every Muslim to fight the occupation of any Muslim land."[81] Despite not claiming any involvement in the attacks in Riyadh in 1995, bin Laden in March 1995 issued a public indictment against the king and the House of Saud. The attack against the Saudi National Guard used by the American offices in Riyadh in November 1995 has raised much controversy regarding bin Laden's role and involvement. The thoroughly researched books by Bruce Riedel and Jason Burke assert that while the attackers appeared to have been influenced by his writings, there was no assistance from bin Laden.[82] The same appears to be true for the attacks in Khobar barracks a little earlier; while Laden was considered the usual suspect, the orchestrators were Shia Lebanese and Saudi Hezbollah.

Also at that stage Sudan's and Turabi's role in his exodus and the pressure against him were blurred, although many attribute this to a clash of ideologies between him and Turabi, which is partially true given the fact that Turabi criticized the attacks of Algerian Islamists. Nevertheless, ideology was not the crucial factor, and of course, it was not the decisive factor for bin Laden's exodus. Bin Laden left Sudan in order to save Turabi's political existence? This is not, of course, to assert that Laden made a sacrifice. Indeed, Turabi as one of the most realistic Sudanese politicians after independence sought to ensure his own political survival. The event that triggered Laden's exodus was the attempted assassination of Egyptian President Hosni Mubarak staged on June 26, 1995, while his motorcade was heading to OAU meeting in the Addis Ababa headquarters. The attack had been plotted mainly by the troika of Mustafa Hamza, Zawahiri, and Turabi in a series of meetings earlier that year.[83] While Turabi and the NIF denied any involvement in the plot, they called the would-be assassins "messengers of the Islamic faith" and accused Mubarak of having "no personal faith in Islam." Egypt and the Sudanese opposition in exile had no doubt regarding the NIF's involvement and warned Turabi that he would be punished.[84] Sudan at that point was internationally isolated, and a further isolation and a war with Egypt could have been disastrous, given the fact that President Mubarak warned Sudan and hinted that all terrorist training camps operating in Sudan would be bombarded and wiped out. Early in 1996, Egypt used the assassination attempt in order to remove Sudanese presence from the Halayeb Triangle, which had been a disputed territory between Egypt and Sudan since 1956.

Bin Laden was the "victim" of the power play that it was beginning within the Sudanese politics. President Bashir appeared not to have any knowledge of the plot and quickly fired the head of the intelligence services Nafi Ali Nafi and tried to regain control over the intelligence that was falling into Turabi's direction. Thus, there was a growing rift within the Sudan intelligence service, between the military and the NIF, with the army regaining control of the service, despite NIF aggravation. In fact, President Bashir was opposed to doing business with bin Laden and al Qaeda and ordered his officers to stop it. It was at that time, in 1995, that street demonstrators in Khartoum demanded "Prison for al-Turabi," for the first time since the 1989 coup.[85]

THE TALIBAN CONNECTION AND THE WORLD ISLAMIC FRONT (1996–2000)

The Taliban connection of bin Laden is a complicated phenomenon and should be understood within the context of their rise and consolidation in Afghanistan. Thus, before expounding into their connection with bin Laden, we shall examine some aspects of their movement. In 1994, Qandahar was under the control of Mollah Akhound, a former Jia Rabbani loyalist.[86] A group of former students of the *mandrassas*, who called themselves Taliban, rose up and responded to the call of local communities for justice against the brutalities of armed groups. It is important to note that the Taliban mainly comprised of the Pashtun ethnic group, which is about 20 percent of Afghanistan's population, and their representation in the Taliban brought hopes of reviving the Pashtun nationalism.[87] The Taliban also advocated a strict interpretation of the Qur'an and directly implementing the laws of Sharia. But for a movement that came mainly as an assembly of minor commanders of the war against the Soviets and former mandrassas students, the main goal and guiding principle was their interpretation of the Sharia laws blended with local customs. In addition, their sense of bringing justice against moral and political corruption gave them a unique attitude of having a divide mission that should not be hijacked by any of the mujahedeen warlords.

The Taliban leader Mullah Mohammed Omar Mujahed is an ethnic Pashtun; he was a local teacher in the *mandrassas*, and his religious thought has roots in the Deobandi school of thought based in India.[88] Pakistan has been also involved in supporting the Taliban by providing military camps, aid, and assistance. The Pakistani connection is also crucial for the later al Qaeda involvement in the country and has been well documented in a series of books and articles.[89] What we need to stress here is that Pakistani leadership, which was heavily involved in the war against the Soviets and felt abandoned after the end of the war, saw in the Taliban an opportunity toward ending the civil war in Afghanistan even through a proxy.

It is important to note that one of the reasons that led to the acceptance of the Taliban and which actually the Taliban took advantage of was the widening gap between the public and mujahedeen leaders. This is a point that had also disaffected bin Laden while in Afghanistan in the later years prior to his relocation to Sudan. This is further pointed out by a document released by the Harmony Project in which the confidential secretary of al Qaeda supports that it was al Qaeda's insistence on taking a neutral stance vis-à-vis the Afghan civil war that prompted bin Laden to disregard `Abdallah `Azzam's advice of amalgamating the Arab *mujahidin* with the Afghans.[90] Thus, Mullah Omar's call for enforcing order and justice within the country through Sharia found support in local communities. Even the fact that he despised the cosmopolitan Kabul and soon moved to Qandahar was also a symbolic move as Qandahar had a religious significance since the Prophet's cloak was kept in the city's mosque.[91] Initially, the Taliban managed to gain some funding and support from local commanders such as Hajji Bashar, yet claims that Rabbani and Masoud provided funding are still unsubstantiated.[92] It seems by all accounts that initial Taliban goals were mostly tactical rather than strategic. As noted above, they sought to provide local justice, rid the roads of commanders who were charging fees and taxes, and install a legal system based on Sharia. Another important issue is that the Taliban were not at least "objected" by American officials at the time[93] (1994); it's worth noting that some voices including General Mirza Aslam Beg accused the United States of even helping to create the Taliban in order to stop the growing influence of the Iranians and other radical forces. It's worth noting that the Haqqani Network as well as other mujahedeen alumni of the Soviet war did not receive the Taliban well. It is important to observe here that the Haqqani were directly collaborating with ISI and the JUI in Pakistan many years earlier, and the relationship between the Taliban and Pakistan shows that the Pakistani government perhaps used Haqqani as a mechanism to project influence to Mullah Omar as the Harmony Project report states.[94] While it is difficult to stress the full leverage of the Pakistani goals at the time of the consolidation of the Taliban, the ISI hoped of (not aimed for) a Pashtun movement taking the governance of Afghanistan. Second and perhaps most important was the fact that the Pakistani saw the rise of the Taliban and the areas that they controlled as safe getaways in order to project their regional business interests. However, the early relationship between Pakistan and the Taliban was not so easy but rather fragile; the Taliban aimed to gain support and retain some independence. A point to be raised here is that the Taliban sought some financial support and donation from Saudi Arabia, while they also hosted Saudi and Emirates princes, which was totally opposite to the Saudi strategy against bin Laden in that period.

For bin Laden' part, soon after leaving Sudan in 1996, his African adventure seemed to be a squandered opportunity at least with regard to his finances. His multimillion dollar investments and companies were seized by the Sudanese government, and he had lost nearly $30 million, which had nearly bankrupted him. His support for Islamic projects such as Turabi's PAIC and for radical groups such as GIA and Zawahiri's had turned Muslim public opinion against them indeed.[95] However, when he moved to Afghanistan, his experiences from Sudan and his opposition against the Saudis made him a fierce symbol of resistance among radical Islamists.

Indeed, for bin Laden his relocation to Afghanistan apart from its practical significance also had religious significance as he felt that he was filling in the steps of the Prophet, who had moved from Mecca to Medina 14 centuries earlier. Furthermore, it was there that bin Laden took his big leap from opposing the United States to killing Americans.[96] But indeed, we need to further assert the fact that his years in Afghanistan were a tactical move in order to assemble radical Islamists who had failed in Egypt, Algeria, and elsewhere; he united them under a global Salafi banner. It was then that bin Laden exerted a prophetic life with the least comforts, sleeping on the floor, eating, and explaining the struggle of Muslims against the Americans in simple terms by staging that the problems the Muslims were encountering from the United Kingdom to Russia and from Nigeria to Philippines were not issues of racial discrimination but an attack against the world of Islam.[97] As it has been confirmed by many accounts, bin Laden started constructing an organization based on his decision-making capabilities mainly consisting of his inner circle, the *shura* council comprising of Afghan Arab alumnus. However, despite his proclamations noted above, bin Laden remained by all accounts a religious nationalist.

The early relations between al Qaeda and the Taliban were marked by mutual suspicion and conflict from the beginning, and remained turbulent throughout the period of the Taliban regime.[98] Bin Laden's proclivity for media statements during the period of his Taliban consolidation had made Mullah Omar suspicious and sometimes even enraged with continuous press statements and media releases against the West. Thus, it is worth understanding at this point that without their relationship with the Haqqani, perhaps it would have been difficult for bin Laden to project influence in other parts of Afghanistan as well. Therefore, the relationship between Taliban and al Qaeda was not what the conventional wisdom calls "bosom buddies," in Fawaz Gerges's words. Indeed, the Taliban aim as noted above was first to pacify the country and gain support among the population who were disaffected with the civil war. In addition, another issue of contention was the Afghan Arab alumni who remained in Afghanistan and still caused troubles to the newly established regime; the Afghan Arabs switched alliances easily and were not a trustworthy partner for the Taliban. But also for al Qaeda leadership, the alliance with the Taliban was an issue of contention as some believed that they were manipulative of the ISI and Pakistan and their motivation was unclear.[99]

However, some analysts including Bruce Riedel attribute the strengthening of relations between the Taliban and al Qaeda to the deepening international isolation of the Taliban regime, particularly after the killings of Iranian diplomats and an Iranian diplomat in Mashaz i-Sharif and the tension between the Iranians and the Taliban.[100] Thus, we cannot be sure whether this was mainly a "marriage of convenience." Indeed, the lines are extremely blurring. In 1997, according to Abdu Walid's memoir, after a meeting between bin Laden and Mullah Omar, the latter pledged the former "to act as if he was in his own country."[101]

Here we should also add as a case in point the follow of Ayman al-Zawahiri in Afghanistan and the motives behind that relocation. Some attribute this move to his continuous reliance on bin Laden's financial contributions, while others to his exhaustion following the fighting against the Egyptian secular government and the public outcry after the 1997 incident with the foreign tourists in Luxor. Others contend that the fact that other radical Islamic groups announced a ceasefire with the government led Zawahiri to Afghanistan. Indeed, the bin Laden-Zawahiri relationship was surely not as it was 10 years earlier when Zawahiri acted as bin Laden's protégé. Furthermore, bin Laden distanced himself from financing attacks inside Egypt in 1994 and 1995. Nevertheless, Zawahiri's decision to affiliate himself with al Qaeda, which was pledging an alliance with the Taliban, was met with dismay among the Egyptian radical Islamists of al-Jihad and Gama'a al-Islamiya. Jihadis feared that unleashed attacks against U.S. targets will result in an American response against all jihadis (and they were not wrong).

In addition, the rift that was evident after the end of the Afghan war in the late 1980s was still the battle of the soul of the jihadi movement, the rift between transnational and local jihadism. Nevertheless, as noted above, this dichotomy is a binary one given the fact that both bin Laden and Zawahiri embraced this strategy due to their failure to conquest the governments of their respective countries. Furthermore, as Gerges supports, the rift between transnational and local jihad "is an unfolding drama."[102] While it is also true that both bin Laden and Zawahiri were accused by fellow jihadis of huge egos, other jihadis with more realistic views advocated that while they were not able even to win the domestic fronts, mainly Egypt and Algeria, the opening of a global war against a superpower would be at least suicide.

The symbiotic relationship between bin Laden and Zawahiri resulted finally in a team in early May 1997; bin Laden and Zawahiri added Khalid Sheikh Mohammed, a close relative of Ramzi Yousef, mastermind of the 1993 World Trade Center bombings. Khalid seemed very ambitious and presented a number of plans to bin Laden for attacks all over the world. It seems that bin Laden's involvement in the planning and organization of attacks against U.S. targets latched onto individuals such as Khalid, who was highly supportive of killings and attacking Americans.[103] By the 1997–1998 winter, the bin Laden-Zawahiri team could count jihadis such as Rifa'I Ahmed Taha, Sheikh Mir Hamza, and Maulana Fazi ur Rahman as members. Together this small group proclaimed the formation of the World Islamic Front. For the first time in the history of the jihadi movement individuals from across the world joined together and proclaimed war against the sole superpower, the United States, and despite the intention to free the Arabian Peninsula from the American occupation, liberate Palestine, and massacre Iraqis after the UN sanctions in 1991, the true motive that united such characters was pure religious nationalism. This nationalism was easily rallied around the intrusion of the United States into Islam's most holy places. This uniting point brought legitimacy to the nationalistic agenda.[104]

It was not until the strikes against the U.S. East Africa embassies that the West realized the significant threat this new group and its nationalistic agenda represented. Al Qaeda had started planning strikes against U.S. embassies in Tanzania and Kenya in 1993.[105] According to then National Security Adviser Sandy Berger, the attacks represented "a watershed event in the level of attention given the bin Laden threat."[106] By the 1998 attacks, al Qaeda had emerged close to the organization the West became aware of in the early 2000s. The East Africa bombings that targeted U.S. embassies in Nairobi, Kenya, and Dar es Salaam, Tanzania, on August 7, 1998, highlighted al Qaeda's militant capacity and global credentials as a nonstate actor. The key al Qaeda operative who coordinated the planning, logistics, and preparation of explosives for this attack was a native of the Comoros Islands by the name Fadil Hurun (also known as Fazul Abdallah Muhammad).[107,108]

One important outgrowth of the embassy bombings for al Qaeda[109] was the ability of the group to operate within weak states and ungoverned spaces. This was especially true in Kenya, where al Qaeda found a space where its plotters were able to set up business structures, lend aircrafts, and send money abroad. In addition, plotters were also able to take advantage of two Islamic Relief agencies operating in Kenya. Somalia proved a different story. In the Somali Civil War al Qaeda faced logistic problems and finally failed to engage there fully.

The bombing of the *USS Cole* in Aden in 2000 has been described—for no obvious reason other than salvaging American pride—as "sophisticated." Aden's natural harbor is large and the port facilities occupy only a small part of it. There are numerous places around the city from which shipping movements could be easily observed. Refueling takes place at a waterborne refueling platform known as a dolphin. According to a U.S. military source, the dolphin used by *USS Cole* was commercially run and lay about 600 meters out in the sea west of the historic Prince of Wales pier and about 100 meters east of CalTex island.[110] The fuel contractor was Arab Investment and Trading, which was owned by a millionaire Yemeni living in

London but also had heavy Saudi investment. At a first view, Yemen had something obvious in common with Kenya: a weak state environment, but also it was a land that bin Laden had ties with and that had the presence of U.S. troops. According to reports, bin Laden had already financed a training facility in Abayan in South Yemen.[111] Authorities were interested in a man provisionally identified as Abd al-Muhsin al-Taifi, a Yemeni national, possibly with Saudi connections, who was wanted for interrogation about the 1998 bombing of the U.S. embassy in Nairobi. However, one of the masterminds and key connections with the al Qaeda and Yemen was Abu Hamza al-Masri and Mohammed al-Harazi. Hamza was the imam of Finsbury Park mosque in London, and the Britons—for plotting to attack American and British targets in Aden. Abu Hamza was the de facto leader of the Islamic Army who had previously claimed responsibility for several incidents in Yemen, which turned out not to have been terrorist acts. He had ties with British Muslims and the Islamic Army of Aden and had been involved in several kidnappings of Britons in Yemen.[112]

AFTER 9/11 AND THE ROAD TO AFFILIATES

The 2001–2003 period found al Qaeda at a crossroads. Leading Islamic figures around the world condemned the 9/11 attack, among them Egyptian Imam Mohammed Tantawni and Saudi cleric Abdul Aziz Abdullah al-Sheikh.[113] In fact, at that time al Qaeda lacked any public Muslim support. Here perhaps was a huge miscalculation from bin Laden and Zawahiri. Drawing from the Russian invasion in Afghanistan 20 years ago, they thought that Afghanistan could result again in a stunning defeat for the remaining superpower, their goal however directed into gaining credibility in the eyes of the jihadi movement. Nevertheless, that goal of bin Laden and Zawahiri maintained one particular dilemma among the jihadis: the passage from *jahiliyyah*, the period of ignorance, to the period of restoration, *hakimiyyah*. As noted earler, several Islamic scholars thought that al Qaeda had distorted Qutb to fit its own purposes.[114]

The deepest schism was within al Qaeda's ranks. A leadership group expressed mainly by the Egyptian Saif al-Adel, echoed Abu Walid's views. Those in the group opposed the attacks, even as it was forced to flee to Iran; it did not remain silent over the actions of the al Qaeda senior leadership. Other issues brought rifts as well with two groups again as has been described by Abu Walid—the hawks and the doves that debated and fought for the acquisition of weapons of mass destruction (WMD); however, this seems to be a debate of a more theoretical nature.[115] No WMD appear to have been acquired. In addition, at least for a while, post-9/11 security measures restricted the mobility, reduced the number of available meeting places, and made long-distance communication between al Qaeda members difficult, and resulted at least in 2002 in a strategic disorientation of al Qaeda; it seemed that old ideological debates and dividing lines started reappearing. Nevertheless, another issue we should keep in mind in this analysis is the fact that after 9/11, independent cell embodies a new breed of post-9/11 terrorist: men animated and inspired by al Qaeda and bin Laden, but who neither belong specifically to al Qaeda nor directly follow orders issued by bin Laden.[116] This fact had proven to be a two-sided coin: On the one hand, as a consequence of 9/11, there was growing "abuse" of the al Qaeda threat in several countries where until 9/11 al Qaeda had no real connections. From Indonesia to former Yugoslavia, governments exploited the "terrorism menace" in order to fit perhaps their purposes and in order to label local threats as "al-Qaeda" affiliated. On the other hand, al Qaeda-inspired independent cell started to blossom, which made counter-terrorism efforts much more difficult in the years to come. The loss of its training camps in Afghanistan and the killing or capture of much of its pre-9/11 senior leadership resulted into a gradual shift toward inspiring and steering jihadist groups, often only loosely affiliated with the core al Qaeda.

One of the key persons in that evolutionary process was Abu Musab al Suri-a, Syrian and a veteran of the Afghan war against the Soviets. He was responsible for the expansion of al Qaeda's geographical base and advocated for a system of loose self-organizing cells without having to seek higher authority; indeed, he was supportive of a system that "individual terrorism" needed to replace the hierarchically orchestrated terrorism of al Qaeda. This was proven by the fact that al Qaeda itself has not been responsible for the bulk of terrorist attacks since September 11, 2001, and a shift had occurred after 9/11 as associated groups slowly and steadily started building a robust network of members, collaborators, supporters, and sympathizers in the West.[117]

In addition, there were attacks staged by al Qaeda associates or affiliates such as Jema Islamiyya in Bali in October 2002 and in Jakarta; by Assiriyat al-Moustaqim in Morocco in May 2003; by the Islamic Great Eastern Raiders Front in Turkey the following November; and by the jihadist cell comprised mostly of Moroccan nationals responsible for the bombings of commuter trains in Madrid (that killed more than 200 and injured over 1,600 others).[118] The Bali plot was characteristic of the years to come for al Qaeda. The plotters were not linked to al Qaeda in the sense that they were not members; they represented a new generation that have not traveled to Afghanistan, have not met bin Laden or any senior al Qaeda members personally, and drew inspiration from their speeches downloaded from the Internet and magazines. Another major attack by al Qaeda was conducted in Madrid in March 2004. This attack was one of the first by an al Qaeda-affiliated groups that was funded with resources obtained from illegal economic activities. One of the plotters, Jamal Ahmidan, was supposedly involved in large-scale tobacco, heroin, and other drugs trading.

As the Spanish authorities investigation showed, none of the plotters had ever traveled to Afghanistan; they had no connections, no middlemen, and no communication.[119] It is important to see that in this attack the common ground was not an anti-Spanish hostility per se. Despite the fact that the then Spanish prime minister Jose Maria Aznar had supported the U.S.-led coalition, the attacker's mindset was to punish anyone in the country who was counted as collaborating with the Americans.

Jihadis also disagreed on the idea of the caliphate. Many followed the notion that this was a war that they could not win and the promise by bin Laden of an Islamic caliphate was a dead end.[120] The critique was intensified by the Egyptian al-Gama despite the claims of al Qaeda that some of them were agents of the Egyptian regime.[121] However, for Egyptian ideologues after having spent years in prison, bin Laden was highly critical of the use of violence as a political tool. Once again the eternal rift within the jihadi movement remained untouched: religious nationalists against transnational jihadis. Despite this binary image, the Egyptian jihadis such as Karam Zuhdi thought that bin Laden was re-applying his own fatal mistake: instead of trying to build a religious order from bottom-up, they preferred to try the way from top-down.

The background of George W. Bush's administration's decision to invade Iraq has been a subject of controversy and it will not be examined here in detail; it was nevertheless a golden opportunity for an ailing movement at that time. The U.S.-led invasion of Iraq, however, opened up new opportunities for would-be jihadis and various groups there and elsewhere in the world as noted above.[122] They have continued to attack the United States and its allies under the banner of al Qaeda, often with only the most tenuous of connections to al Qaeda central or the original leadership.[123] Some analysts have argued though that the vague picture of al Qaeda shortly before the Iraqi invasion and soon after have contributed toward noneffective responses against it at that time. In fact, the period between 2001 and shortly before 2003 was one of the golden opportunities that the United States had into cracking down al Qaeda once and for all.[124] The persistence on our behalf to the loss of Iraq is essential since it was the first time that al Qaeda attacked Muslims in Muslim lands, which as it will be shown had bitter consequences for the group.

We should also bear in mind that provoked horror and anger among the Muslim world was the leaking of information about abuse by the CIA tactics documented in Abu Ghraib.[125] This seemed to have consequences for the United States especially in Iraq and in the years to come. For example, Jason Burke describes how a moderate Iraqi Abu Mojahed turned into a radical within few months of the American invasion.[126]

The leadership of the old al Qaeda started referring to the looming Iraq War in early October 2002. Moreover, in rural areas of Iraq, local tribes such as those in Fallujah were Sunni conservatives practicing a strict form of Islam, which made them far different from other more urbanized tribes of Iraq. The insurgent movement that emerged postwar constituted a largely indigenous force, with foreign elements playing regular—and deadly—cameo appearances as "force multipliers": those carrying out comparatively rare but highly destructive suicide attacks. Nevertheless, at least in the beginning of the insurgency, as Bruce Hoffman observed, there was no evidence of any direct command-and-control relationship between the al Qaeda central leadership and the insurgents. If there were al Qaeda warriors in Iraq, they were likely cannon fodder, possibly recruited through al Qaeda networks and routed to Iraq via jihadist "rat lines," rather than battle-hardened, veteran mujahideen.[127]

Fallujah became the heart of the Islamic insurgency shortly after the battle of March 2004, which resulted in a defeat for the U.S.-led coalition.[128] It can be thus said that this was a turning point for the future of the jihadi movement in Iraq at least for the following years. It was a turning point in the sense that Islamic militarization and mobilization reached levels that the Muslim world had never seen since the 1967–1973 period. A particularly important guidance document, titled the "Camp al Battar [the sword] Magazine," was released around March 31, 2004. Reportedly written by the late Abdul Azziz al-Moqrin, the reputed commander of al Qaeda's operations in the Arabian Peninsula, it sheds considerable light on the current pattern of jihadist attacks in Saudi Arabia and Iraq.[129]

Following the 9/11 strikes, the debate among jihadi circles took another shape on what to do with the occupation of Iraq by a foreign power. Despite the fact that the existence of two distinct approaches seems binary and does not reflect reality at large, the truth of the matter is that the most obvious tension was among the global and local approach. This dichotomy was best represented by Abu Musab al-Zarqawi in Iraq, who advocated in a sense the local approach, and Abu Musab al-Suri, the Syrian jihadist with Spanish citizenship who was called the architect of the new al Qaeda.[130] Al-Suri was adamant that jihad should be continued and he praised bin Laden for carrying the September 2001 attacks calling it "heroic and glorious." This is not to suggest that al-Suri and Zarqawi were at odds, but they had different approaches to jihad.

In 2003, hostility arose within Iraq's Sunni Arab community at the prospect of a Shia-dominated government. The hybrid al Qaeda in Iraq (AQI) quickly took advantage of the situation and sparked an unrest. The foreign fighters, of which Zarqawi was the recognized leader, represented somewhere between 5 and 10 percent of the total insurgency.[131] It is also important to note that the new thinking in al Qaeda was that foreign fighters that came to Iraq from Saudi Arabia were not members of QAP or the newly founded al Qaeda in the Arabian Peninsula. AQI and AQAP were not connected operationally.[132] There was also discord because of the 2003 Riyadh bombings. Senior members of AQI believed that the events in Saudi Arabia diverted media attention away from the developments in Iraq. During the Iraq War, Zarqawi became a lighting rod for the global jihadist movement, attracting recruits from around the world.

Zarqawi had come to Iraq after the battle of Tora Bora. At the Battle of Tora Bora, Zarqawi escaped the encirclement and was believed to have fled to Iran and later Iraq. Zarqawi had tremendous capability for building a vast network comprised of jihadis across several nations. Once in Iraq, Zarqawi was underestimated as a threat. This proved to be another gross miscalculation for the then U.S. administration.[133]

Up until 2004, Zarqawi believed that bin Laden did not concentrate enough on the Arab-Israeli conflict, and instead focused too much on wars elsewhere—in Yemen, Sudan, Afghanistan, Chechnya, and Bosnia. However, in 2004 Zarqawi renamed his organization al Qaeda in Mesopotamia and formally pledged allegiance to Osama bin Laden.[134] The disagreement over the AQI and al Qaeda goals in Iraq was of central importance and was demonstrated in a letter of al-Zawahiri to Zarqawi in summer 2005 in which he expressed disdain for the latter's indiscriminate attacks on Iraqi civilians, including Shi'a Muslims, and called for Muslim unity.[135] The letter showed the wider picture: it was the unmistakable evidence of the significant differences in strategic thinking and priorities that existed between al Qaeda central and Zarqawi's al Qaeda in Iraq.[136] For Zawahiri the strategic target was to expel the United States from Iraq, establishing an Islamic authority and extending jihadi to secular Muslim countries.[137] In addition to Zawahiri, a Libyan militant named Abd al-Rahman, who had fought in the Algerian front in the 1990s, sent a letter to Zarqawi outlining him his firsthand experiences and how the Algerian jihadis lost the battle.

The Zarqawi case is deductive for the future of al Qaeda-affiliated movements: its loose character after 9/11 led to small groups that have been inspired by al Qaeda central but they had their own agendas and priorities; nonetheless, some of them like Zarqawi balanced between global and local jihad. As Gerges observes correctly, the Iraqi experience was a lost golden opportunity for al Qaeda since it failed to make inroads into the neighboring Arab countries, which in part explains its failure to gain foothold in the so-called Arab Spring later.[138] Anbar in Iraq is an identical example. It served as a crucial portal through which to infiltrate Iraq from either Syria or Jordan. Indeed, many foreign fighters who entered Iraq passed through Syria.

The example of AQI's attempted infiltration of the local society with marriages is identical. Moreover, the harsh tactics such as breaking the fingers of cigarette smokers and murdering women who refused to wear the niqab naturally combined with the attempt to gain foothold into Anbar's lucrative illicit economy alienated locals while several of them were found dead after voting in the 2005 national assembly elections.[139] Indeed, the case of Anbar showed that in large part local groups risked the support of their local communities. Moreover, like in the 1990s, when al Qaeda failed to gain strong foothold in the Balkans, Somalia, and Caucasus, cases like Anbar showed how resistant Muslim populations were to pan-Islamic ideologies.[140]

For Zarqawi, the pursuit of the Iraqi caliphate had a historical impetus; in 1802 the first major operation of Wahhabis outside the Arabian Peninsula was against Shi'a shrines.[141] Zarqawi was also greatly inspired by the twelfth-century Arab sultan Nur al-Din Zangi, who pursued two missions in life—namely, drive out the crusaders from Arab lands and crush the Shi'a rulers. His anti-Shi'a stance, however, was also shared by al-Suri, who pointed to the "negative influence" that Shiite groups like Hezbollah have had on the Palestinian struggle.[142]

At that time in Iraq, a large part of the security forces and police were Shi'a and after the invasion they allegedly collaborated with the United States. Hence, Zarqawi began turning his intentions into actions when after the summer of 2003 to spring of 2004 senior Shi'ite clerics were killed. He was supported by a leading Abu Anas al-Shami based in Fallujah, who claimed that anyone collaborating with the Coalition Authority in Iraq was a non-believer.[143] Hence, the tactics and strategy of AQI were somewhat different from al Qaeda's. For example when they found Sunnis who felt existentially threatened by Shi'a militias or military forces, they offered help from its zealous and highly trained leaders and fighters. In communities not eager for such help, or that resist AQI's efforts to impose its religious code, AQI used violence to terrorize Sunnis into participation.[144]

Zarqawi's tactics of kidnappings, beheadings, and blind suicide bombings led to further alienation from bin Laden and Zawahiri. As the divide grew, bin Laden and Zawahiri's hopes and expectations for the Iraqi front diminished. The best illustration of Zarqawi's estrangement strategy was the November 2005 coordinated bombing attack of three hotels in Amman, Jordan, where innocent civilians lost their lives. His recruitment tactics were focused mostly on the Iraqis in the organization who may not have been pursued by other organizations but would support the violence tactics. In many areas the recruitment process was like that of any street-gang, where the leaders combined exhortation and promises with exemplary violence against those who obstinately refuse to join.[145] His strategy of sectarian cleansing swept through Iraq, further polarizing the Sunni and Shi'ite communities, which resulted in a kind of public apology on bin Laden's behalf in an audiotape in 2007 where he admitted that AQI has made mistakes. Moreover, the Muslim scholar al-Maqdisi, while having warned that fighters should be extra careful in perpetrating these attacks, singled out his former student al-Zarqawi for special criticism for wreaking havoc among Iraqi Muslims.[146]

With the use of camcorders and the Internet, Zarqawi was able to mount international media events at the tactical level, which had a tremendous strategic impact along with his massive suicide bombing campaign that changed once and for all the face of Islamic terrorism.[147]

By early 2006, a deepening rift between native insurgents and the foreign fighters became increasingly evident; thus, the story of Zarqawi's death is well documented elsewhere and his presence perhaps would only deepen the schism. Some of the Iraqi insurgents resented the role of the foreign jihadis in that the latter alienated much of the public through their unrestrained attack.[148] The U.S. air strike that killed Zarqawi on June 7, 2006, deprived AQI of its strategic leader and left the individual under the alias of Abu Hamzah al-Muhajir in charge.

Zarqawi's strategy bears a lot of responsibility not only in his anti-Shi'a notoriety but also in the way he handled relationships with locals as outlined above. Zarqawi relied on fear, intimidation, and brute force in order to enforce his strategy.[149] The AQI's story is identical in order to show how the core al Qaeda split up into five regionally defined clusters, whose centers of gravity are in Iraq, Saudi Arabia, Afghanistan/Pakistan, Southeast Asia, and Europe/North Africa with the Arabian Peninsula and North Africa/Sahel region being our centers of focus in this book.

Since roughly 2006 the balance has shifted from Iraq to mainly the Arabian Peninsula. The loss of Iraq had damaged al Qaeda's profile in the Muslim world notwithstanding blurring the lines between the far/near enemy binary, which is an issue to hold for further analysis.[150] It was the first time after 2006 that al Qaeda's character was confused. Perhaps this is due to the influx of a second wave of jihadis that made no distinction between the far and the near enemy. It was the first time in the mid-2000s that al Qaeda had made no distinction between Muslims and Westerners despite some public denunciations. The other issue that is also important is that members of the AQAP believed it was preferable for Saudi jihadists to stay and fight in the country they know the best, which also caused resentment among al Qaeda's leadership.[151] Despite the fact that European countries seemed to be described increasingly often as enemies of al Qaeda and al Qaeda cells have been evolved in the early 2000s, the issue of the next chapters will be the Arabian Peninsula, which seemed the new spotlight for the transformed al Qaeda.

3

Al Qaeda: The Violence Examined

On May 22, 2013, Michael Adebolajo and Michael Adebowale drove a car into Private Lee Rigby and wielded a meat cleaver in broad daylight on a street in London.[1] The act, according to Adebolajo, was "an eye for an eye" retaliation for the many deaths Muslims had endured at the hands of the West.[2] In an on-the-scene smartphone-captured speech, Adebolajo waved the hacking instrument as he continued a rant, giving no specification of the category of deaths such as those that occurred over the fight for Palestinian homeland or the demand for the removal of any Western presence on the sacred lands of the Two Rivers.[3] The reasoning was general but the act was specific.

The specificity seemed to intensify the viciousness of the broad daylight assassination. But more than intensify the viciousness of one violent event, the specificity signaled a transition in the direction and tactics used by attackers who have a purported connection to al Qaeda. The attack and the attackers exhibited violence and bravado that has become more prevalent over the last 20 years. For instance, in 1993, the first World Trade Center bombing placed civilians eating lunch within U.S. borders in peril.[4] By 1998 the bombings were simultaneous and the destruction was devastating. This was especially true for the families of the 223 killed and over 1,000 injured in the Dar es Salaam, Tanzania, and Nairobi, Kenya, U.S. Embassy bombings.[5,6] The massive blasts' viciousness played on the psyche of the international community because it served as an example of the change in al Qaeda capability to inflict harm. The international community responded by initiating several defensive efforts. Chief among them was reinforcement of protective barriers for critical infrastructure in an effort to mitigate land attacks. Al Qaeda adapted strategy that circumvented those barriers with airplane missiles on September 11, 2001.

The term *vicious* was used in the media to describe the September 11 attacks; al Qaeda took this term as a badge of honor, particularly when describing the devastation wrought from the aftermath.[7] The victims selected were eventually deemed shrewd because of the significant debate it caused on who is an appropriate target for such attacks. Both Sunni and Shi'a clerics held this debate and al Qaeda changed the philosophical dynamic of the terrorism industry.[8,9,10]

But by 2003 when Zarqawi moved into Iraq, he brought the drama of shock and awe with a vicious attack's visual effect readily available in the international community's living rooms. The best example of that was the May 7, 2004, beheading of Nicholas Berg.[11] Zarqawi recorded the event and distributed the tape on the Internet.[12] The worldwide response was one of horror. The worldwide media response was one of absolute intrigue. Recording executions today does not have the same response that became prevalent when Zarqawi started the trend. He did foreshadow the AQI/ISIS propensity for shock and awe, which leverages the chaos theory initiated by Zarqawi. The post-2012 period of attacks and advancement appears to implement Zarqawi's plan detailed in a letter seized in 2004. In the letter Zarqawi expresses intentions to cause sectarian strife; remove the Shiite "prowling serpent"; undermine the Iraqi government, soldiers, and police; and bring the Kurds to AQI's way of thinking.[13] Abu Akbar al-Baghdadi's calculated plan of chaos is well on its way to fulfilling all of these, and more.[14,15,16]

The technique of highlighting individuals with whom the viewer could form a bond did not become a staple for al Qaeda. Instead there was continued reliance on the viciousness of large-scale attacks. In particular, al-Baghdadi's troops focused on large-scale executions of Shiites during 2011–2014. One such mass killing made available through a posted video presented Iraqi soldiers forced onto trucks and then made to lie in shallow ditches.[17] ISIS members then proceeded to fire at the prone men, killing them all. According to the tweet announcing the event, a total of 1,700 soldiers lost their lives this way.[18] It is quite likely the taped executions were conducted to demonstrate ISIS's ability to do whatever it wanted, as its area of control extended into more and more of Iraq and Syria. The ultimate goal was to instill fear.[19] This was evident by the reports of fear in Baghdad as ISIS announced a "wave of suicide bombings" that would precede a forward push that would end with attacking Baghdad.[20,21]

In February 2014, Boko Haram, al Qaeda's Nigeria affiliate, initiated coordinated attacks that targeted universities, hospitals, and remote villages.[22] By May attacks were launched using chainsaw machetes and car bombs.[23] Between May 7 and June 2, 2014, Boko Haram killed 654.[24] More than

3 million people abandoned their homes and land to seek refuge elsewhere.[25] The group's attacks drastically changed from 2006 through 2012, demonstrating the change in approach to violence it learned from al Qaeda training.[26,27] Al Qaeda has exploited the social transitions of that change in violence by leveraging the impact of political, social, and cultural underpinnings.[28] But one fact was often overlooked as each of the attacks occurred; each individual perpetrator had to make a conscious decision within the quiet of their own soul to participate.

The road to that decision is not widely understood, but must be to analyze the process followed to execute attacks to become more vicious.[29] That viciousness is wielded like a tool used to leverage the fear produced as al Qaeda advances through towns and villages toward its next targets.[30] This was demonstrated in the June 2014 fast-moving strikes and attacks of ISIS on Mosul, Tikrit, Fallujah, Ramadi, and Baiji. ISIS, which started taking control of towns and villages in conflict-ridden Syria in 2013, followed those successes with towns along the Tigris and Euphrates rivers in Iraq.[31] All the conquered towns help ISIS move toward its goal of creating one region between Iraq and Syria, one that "smash[es] the Sykes-Picot border."[32] At each town ISIS enforced a draconian set of laws they define as Sharia. In Raqqa they sent child soldiers to the front, beheaded or executed by firing squad those deemed in violation of their defined Sharia law, crucified those who do not submit, and then deposited violators' bodies in mass graves—with no chance of a proper Islamic burial.[33] In Mosul they issued a Twitter statement saying the goal was to "cleanse it of apostates."[34] This cleansing required "Shias, heterodox, Shia Alawites, Christians and members of other minorities" to agree to one of three options, "conversion to Islam, acceptance of the new rules or death."[35] Al Qaeda Sharia law is in violation of the Qur'an's Sura II, verse 256, "There is no compulsion in religion," and the Christians and Jews are considered "people of the book" as specified in Sura II, verse 62:

> Indeed, those who believed and those who were Jews or Christians or Sabeans [before Prophet Muhammad]—those [among them] who believed in Allah and the Last Day and did righteousness—will have their reward with their Lord, and no fear will there be concerning them.[36,37]

ATTACK TARGETS

The government's military unlucky enough to be in the path of the ISIS onslaught was so consumed with fear of the oncoming "doom" that a significant number abandoned their posts and uniforms in order to flee. As ISIS neared towns, they threatened local police and soldiers and warned local leaders. For those who did not respond appropriately, suicide bombers killed the "recalcitrant."[38,39,40] Captured Shi'a soldiers were reportedly victims of mass executions and beheadings. ISIS reportedly rounded up the soldiers from the Iraq army and shot those who were Shiite. Bodies of some were "dumped in the Tigris River."[41] The heads of some of the dead bodies were severed; one was even kicked soccer ball style in honor of the World Cup games.[42] More than half a million residents fled the cities seeking refuge anywhere else but home.[43] Dislocation is the preferred alternative to adding to the mounting casualty count for the year.

Casualty counts have been conducted in Iraq since 2003.[44] Started in 2003 to ensure accurate reflection of deaths occurring in the war-torn nation, the count provides monthly totals based on daily database entries. These entries reflect the clashes between not only U.S. troops and insurgents but insurgents and civilian residents as well. Patterns have emerged where increased activity are noted in the spring and less action in the winter. But even when these expected fluctuations occur, there are strikingly acute points when the increase in deaths reflects significant increased action. Using the first five months of each year, we can see this over the 2003–2014 time period. Whereas the 2003–2006 January–February time period historically showed casualties that doubled or tripled by April or May, in the 2007–2008 U.S. troop surge period, the Iraq casualty numbers significantly reduced.[45,46] By 2009–2012 the numbers were truly trending downward.[47] But the knowledge of imminent U.S. troop withdrawal emboldened ISIS attack planners and the casualties strikingly increased for the same January–February period from 2011–2012 to 2013–2014. Compared to 2011, just two years before the increase, the body count is often threefold, from 389 in 2011 to 1,076 in 2014.[48] The April–May time periods show similar spikes compared to 2011–2014.[49] For those time periods the numbers jumped from 289 and 381 respectively (April–May) in 2011 to 1,013 and 1,027 in 2014.[50]

But the "numbers" represent people, and the reports of casualties are families whose lives have been drastically altered by how the people died. Reports of beheadings, point-blank murder, or torture and then murder precede the ISIS as they tighten the tentacles to move in on the people of Mosul, Tikrit, and Fallujah.[51] There were also reports of shakedowns for protection money already occurring in the city of Mosul, shakedowns reminiscent of mobster-organized crime tactics.[52] A suicide bomber targeting local Shi'a leaders reportedly hit Sadr City. The death toll from that ISIS calling card was estimated at 15 or more with 34 wounded.[53]

THE BACKDROP

When Abdullah Azzam first outlined al Qaeda in 1987–1988, he saw an organization that acted as "a rapid reaction force" defending oppressed Muslims.[54] The definition of oppressed Muslims is not specifically identified as much as the concept of regaining territories lost "into enemy hands." The land becomes the central focus, with the moniker of "sinner" attached to guidance on who should participate and the ferocity with which to retake the lands.[55] "All Muslims are sinners as long as any country that was once Muslim is in non-Muslim hands."[56] The battle for the whole of "all lands" needed the counter of identifying why the land had to be retaken to begin with—in essence he was justifying a world battlefield rather than previous battlegrounds drawn because of UN Resolution 181 and Palestinian partitioning.[57]

Under that earlier focus, Hezbollah and Hamas were considered the most influential militant groups, demanding the removal of Israel and creation of a Palestinian state. When Yasser Arafat declared the Palestinian state in November 1988, his act was considered bold but it was still a stand within the accepted stratagem of Palestine and Israel coexisting.[58]

Abdullah Azzam altered the discussion four years earlier by not centering on Palestine. Rather he stated and established a call to arms for the larger "struggle." His declaration of war in his 1984 *Defense of Muslim Lands* was bold and imaginative. It harnessed the entire Muslim population as cadre, using one unifying factor—Islam.[59] It was also a precursor to Osama bin Laden's 1996 and 1998 declarations of war against the United States and its allies.

During the 1979–1988 fight for Afghanistan, the international community framed the struggle in the context of a removal of an invading force. But Azzam's treatise "The Defense of Muslim Territories" started transitioning the focus to one of believers versus non-believers. This began the transition of message control from the superpowers to the jihadists, permitting the change in the central focus of the fray to create a ground swell for the future fight that toppled a superpower. It opened the flood-gate of fighters from across the world. There is nothing new about fighters from other countries supporting a fight/cause that might not be described as "their own." Americans went to England before the United States entered World War II, and several countries had citizens support Spain's Franco. Success fired the imagination of Afghanistan's fighters and buoyed the arguments Azzam put forth in his 1984 treatise. Azzam stated that "every Arab who wants to wage jihad in Palestine may start there, but those who cannot should go to Afghanistan."[60]

By thus redefining the Palestinian struggle, Azzam not so much dismissed the earlier attempts of framing the struggle through the fight for the Palestinian state as much as he extended Palestine's borders to that of Afghanistan through the defense of Islam. The land is the concrete/tangible representation, but the religion is the mesh that weaves through each "neglected" concrete structure. Azzam takes his generation to task for the sin of neglecting "contemporary issues like Afghanistan, Palestine, the Philippines, Kashmir, Lebanon, Chad and Eritrea." In that tasking, Azzam starts with a struggle for land. He off-handedly accuses the previous generation of "allowing" former Muslim land "to fall."[61] He keeps his eye on the prize of Palestine but places more in his basket than just Palestine. The land meant more than Palestine and the removal of Israel from the region. He insists that former efforts were inadequate as he frames the newer discussion and its potential. Afghanistan and its civil war are critical because they provide the controlled violence of a structured war to launch the great goal—the global Islamic effort.

When bin Laden outlined a plan to use jihadi funds to train members in terrorist tactics to achieve this goal, Azzam refused. He seemingly differentiated his rapid response force from a terrorist tactics organization.[62] The training camps Azzam and bin Laden had initiated for training in Afghanistan civil war were destined from different end goals after the civil war ended, depending on who won the argument.

Azzam's timely death made the point moot, and the cadre of individuals that has evolved easily made the transition to terrorist tactics because of the training that began in the camps of Afghanistan and Pakistan, and is now conducted through *Insight Magazine* and online social media.

Does the transition mean the countries themselves are no longer of import? On the contrary, the land remains the focus, and it is the land for which policy development and action considerations remain center stage. While rhetoric and slogans abound, it is important to watch the transitions that have occurred in the execution of tactics and the attitude toward the former colonial powers that were and still remain in the region. France and Britain are easy targets because of Algeria and the countries where al Qaeda is currently demonstrating strength. Using those we can see a trajectory toward future growth not only in Africa but in China and (given some new overtures) in Japan as well.[63]

These considerations of land, policy, rhetoric, and slogans help frame the examination of the violence, and the ferocity associated with it, from an organizational perspective. Caruso et al. propose that al Qaeda positions itself as a "contest organizer."[64] According to Caruso, organizations make the rational decision to participate in the competition for al Qaeda approval and recognition. Part of that competition is to execute attacks that demonstrate certain characteristics, like a "self-starter" capability. The competition aspect of this hypothesis assumes a limited number of openings that achieve al Qaeda approval.[65]

The Heart of the Matter

When the fighters left Afghanistan for their home countries, they took with them a desire, and a mandate, to continue the struggle. Azzam was dead and the organization that remained had been given license to kill. Bin Laden wanted the same successful regime-changing result that had occurred in Afghanistan to occur in Yemen, Chechnya, the Philippines, and Pakistan. Bin Laden, and Ayman Zawahiri, militarized the jihad movement, creating fighters adept in "weapons handling, battlefield maneuvering and explosives."[66] One such fighter, Abu-Jandal, had an "emotional" journey to jihad. A member of the generation after Kamal el-Said Habib, Abu-Jandal was aware of the Islamic Ottoman Empire and the West-backed regimes of the Middle East. To him the West had brought shame to Islam. But he also watched the successful establishment of Islamic governments in Iran, and even Sudan and Afghanistan. He did not want to miss an opportunity to be a part of that "revolution."[67] He ran away from home to join "a mission of martyrdom."[68] He was stuck in Yemen for a year but listened to the news of the successes that were occurring without him.[69] But he also saw accounts of children dying and women and old people suffering violence in Bosnia-Herzegovina. He had to take up the sword to defend them.[70] Was he like the young in 1930 helping Spain, or the respondents to the call to free Afghanistan from the Soviet Union just years earlier? He fought in Bosnia. He defended "the weak and oppressed" of Somalia.[71] As they returned, they looked at the homefront differently. Many did not even want to go home. They knew they had the power of change. In Afghanistan they were trained on and equipped with firepower hardware from the West.[72] After Afghanistan, some of the al Qaeda-associated veterans of that conflict headed to other nations to fight the revolution there. Some headed home to fight for change there. Those fighters who did return to their home countries had a goal of inserting chaos into whatever situation they found with the hope of achieving the destabilization results achieved in Afghanistan. If they could oust what was at that time one of the two world superpowers, then challenging their own governments was no problem.

When they returned home they fanned the fires of unrest, hoping to spark great rebellions.[73] Countries like Iraq, Yemen, Syria, and Mali did not immediately respond with open rebellion. So, to achieve its desired end, al Qaeda stirred the fire of discontent important to achieve a steady stream of dissatisfaction with the young, who could eventual function as lower level personnel. Helped by the U.S. policy that was framed as continuing colonial control and contrary to the Qur'an, these areas became areas of growth. Al Qaeda and its affiliates learned to fan the flames of discontent from both the stance of the U.S. occupation and the failed or fragile governments' unresponsiveness to the needs of the people. The United States was the "colonial occupier" and the failed states showed how a secular government failed the ummah.

These two stances created an atmosphere of discontent that the Afghanistan warfare returnees could exploit, a role they were trained to leverage. Over time other countries like Nigeria, Niger, Mali, and Mauritania have responded to that same "break colonial control" message, offering additional opportunities for al Qaeda to market its violence products.

Al Qaeda's requirement to develop "product," that is fighters, changed over time. Initially the number was contingent on the number of physical training facilities. But the United States and its allies began to exert external pressures that resulted in the loss of those camps and the critical personnel who staffed them. Al Qaeda had to find alternate approaches to attacks and management controls. This forced al Qaeda to morph into a resilient organization that can withstand those forces initiated from the West, including increasing its use of low-technology explosive devices to counter the high-technology firepower used by the West. Al Qaeda did incorporate high technology for electronic communication in order to more easily connect to target audiences.

During his trial, Michael Adebolajo insisted that he had cut Fusilier Rigby's throat, after ramming him with a Vauxhall Tigra, in retaliation because "your people have gone to Afghanistan and raped and killed our women."[74,75] Nowhere does he refer to the colonization remnants that are reflected in Nigerian life; instead the only country mentioned is Afghanistan. His intentional decision to perpetrate violence navigated a conscious decision-making process that did not steer in the direction of personal/individual heritage. The question is, are others navigating the same or similar decision-making processes using the same route? Radicalization is an external process; the internal process is the counter that must be understood.

Adebolajo's entire speech is faintly reminiscent of one given by Ayman Zawahiri at his December 1982 trial for aiding/supporting the assassination plot of Anwar Sadat. Zawahiri, too, claimed, "[W]e are not sorry, we are not sorry for what we have done for our religion, and we have sacrificed, and we stand ready to make more sacrifices!"[76] Zawahiri lashed out at the Nasser leadership, not only because of the Jewish presence in the region but also because of the torture inflicted on him and his fellow defendants.

Zawahiri had gone into prison as a quiet supporter; he emerged a hardened zealot bent on exacting revenge for the wrongs he insisted the regime had inflicted.[77] Low-technology tactics, particularly improvised explosive devices (IED), were initially employed out of necessity, but IEDs became a staple when they proved extremely successful against the West's high-technology-dependent countering tactics. IEDs could be employed in the urban environment of Iraq and Afghanistan, locales that did not readily accommodate U.S. armored personnel carriers.

As al Qaeda employed these low-technology devices to destroy equipment and people in Afghanistan and Iraq, they also conducted reconnaissance on critical infrastructure within the bounds of the United States.[78] This ranged from railroads to natural gas deposits to crucial bridges that cross over essential submarine fiber-optic cable.[79] Low-technology IEDs accurately positioned and then exploded against these vital vulnerable structures would also be classified vicious as they could devastate lives, incomes, and business economic contributions within the region of attack. Al Qaeda personnel have possessed the skills to conduct such attacks as far back as 1994. In that year, Khalid Sheikh Mohammed, an engineer who worked in the Qatar water industry, planned attacks for an operation that came to be known as Operation Bojinka, a precursor for the September 11, 2001, attacks.[80] Since then al Qaeda has made it a point to recruit highly trained technical personnel. Among those al Qaeda approached were nuclear physicist Adlene Hicheur, biology student Samir al-Baraq, and biologist and chemist Abu Khabab al-Masri.[81,82] Its success with cyber experts has also long been keenly felt with young people like Younes Tsouli and Abu Anas al-Libi.[83,84] Al Qaeda has resources available to it that include not only its own electronic army but also the Chinese cyber hackers and Tunisian cyber army.[85] One of the most recent was Boko Haram's unauthorized electronic entrance into the Nigerian elite secret spy agents' personnel records.[86] The hackers then made all the agents' personal data public, thus compromising each of the agents and their families, making them vulnerable to any who may want revenge.[87] Al Qaeda is well aware of the Western world's dependence on information technology to control infrastructure necessities such as water, electricity, financial systems, and hospital data sharing.[88] Compromise of such structures could cause "violent" harm in that the cyber attacks would intentionally use electronic injurious force against a person or an organization, leading to havoc across critical systems.

REGIONAL USE OF VIOLENCE

An assessment of al Qaeda, ISIS, AQAP, and AQIM violence by organization and country reveals several critical points. Organizationally speaking, from the beginning al Qaeda central focused on plans and events that minimized Muslim civilian casualties and maximized conventional media response. Western response to counter al Qaeda attacks centered on leadership like Osama bin Laden and, to a lesser extent, Ayman al-Zawahiri. There was a firm belief that removal of reported critical personnel and pummeling suspected places of refuge were key to dismantling the organization.[89] ISIS, and its Zarqawi-initiated predecessor Tawhid wal Jihad, created a reign of terror that made al-Zawahiri respond with a letter of chastisement for the loss of civilian life Zawahiri felt was unnecessary.[90] Zawahiri cautioned Zarqawi against the vicious attack method, advocating persuasion instead. Zawahiri felt persuasion was the more productive approach with civilian populations.[91,92] While under the al Qaeda banner, the senior-subordinate relationship with al Qaeda central was often tense. But that is no longer a concern since ISIS no longer considers itself part of al Qaeda. The declaration of the caliphate negates the need for any such organization. As a matter of fact, under the new rules instituted by ISIS, organizations like its previous iteration (Tanzim Qaidat al-Jihad fi Bilad al-Rafidayn or al Qaeda in Iraq) would face harsh punishments.[93] It must have been infuriating for Zawahiri to have Abdul Majeed Aleftara Rimi, one of Yemen's top imams, urge Zawahiri to declare allegiance to the very man he had denounced just a few months earlier.[94]

But the affiliate relationship existed during the formative period and was pivotal to orchestrating the series of events that led to the new caliphate even existing. Immediately after declaring the caliphate, however, ISIS closed the door on new entrants who might try the same tactic.[95] ISIS clamped down on all who might offer dissent against the new regime, instituting strict guidelines of behavior and interaction, making it clear that violators faced severe consequences of not adhering to those rules and guidelines.[96] There is no effort to win the hearts and minds of people through a justification of violence used to implement ISIS version of Sharia law.

AQAP, on the other hand, remains cognizant of the people and the support that can be crucial to governance longevity.[97] AQAP's predecessor organization in Saudi Arabia could not muster a wide support for violent tactics to remove the sitting monarchial government. Without popular support, AQ in Saudi Arabia leadership fled to Yemen when the Saudi Arabian monarchy effectively countered their tactics. That escape to Yemen did not diminish the hope of removing the Saudi Arabian ruling family. It simply created an effective buffer space for retooling the AQ of Saudi Arabia into a merged AQY plus AQ of Saudi Arabia to become AQAP.[98] AQAP also had a less-productive economy in Yemen than ISIS had in Iraq. Using violence to extort protection money would not have been fruitful. The Yemeni people were also tired of violence from the Houthi and al Qaeda in Yemen and Ansar al-Dine. AQAP strategically executed its violence, concentrating on suicide bombings, assassinations, and other targeted attacks that minimized Muslim population casualties.[99] AQAP is credited with kidnapping the Iranian diplomat Nour Ahmad Nikbakht; planning the 2009 Christmas Day attempted suicide bombing of Northwest Airlines flight 253; attacking the Italian, British, and U.S. embassies; and killing 90 Yemeni soldiers.[100,101,102] AQAP, guided by its Emir Nasser al-Wahayshi, is loyal to Zawahiri and his philosophy.

AQIM, on the other hand, is an outgrowth of the Algerian Groupe Islamique Arme's (GIA) struggle against France and the government it wants to replace with an Islamic state. AQIM introduced coordinated suicide bombing attacks as a tactic in Algeria, escalating the country's violence tremendously. Over time AQIM increased direct violence against political or government entities and then transitioned to other illegal activities, ones that generated needed revenue. Instead of executing violence against establishment representatives, AQIM expressed their disdain for descendants of the colonial era and started a campaign to selectively kidnap visitors of

Northern Africa who were from countries known to pay ransom. AQIM saw this as a guaranteed revenue stream to replenish al Qaeda coffers on a constant basis. This guaranteed funding was supplemented by revenue from drug trafficking and transportation of contraband (both human and product). Recent AQIM violence have centered on the results achieved by groups associated with AQIM. AQIM is training organizations like Boko Haram, infiltrating already existing conflicts like that in Mali, and training personnel to execute missions and attacks that employ the highly successful violent tactics used by AQIM experts.[103] Among its trainees are personnel from counties like Mali, Pakistan, Algeria, and Mauritania.[104]

What Violence Tells Us

Al Qaeda is in the business of terror with its "fear" as its chief product. It uses several tools to create an environment that makes fear a desirable product to achieve its desired end. Violence is just one such tool. When al Qaeda's initial investors seeded the organization, they recognized it was a long-term endeavor. Those initial investments paid off with the current configuration of al Qaeda a modification of the initial and the organization considered the most recognizable competitor in the terrorism business. Its strengths, weaknesses, opportunities, and threats have been identified, and its mission[105] value function that results after merging the trust in Islam with the specifics of event execution is as follows:

$$V_m = f\{(c + t + m_q + m_f)\}^I$$

where:

V_m = Islamic business value of the mission
c = cost of the mission
t = time from planning through mission execution
m_q = quality of the mission execution
m_f = quality of the mission functionality to the jihad
I = Islamic perspective

Mission cost is the total of the financial resources needed for the mission; time includes planning as well as execution time; and the quality of the execution and functionality are subjective.[106] While cost and time are finite, the exponent I applies the subjective assessment of the impact of Islam on the mission. With this functionality to the jihad also includes the profit, future ability to leverage this event, and perceived and actual return on resource investment to execute the mission.

The business value function includes the result raised to the power of the projected influence exerted by Islam on all factors. Mission functionality captures factors like profit, marketability, and improved investor return on investment. Grounding al Qaeda in Islam, bin Laden and Zawahiri structured the organizational relationships so that they represented a contract with each of the individuals and the individual's spiritual commitment. But al Qaeda's adherence to the mission function, that is, the ability of the mission to further jihad either from a uniqueness perspective or through media response, demonstrated that a metric is used to determine successful use of the violence. This was particularly evident when ISIS issued its second annual report.[107] The report identifies areas of performance and areas of "improvement statistical."[108]

Given the ISIS reports, using return on investment (ROI) as a metric follows the group direction and offers the ability to apply business tactics to al Qaeda, or al Qaeda-like organization/business entity. The metric could then be used in a terrorism-monitoring tool that would track the "business ramifications" of an event, whether it is violent or nonviolent. This would permit assessment of recruitment campaigns, video distribution, establishment of food distribution points, or the abduction of women and girls from their homes or schools. This information would be available to all including group constituencies. This Terrorism Venture Index can act as a platform that maintains general descriptions of the national, regional, and local economic impact of events (violent and nonviolent). It can also track trends within the industry and note shifts in business operation and performance.[109]

Quarterly statements, always with the caveat that these are estimates, can facilitate comparisons, trend analysis, and valuations. Each organizational assessment can remain as unbiased as possible with tangible asset inclusion in valuation. Among the assets that can be included are personnel, real estate, office equipment, and weaponry. Each category can of course have subcategories, so that personnel can include estimates on numbers, areas of expertise of known members, and affiliations of those personnel. These affiliations are separate from the organization-to-organization affiliations. Both would be included. Indices for other areas of review can include civilian deaths, business closures in area of operation, jobs lost, schools closed, and children not receiving education.

All could be maintained within a New York Stock Exchange index environment. A classification coding similar to the North American Industry Classification System and/or the Kompass International Neuenschwander SA can act as the central repository to access all organization-related data. Graphs and data assessment displays and reports can be generated. The information may offer a means to balanced, non-emotive, assessments of gaps, opportunities, and policy directions.

Underlying this mission analysis is an assumption that the "violence" designed to occur during the mission/event/attack is an element the terror group believes it controls. The ISIS annual report offers some insight into

Kompass International Neuenschwander SA (Proposed)

Al Qaeda
Bait al Ansar
Peshawar, Pakistan[1]
www.alneda.com[2]
www.jihadunspun.com

Products and Services
Nature of Business
Activities
Disruption; Fear; Technical and physical threats to objects, security, citizens;
Anti-security/theft services; Informational services; Fear consultations;
Special explosion techniques and services, Research and development for
security threat devices.

P – Producers
D – Distributors
S – Service provider
E – Export
I – Import

P/D	Disruption
D	Fear
E/I	Technical and physical threats
P/D	Fear consultations
S	Anti-security/theft
P/D	Research and development

[1]Abedin, M. (2004) "The Essence of al Qaeda: An Interview with Saad al-Faqih" Spotlight on Terror
Vol. 2, Issue 2. The Jamestown Foundation. Online Reference to al Qaeda guest house. http://
www.jamestown.org/publications_details.php?volume_id=397&&issue_id=2907
[2]Use of original known al Qaeda websites rather than any known current ones is intentional. This
display is for demonstration purposes only.

Figure 3.1   Proposed International Community Industry Code Entry

the validity of that assumption. If this violence is a tool that can be controlled, then it can be examined for its efficiency and effectiveness. Identifying that efficiency and effectiveness may offer a key to unlocking our
understanding of the impact a relationship, whether former or current, with
al Qaeda may have on a group's use of resources, and the ability to adapt to
changing circumstances. As the ISIS/al Qaeda phenomenon evolves, that
efficiency and effectiveness assessment may also expand to the financial
and psychological "violence" of cyber and WMD attacks. These can be studied as additional data become available.

Kimble, testing the feasibility of such efficiency and effectiveness assessment, has already conducted one initial and one follow-on study.[110] Kimble mined the open-source Global Terrorism Database (GTD) for data on attacks executed by 18 specific organizations between 1990 and 2012.[111] The 18 organizations were selected from the Al Qaeda and Associated Movements Matrix Exercise provided by Zimmerman in *The Al Qaeda Network: A New Framework for Defining the Enemy.*[112]

Kimble's analysis appears to accommodate the fluid relationship that exists among the organizations by retaining unique datasets for predecessor groups, prior to the groups' evolving to al Qaeda affiliation.

Table 3.1. Efficiency and Effectiveness Assessment Organizations

Organization	Relationship	Notes
Al Qaeda in the Arabian Peninsula	Affiliate	Al Qaeda in Saudi Arabia and al Qaeda in Yemen data were also separately reviewed
Al Qaeda in the Islamic Maghreb	Affiliate	
Al Shabaab	Affiliate	
Al Qaeda in Iraq	Affiliate	
Islamic Emirate of the Caucasus	Affiliate	
Haqqani Network	Associate	
Jundallah	Associate	
Tehrik-e-Taliban Pakistan	Associate	
Abu Sayyaf Group	Associate	
Groupe Salafiste Pour la Predication et le Combat (GSPC)	AQIM Predecessor	Data for years prior to AQIM analyzed
Lashkar-e-Jhangvi		
Lashkar-e-Taliba		
Boko Haram		
Ansar-al-Islam		
Tawhid al-Jihad	Al Qaeda in Iraq Predecessor	
Jemaah Islamiyah	Associate	

Source: Courtesy of David Kimble.

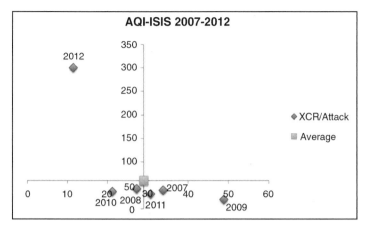

	2007	2008	2009	2010	2011	2012
Leadership Change	-	-	-	X	-	-
Key Personnel Addition	-	-	-	-	-	-
Key Personnel Subtraction	X	X	X	X	-	-
Internal Dispute	X	-	-	-	-	-
US/Western Pressure	X	X	X	X	-	-
Local/Regional Pressure	X	X	X	X	X	X

Figure 3.2   AQI-ISIS Efficiency and Effectiveness Factors (*Source:* Courtesy of David Kimble)

The initial assessment examined the efficiency and effectiveness for groups defined as having received "both resources and guidance from al Qaeda Central" to determine if a correlation existed between receipt of resources and guidance and group efficiency and effectiveness.[113] Looking at the resources and guidance as input and the attack results as output, the initial study indicated some positive correlations existed. The groups also appeared to fall into three categories: those who could sustain moderate or high efficiency, those who could not, and those who fluctuated. Examination of those who displayed variations in the ability to sustain increased efficiency and effectiveness prompted the follow-on study. In the follow-on study, internal and external pressures like leadership change, key personnel additions or subtractions, and internal disputes were identified for each of the groups. The efficiency and effectiveness rates for each group were again examined in relation to these additional factors. The original results were reinforced with focus on factors like leadership.[114]

Kimble offers one data analysis to glimpse at possible new paths to analysis patterns for terror groups, but as Michael Adebolajo and Michael Adebowale have demonstrated, non-group-affiliated events must be studied as well. Several have already been conducted, one even looking at the definition of a "group" and "lone actor."[115] In *Tracing the Motivations and Antecedent Behaviors of Lone-Actor Terrorism* from the International Center for the Study of Terrorism, Paul Gill indicates that so-called lone-actors reflect ideological subgroups.[116] The report traces some of the network relationships lone-actors develop prior to actually executing a violent event. These relationships and their group dynamics can work with results from analyzed data related to organizational event and activity output.

Significant data are available to assess violence as a controlled tool. Some of those data are perpetrator generated. Abu Bakr Naji offers one approach when he discusses violence as a tool and the opportunities it offers against the West in his *Management of Savagery: The Most Critical Stage through Which the Umma Will Pass*. Well versed in Western culture, Naji uses this knowledge to outline approaches that can leverage Western weaknesses. ISIS appears to have read, digested, and implemented the advice provided in Naji's document. ISIS could be said to have implemented phase two when they coopted the civil disturbances in Syria and Iraq. Phase three, the caliphate, occurred when, with no impediment in sight, ISIS moved through Mosul, Fallujah, and Tikrit with relative ease.[117,118,119] Violence, as prescribed by Naji, is a fundamental tool for achieving the goal of the caliphate and avenging the "wrongs" imposed with Sykes-Picot and its associated agreements and is a "justifiable" action.[120] It must be recognized that ISIS violence is not going totally unanswered. The Kurdish fighters in semi-autonomous northern Iraq have engaged in a back-and-forth territory control since 2013.[121] ISIS has tried to take control of several western Iraqi towns that Kurdish forces control. This has incensed the Kurdish leaders and military commanders. These "peshmerga" (those who face death) are intent on fighting diligently to avoid that loss of control.[122]

ISIS's controlled approach to the violence tool is seen in its continued and escalating use of that tool. As media coverage focuses on beheadings, mass killings, and abductions, ISIS repeats the process. Counting the number of attacks and examining the weapons used for those attacks offers one response. However, it does not address the nuances of each type of attack. Differentiation between AQAP's printer bomb, underwear bomber, and Charlie Hebdo attack and ISIS's conscription, extortion, beheadings, and Jordanian pilot burning are critical to strategic understanding and effective response.[123,124] ISIS burning of the Jordanian pilot was ferocious. For instance, when Boko Haram, the ISIS of North Africa, advance across their targeted regions, fear grips the people who live in those regions. That fear overwhelms the people of towns like Baga who flee before Boko Haram arrives. Boko Haram's violence creates a buffer zone that precedes the violence perpetrators. That is because Boko Haram's reputation for viciousness justifiably panics villagers or townspeople who flee in advance to avoid the mayhem and protect their lives. They recognize that the under-resourced Nigerian army, which will probably be overwhelmed without much resistance, is not a protection mechanism on which they can depend.[125,126] The viciousness of the violence offers a mechanism for Boko

Haram to present its constituents with an external face that is comparable to that of ISIS. Boko Haram now has a death total that is over 10,000 and a homeless tally of over 1.5 million. They have shot down a Nigerian attack jet and videotaped the beheading of the aircraft's pilot.[127] Boko Haram has even extended the violence to cyberspace by hacking the personnel records of 60 Nigerian secret service staff and publicizing the staff's personal data.[128] The release of the data placed each of the secret service staff at risk of physical violence.[129] With this incursion, the definition of violence is meant to include the harm exerted through nonphysical contact with its victims.

SUMMARY

The next step is to reconsider the definition of violence to expand it beyond the idea of extreme physical force. If violence is accordingly redefined then assessment of the physical violence factors may identify characteristics that could offer insight into the type of cyber attack al Qaeda-ISIS-et al. might execute. Most Western experts dismiss the possibility of al Qaeda-ISIS-et al. conducting a massive cyber attack.[130] Response for a WMD attack may have a more substantial chance of response identification given the data stored on a captured ISIS laptop. On the equipment was a fatwa justifying killing all non-believers if need be and a document that suggested ways to spread bubonic plague (an agent that could produce high numbers of casualties).

Finding new approaches to terrorism will improve if the violence research data are assessed with methods that incorporate suggestions from the very targets the violence campaign recruiters seek to win. The target constituency has never received a message or offer of support, other than "you go to jail" or "you could wind up dead." To the young the first may be taken as a challenge and the second as implausible. It can be seen as an exciting adventure—one that starts on a plane to a place you don't know and ends on a roller coaster ride you have never, in your wildest dreams, thought could happen. They want to help liberate people.

ISIS wants to viciously institute a new world order, a world order as defined by terrorist industry's ideologues who reject anything outside the Qutb-prescribed sixth-century parameters. But to achieve that old world, current implementers like Abu Bakr al-Baghdadi have leveraged modernity (like YouTube videos and ISIS-owned media outlets) to condemn the West and recruit our young against us—all while touting the old-world constraints.[131]

4

──❦──

The Funding and Finance
of al Qaeda

Al Qaeda's original fundraising model was an outgrowth of the one used by rebels to support their activities combatting the Soviets in Afghanistan. That model relied on commitments of faith and funding from trusted external sources.[1] There was no significant reliance on state-derived funding.[2] Rather there was an alternative source that emerged, which focused on religiously motivated givers. These givers were sympathizers to the al Qaeda cause and its jihad intent. They ranged from supportive individual donors to sympathetic individuals who funneled monies to al Qaeda from complicit (and sometimes noncomplicit) charitable organizations. But as countries like the United States and Saudi Arabia applied external pressures, these avenues of funding started to diminish and in some cases disappear. More secure and controllable funding sources became a priority.[3] These more controllable sources were ones that diverged from a religiously empathetic focus to ones that traveled more secular non-ideological avenues. These new avenues were more difficult for legal authorities like Western governments to breach. Among the avenues pursued were illicit drug trafficking, kidnapping, and security for criminal activities.[4] No longer dependent on "hand-outs," al Qaeda and its affiliates and associates now have funding surety because of a steady funding stream based increasingly on a "crime-terror nexus."[5] The result is a former affiliate, ISIS, reportedly worth over U.S.$2 billion and a current affiliate, AQIM, considered of the richest terrorist organizations in the world.[6,7] How did they get to this point?

While we often focus on the leaders, what roles do the everyday foot soldier play in this transformation?

BACKGROUND ON EARLY FINANCING AND FUNDING

From the very begining, it was difficult to determine al Qaeda's net worth.[8] Early estimates of that net worth focused on bin Laden's personal wealth.[9] The assumption was that bin Laden would make all of his wealth available to the nascent group.[10] Best available data indicated that by the time bin Laden left Sudan in 1996, his net worth had plummeted to almost nothing.[11] But it was certain al Qaeda continued to receive monies; it was just uncertain from where. The 9/11 Commission itself admitted that its efforts to identify that source was stimed by a dearth of credible evidence regarding al Qaeda activities. The commision attributed that lack to what was then a scarcity of hard intelligence regarding the source of al Qaeda finances.[12] According to a CIA report, al Qaeda's financial requirements before the September 11, 2001, attacks amounted to U.S.$30 million annually.[13] This money was earmarked for carrying out attacks, for the maintenance of its quasi-military apparatus, for training and indoctrination of its members, for contributions to the Taliban regime, but also for the occasional support of associated terrorist organizations. It is currently very difficult to make a reliable estimate of the operating cost of al Qaeda, as it now acts through a large number of cells and satellite terror groups that are more or less autonomous.

The history of Osama bin Laden cofounding al Qaeda with Abdullah Azzam, and his efforts in helping to run the Maktab al-Khidmat lil Mujahideen al-Arab (MAK), or the Afghan Services Bureau in 1984 in Peshawar, Pakistan, is well documented. For years, since the installment of Arab Mujahideen forces in Afghanistan in 1980, wealthy Saudi businessmen, bankers, and institutions have forged the financial backbone of al Qaeda by transferring or facilitating the transfer of such funds to charities or fronts of the terrorist organization.[14] Legitimate organizatons, whether charitable or for-profit, offered cover for al Qaeda fundraising activities, which ultimately led to a considerable network that stretched out across the Muslim world.[15]

The early al Qaeda leadership had two committees in this structure that dealt with funding: the finance committee and the foreign purchases committee. The finances committee dealt more with long-term funding planning and developing financial resources to meet al Qaeda's payroll and fund its operations and those of its various affiliates. The other committee was supposedly more involved with logistics and purchases of equipment.[16]

For many years, U.S. agencies believed that bin Laden financed al Qaeda's expenses through a vast personal inheritance or through the proceeds of the sale of his Sudanese businesses. According to estimates, from 1970 until 1993 or 1994, Osama bin Laden received about a million dollars per year—adding up to a significant sum, to be sure, but not a $300 million fortune.[17] However, in 1994 the Saudis had frozen all his accounts and his family found a buyer for his share in the family business. This was partially a result of his earlier break with Prince Turki al-Faisal. At around the same time, the Saudis had issued a royal decree banning the collection of money in the kingdom for charitable causes without official permission. King Fahd set up a Supreme Council of Islamic Affairs (al-Majlis al-A'la lil-Shu'un al-Islamiyya), headed by his brother Prince Sultan, to centralize, supervise, and review aid requests from Islamic groups.

For example, according to some reports, al Qaeda did not have the necessary resources to carry the 1993 World Trade Center Attack. The most reliable scenario supports that Khalid Sheikh Mohammed, Ramzi Yousef's uncle and one of the architects of the 9/11 attacks, provided the bomb money for his nephew.[18] After his capture in 1995, Ramzi Yousef conceded to investigators that a lack of funding forced his group's hand in plotting the destruction of the World Trade Center. Running short of money, the plotters could not assemble a bomb as large as they had originally intended. The timing of the attack was also rushed by a lack of finances.[19]

Much controversy has surrounded bin Laden's assets (a purported source of money for al Qaeda) during the period he was in the Sudan. Bin Laden was reputed to own 35 companies in Sudan when he lived there from 1992 to 1996, but there is uncertainty that all 35 were actually owned by him, particularly the small or not economically viable. According to Peter Bergen, "[i]n the Sudan alone, bin Laden owned the most profitable businesses in Sudan, including construction, manufacturing, currency trading, import-export, and agricultural enterprises. These businesses were run on a commercial basis, and at least some profits were used to support 'local Al Qaeda cells that in essence became entirely self-sufficient, self-reliant terrorist entities in the countries within which they operated."[20]

The network of businesses controlled by Osama bin Laden included:

- Al Shamal Islamic Bank, funded and controlled by wealthy Saudi businessmen and bankers including Saleh Abdullah Kamel, Mohammed al-Faisal, and Adel Abdul Jalil Batterjee
- An import-export firm
- Several agricultural companies
- A construction company settled in connection with his family Saudi conglomerate (Saudi Binladin Group) to build roads and airport facilities in Sudan

Several analysts pointed out that his businesses were inclined more toward repaying his hosts Hassan al-Turabi and Omar Hassan al-Bashir. While this argument has merit, it does reflect the wider picture on bin

Laden's finances. It is perhaps odd for a man like bin Laden to have his personal funds in a project that would not refinance future operations.[21] There is also the speculation that bin Laden left Sudan almost bankrupted after the Sudanese government apparently expropriated his assets and seized his accounts. This theory concludes that he left Sudan with practically nothing. The 9/11 Commission reported that the Sudanese government closed bin Laden's businesses within the borders of Sudan but information indicating there may have been some worth to outside holdings has come to light.[22]

After bin Laden moved to Afghanistan in 1996, his financial situation was dire; it took months for him to get back on his feet. While relying on the good graces of the Taliban, bin Laden reinvigorated his fundraising efforts and drew on the ties to wealthy Saudi nationals that he developed during his days fighting the Soviets in Afghanistan. But again this is subject to much controversy as his ties with some of the Saudi financiers had disrupted. However, it is true that prior to moving to Afghanistan, bin Laden's personal wealth was much less than before entering Sudan in 1992.

In an unpublished interview in 1996, bin Laden stated that an emissary from the Saudi royal family had offered his family 2 billion Saudi riyals (about $535 million) if he abandoned his "holy war" and that he rejected the offer.[23] Resulting from confessions of Omar al-Faruq, former al Qaeda representative in southern Asia, to the U.S. authorities in 2002, we learned that the Saudi support to fundamentalists was not only proven but organized. What needs to be underlined here is that probably while official Saudi policies discouraged any assistance to bin Laden, Saudi Arabia offered support to the Taliban regime, which suggests a controversy.

An interesting case that revealed, on the one hand, an "undiscovered" link to 9/11 financing and, on the other hand, the high complexity of tracing terrorism funds is the Spanish connection. The Spanish connection is found in pre-9/11 al Qaeda finances since the group had connections all over Europe.[24] In 1999, business associates of al Qaeda began investing in companies based in Spain. They were transferring money through the Islamic Banking System, namely, the al-Rajhi Bank, National Commercial Bank, Faisal Islamic Bank, and Saudi American Bank.[25] The main hand behind this scheme was that of a man called Muhammad Galeb Kalaje Zouaydi, who also sustained Islamic charities connected to al Qaeda.

As far as costs and financial expenses for the attacks is concerned, it was clear that shortly before al Qaeda's official existence, Khalid Sheikh Mohammed and Wali Khan Amin Shah had been in charge of the logistic part of operations. They used the Al Ansari Exchange Establishment (AAEE) to move funds for the Operation Bojinka plot in 1995, which showed Sheikh Mohammed's central role in the organization's funding schemes and then to committee structures.[26]

Moreover, while the operational cost of the *USS Cole* bombing in 2000 is estimated between $5,000 and $10,000, and the cost of the Djerba suicide attack in 2002 is estimated to be $20,000, other actions around the world have turned to be much expensive. The Bali bombing is estimated at $74,000, the Limburg attack at $127,000, not to mention the September 11 attacks, whose cost was largely above $500,000.[27]

As far as the 9/11 execution and costs incurred in the attacks are concerned, the main transfer system used by al Qaeda was the formal banking sector, especially U.S. banks, and was overseen by Mustafa al-Hawsawi. Each operation had it own finance support team, as with the 1995 Operation Bojinka attempt to down a dozen U.S. airplanes. Mohamed Jamal Khalifah reportedly led that finance support team.[28]

Estimations vary, but around U.S.$300,000 were deposited in U.S. banks, all of which was spent before the attacks except U.S.$36,000. About U.S.$130,000 of the funds the hijackers used came through bank-to-bank transfers (including through MSB correspondent accounts at banks) and the rest was deposited as cash.[29] The main source of funding for 9/11 was largely unclear and still is. However, U.S. authorities believed that among them was the Benevolence International Foundation (BIF), listed among the top 20 al Qaeda financiers, known as the Golden Chain.[30]

AFTER 9/11

The Patriot Act of 2001 gave the U.S. government new international anti-money-laundering tools or "special measures" to "restrict or prohibit access to the US financial system for states and individual foreign financial institutions that lack adequate anti-money laundering controls."[31]

Some have been designated by the U.S. Treasury and the United Nations Al Qaeda and Taliban Sanctions Committee. By June 10, 2002, $112 million had been seized from all terrorist organizations (including al Qaeda), $34.3 million blocked domestically, and $77.8 million internationally.[32] In addition, the May 2003 terrorist attacks in Riyadh pushed Saudi law enforcement efforts to have al Qaeda's cadre of Saudi facilitators reduced and seized.

According to most analyses, al Qaeda's decentralized structure led to interlinked independent entities.[33] Despite the watershed after 9/11 and the capture of several leaders, the organization showed remarkable resilience and adaptability. For example, after al-Hawsawi was captured, his role was quickly assumed by Abdullah Ahmed Abdullah, with no real evidence of loss of capability.[34] Moreover, the structural evolution of al Qaeda after 9/11 included cells totally independent from central authority, which in turn meant that they are responsible for funding and financing their own activities.

By most accounts al Qaeda central has its own fundraising as well as the cells, but the cells do not receive large amounts from large "well known" charities or organizations.[35] The logic of self-funding that perpetuates cells' financing structure includes common crime as it will be seen further on. Most typically, costs for a cell member may include living, travel, and communication costs that are mostly covered by these illegal activities.

Since core leadership probably does not provide support to local affiliates, focus is better placed on the so-called common crime used to create funding streams. Despite the fact that cells may receive funding from other traditional sources such as charities, al Qaeda-affiliated groups must have their own revenue streams, whether from illicit drugs, kidnapping, or human trafficking.[36] This is further highlighted by the fact that after the AQI merger with al Qaeda, the *New York Times* reported in 2006 that the U.S. National Security Council believed that the insurgency in Iraq was self-financing.[37] In 2007, the *Los Angeles Times* reported that the U.S. intelligence community believed that AQI's criminal enterprise was so lucrative that it was able to send excess money to al Qaeda's senior leaders in the Pakistan border region in 2006.[38] As al Qaeda has decentralized after 9/11, some of the core al Qaeda financial activities have allegedly been transferred to Africa, the Middle East, and Asia as these areas are regarded as having weaker institutions and financial regulatory measures in practice.

After the Iraq War, an al Qaeda branch began to operate in Saudi Arabia, which remained relatively in low-density activities until 2009 when Yemeni and Saudi cells merged to form the AQAP (al Qaeda in Arabian Peninsula). In 2006 the GSPC followed suit, becoming al Qaeda in the Islamic Maghreb. Al Qaeda also announced its unification with the Libyan Islamic Fighting Group and with a segment of the Egyptian al-Gemaah al-Islamiyah. In past years, according to various sources, an affilate would request funds for attacks, but the requests went unfulfilled. Frustration with the situation must have been high because Mustafa Abu al-Yazid raised the issue in a June 2009 forum, saying, "[M]any of the mujahidin have been inactive and failing to participate in jihad through lack of money."[39]

TRADITIONAL SOURCES OF AL QAEDA FUNDING

Charities and Donors

Charitable contributions are fundatmental to Islam. Depending on your earnings, you could be subject to up to 2.5 percent of those earnings, or zakat. *Zakat* belongs to one of the five pillars of Islam and constitutes a religious duty for the Muslims. According to the Quran, only the poor and needy deserve zakat.[40] Basically, zakat takes three forms, depending on its recipients, Feesabeelillah (in the way of Allah), Lil-Fuqara (for the poor), and Lil-Masakeen (for the needy). The al Qaeda network extensively utilized the weakness of legal rules to rely on funds diverted from the zakat and other direct donations through Islamic banks, and since 1998, Osama bin Laden made regular calls to Muslims to donate through the zakat system to his organization. Al Qaeda's strategy for receiving charities before 9/11 penetrated specific foreign branch offices of large, internationally recognized charities. Their main goal was to divert money from the charities' legitimate humanitarian or social programs toward their own illicit activities.[41]

These large international Gulf charities donated money to end recipients, usually smaller in-country charities, whose employees may have siphoned off money for al Qaeda. On the other hand, there were cases where entire charities from the top-down may have known of and even participated in the funneling of money to al Qaeda. Whatever their direction, charities are quite helpful for terrorists since they act as a conduit for funds and recruitment. They may also have infrasturcture to ease logistical requirements, when needed.

Two of the charities that have come to the attention of the U.S. Justice Department are the Muslim World League (MWL) and the Qatar Charitable Society (QCS). These charities belong to the first category where al Qaeda has penetrated or at least managed to have direct contacts with key people within them. Another thing to bear in mind when assessing the complexity of the picture regarding charities and terrorism is that these organizations may not be subject to state governance. These are especially difficult to eliminate.[42] Second, closing down charities may perhaps directly affect people in need and divert money to illegal charities that are controlled by al Qaeda. Indeed, many of these charities were not specifically created to fully fund al Qaeda, but have since become supportive of its cause.

Other well-known charities linked with terrorism include the International Islamic Relief Organization (IIRO), a Sunni charity based in Jeddah, Saudi Arabia, and the Benevolence International Foundation (BIF). IIRO started in 1978 and has a Sanabil al-Khair private endowment that ensured a dependable finding stream.[43] Working with the Global Islamic League, the IIRO has a broad activity list.[44] Per the CIA, that broad activity list included pre-9/11 al Qaeda training camps. IIRO's current leadership has worked to eliminate ties to al Qaeda. However, its Secretary General Dr. Adnan Khaleel Pasha reportedly continues to support Hamas activists.[45]

In 1987, an organization known as "Lajnat al-Birr al-Islamiyyah" (Islamic Benevolence Committee, or LBI) was founded by Adel Batterjee in Saudi Arabia and Peshawar, Pakistan.

The BIF, also based in Saudi Arabia, reportedly supported al Qaeda, along with other groups like fighters in Bosnia and Chechnya. Benevolence was initially two separate organizations, but by 1992 both were merged into one as the BIF.[46] During that same time period, the BIF opened offices across Southeast Asia, Europe, and the United States. It was not until 2001 that the U.S. Treasury made a case for designating the BIF as a terrorism financier.[47]

Enaam Arnaout assumed BIF's management while he had worked in the mid- to late-1980s for Mektab al-Khidemat. Allegedly, the BIF had established connections with the Texas-based Holy Land Foundation for Relief and Development (HLF).[48] The case of Arnaout reveals how funds were allocated for BIF with final destination al Qaeda's operational cells. Once the full amount was pulled out for the charitable project, a small percentage (around 10 percent) of the cash was skimmed off the top and physically passed to an al Qaeda operative who deposited this clean money into al Qaeda's accounts in the Middle East or dispersed it to operational cells in other parts where al Qaeda operates, such as Bosnia.[49]

One of the most significant charitable supporters is the al-Haramain Islamic Foundation (al-HIF). Based in Jedda, al-HIF is said to have funded missionaries and new mosques across Africa, Southeast Asia, and the Balkans.[50]

Al-HIF presence in Somalia includes al Qaeda affilates. Together they fuction as al-Ittihad al-Islami (the Islamic Union). According to post-9/11 reports,[51] al-HIF's founding managing director Shiekh Aqeel al-Aqeel has close ties with the Saudi Ministry of Islamic Affairs. Despite closing several of its offices around the world, the organization continued to operate in Yemen, Nigeria, and Bangladesh.[52] As late as 2009, the group was accused of contributing $15 million to jihadist groups like the Tehrik e-Taliban (TTP), the organization accused of assasinating Benazir Bhutto.[53]

Another charitable organization the "Blessed Relief" charity, also known as the Muwafaq Foundation, was established in 1991 by Yassim al-Qadi, who was subsequently identified as an associate of Osama bin Ladin. Yassin al-Qadi, a Saudi businessman from Jeddah who had business interests around the world, was accused in 2002 as having connections with al Qaeda after the Swiss government blocked 23 bank accounts belonging to him.[54] His investments in property acquisitions within the United States meant that perhaps al Qaeda donors were investing through him in real estate. Moreover, his name appeared in relation with the Koranic Institute, the International Islamic Welfare Organization, and a software company, which all had al-Qadi in common. The case of al-Qadi proves and shows the difficulty of containing al Qaeda and terrorism-affiliated individual funding. Other individual Saudi wealthy donors whose names have appeared in relation with al Qaeda include Khalid bin Mahfouz, banker; Saleh Abdullah Kamel, banker; Abdullah Suleiman al Rajhi, banker; Adel Abdul Jalil Batterjee, businessman; Mohammed Hussein al-Amoudi, businessman; and Wa'el Hamza Julaidan, businessman. Of course, this is a nonexhaustive list, as there were also Farhad and Junaid Dockrat, two South African al Qaeda financiers. Farhad funded al Qaeda and the Taliban through an al Qaeda charity that was on the UN 1267 committee's terrorism list, and Junaid raised $120,000 for then al Qaeda operations chief Hamza Rabi'a.[55]

The Revival of Islamic Heritage Society (RIHS) was labeled as a terrorist organization. RIHS was a Kuwait-based charity with offices in Pakistan and Afghanistan. RIHS has been accused of helping the al Qaeda-associated Lashkar e Tayyiba (LeT). This Pakistani terrorist organization has been accused of being involved in the 2006 Mumbai train attacks linked to the *al Qaeda* network and the 2001 Indian parliament attack.[56] It is said to have also provided the funding needed to coordinate the 2005 Jamaat Mujahidin Bangladesh (JMB) attacks.[57]

It is important to notice here that Saudi efforts to contain terrorism within their own territory have proven doubtful and weak, which perhaps contributes to AQAP funding as well. However, as noted above, cells do not receive funding from large charities. In 1999, the kingdom approved amendments to existing money-laundering laws intended to bring them into compliance with international regulations, but these amendments have not been implemented.[58] Additionally, the measures taken by the Saudi government after 9/11 did result in a severe blow to al Qaeda's illicit financing activities. It was only the 2003 attacks inside Saudi Arabia that brought a clear change of mind for Saudi authorities. They began to combat terrorist financing and considered *al Qaeda* as a threat to the regime itself.

NEW PATTERNS

Drugs Trafficking and Other Common Crime

In the first one, the convergence between terrorism and organized crime would be little less than a *contra natura* option. According to the second one, on the other hand, this deals with a spontaneous, quasi-natural tendency.[59] Al Qaeda has in the past preferred to limit its interaction with crime networks to the minimum and to run its own criminal enterprises, when necessary. Theoretically, this is a potential form of collaboration from purely practical interests and entails a material or economic transaction exchange. Another one deals with the situation when a terrorist group provides support to a terrorist structure, due to ideological or religious affinity. The second form of collaboration stems from buying weapons, explosives, or false documentation from criminal gangs and is a resource that terrorists can make use of when they are short of the capacities or opportunities necessary to obtain these products by their own means. Most importantly, since the decentralization of the group, al Qaeda cells have been involved in illicit and illegal activities in order to finance their activities and achieve financial independence from al Qaeda core. Another issue that we should bear in mind regarding al Qaeda cells is that their nature of crime depends largely on the agenda of the group. Since these groups rely mainly on self-funding, the territorial area of their action partly defines the nature of their "economic activities."

It is equally important to notice that there is no conclusive evidence of senior-level al Qaeda members directly involved with or motivated by organized crime to date. Hence, as Lorenzo Vidino, author of the new book *Al Qaeda in Europe*, writes: "They do not need to get money wired from abroad like 10 years ago. They're generating their own as criminal gangs."[60]

As far as the Sahel-Sahara region is concerned, it is an area where transnational crime has flourished for years. This region is one of world's most sensitive and volatile regions due to its ethnic mixtures, cultural backgrounds, unchecked population growth, and the fact that most of the countries in this zone are at the bottom of most development indexes such as the UN Human Development Index.[61] Therefore, it is no surprise that this region presents an unparalleled opportunity for the growth of criminal networks and terrorist groups. Most common crimes that allegedly involves al Qaeda are smuggling of cannabis resin and cocaine and kidnapping for ransom.

When examining the organized crime-terrorist nexus in the region, we should not neglect the fact the most possibly in regions highly associated with such crimes, the erosion of the customs services because of corruption and collusion between smugglers and state officials has contributed as well. State authorities are perhaps involved in this game, which gives them the opportunity to generate funding and play off political enemies in respective regions. Wolfram Lacher suggests that, in the case of Mali, individuals with drug-smuggling connections successfully petitioned the Malian leadership to create the Taoudeni adminstrative region, along with associated districts, prior to the 2012 rebellion.[62]

To begin with, drug trafficking has been known since the poppies production by the Taliban and other jihadist groups with a presence in Afghanistan and Pakistan since the mid-1990s. However, Afghanistan is not the only place where allegedly al Qaeda has established connections with drug trafficking. There is massive use of West Africa as a cocaine stockpiling location notably in Guinea and Guinea-Bissau, as well as Togo, Benin, and Ghana. European and Latin American law enforcement agencies have confirmed seizures of cocaine shipments from and bound for Africa that allude to the size of the economic activity: in 2006, the Spanish and British navies operating in international waters seized 9,800 kg of cocaine on five fishing boats departing from African ports, against 3,700 kg seized on a single ship in 2005.[63] As the United Nations Office on Drugs and Crime estimates, cocaine trade from South America to Europe via West Africa expanded rapidly in 2005–2007 and roughly $1 billion in Western Europe—transited through West Africa in 2008.[64] This rapid growth in conjunction with several events contributed to an eager hypothesis that AQIM is collaborating with the Colombian drug lords.

New York tried to test that hypothesis when it "charged three Malian nationals with narco-terrorism offenses that appeared to establish a link between AQIM, the Colombian FARC, and cocaine smugglers."[65] The charges were brought after an undercover operation appeared to confirm the tie when the three Malian nationals boasted they could assure the cocaine shipment would make it across the Sahara because AQIM protection could be arranged. However, there was no proof the statement was more than a boast and the terror network connection charges were dropped.[66]

Another case was the discovery of a Boeing 727 carcass that had either crashed on takeoff or been set on fire near the town of Tarkint in the Gao Region in November 2009. This was linked with the other cocaine route via airport transfers of Bamako, Ouagadougou, and Niamey. However, it remains unclear if this was an isolated incident. In addition, the concept and its connection to al Qaeda has been a subject of tabloid fodder. In April 2013 the UK tabloid *Sunday Mirror* broke another story that has been widely reproduced as proof for AQIM involvement in cocaine smuggling. The story was based on a cocaine shipment of 168 kg from Senegal that had been seized at a UK port. The tabloid turned the seized quantity into a shipment worth £168 million and added allegations that AQIM had been involved.[67] This was like differentiating fact from fiction, or even determining if the fiction as any kernel of fact complicates the matter.

Then there are the consequences of movement of individuals or factions within the jihadi network. It has been reported that individuals and factions within AQIM subsequently became associated with the Movement for Tawhid and Jihad in West Africa (MUJAO) when the latter group emerged in late 2011. The MUJAO's Mohamed Ould Ahmed Deya "Rouji," Cherif Ould Taher, and the Sultan Ould Badi are reportedly linked to drug smuggling.[68] It does not appear to be a strategic source of revenue in order to generate resources. It may be part of a larger plan or only for the financial gain of the leaders.

When these illegal sources of income are examined, they appear to offer little risk on the part of the terrorist network participants. It could be that groups like MUJAO and AQIM are risk averse. That is they are unwilling to become involved in a crime that contains large risks. One aspect of those risks for West African coastal states is the flexibility needed to route through these states. Cocaine can take maritime, air, or overland routes depending on the current enforcement efforts. Indeed, what seems to be the most possible explanation that includes al Qaeda-affiliated activity in the Gulf of Guinea involves a network of mainly Nigerian and Ghanaian or Malian nationals who are paid in kind by foreign cocaine-trafficking operators for the provision of logistic services.[69] In addition, the trafficking operators network perhaps exists through the auspices of the jihadists of the Sahara who have for some time been applying charges to the cocaine traffickers who cross the territories that are under their control.[70]

As suggested above, it seems that there is no direct connection of strategic alliance between the Colombian FARC and the AQIM, but only a "marriage" of convenience. On the other hand, when examining the FARC-AQIM relationship and AQIM's involvement in drugs, we should

bear in mind that any potential "official" involvement would expose al Qaeda operatives to risks of detection or arrest.[71] Furthermore, it is highly debatable if drug traffickers prefer to pay bribes to AQIM and risk being targeted as well. Substantial post-9/11 intelligence collection efforts have failed to corroborate rumors of current narcotic trafficking.[72]

Tobacco smuggling is probably the most lucrative form of trade of the many kinds that are practiced in the region, above the smuggling of fuel, the arms trade, and even drug trafficking.[73] The total value of the illicit tobacco trade in North Africa is thought to exceed $1 billion (£632 million). The United Nations Office on Drugs and Crime (UNODC) estimates that Africans smoke 400 billion cigarettes a year, of which 60 billion are bought on the black market. Mokhtar Belmokhtar made a fortune through a different commodity: smuggled cigarettes. Such was the volume of his trade that he earned himself the sobriquet "Mr Marlboro."[74] Mr. Marlboro and AQIM clean up, either by charging a "tax" for the safe passage of the cigarettes along the salt route or by facilitating their transport, using 4×4s, trucks, motorcycles, and even bicycles.

Another alleged source of revenue for al Qaeda-related cells involved human trafficking and kidnappings. According to estimations by international organizations such as the the International Labour Organization (ILO), 200,000–300,000 children are trafficked each year for forced labor and sexual exploitation in West and Central Africa. It is important to notice here that AQIM and possibly its criminal network contractors are benefited by both kidnappings and human trafficking. Compared to Yemen and Saudi Arabia, the region offers practical advantages for human trafficking: there are many individuals working in agriculture activities without family connection to the owners of the farm.[75] This means that the strict family traditions practiced in the Arab world are not in play in these regions. It would be much easier for AQIM or any other criminal network working with AQIM to pay local providers of humans. We should also bear in mind that the West Africa/Sahel region is constantly "providing" sexual labor to other worldwide routes and mainly Europe. Sexual workers in many European countries came from Nigeria, Mali, Gabon, Benin, and Burkina Faso, among others.[76]

Human trade has involved, among others, the Algerian GIA; Yemaa Islamiyya, the most powerful terrorist structure in Southeast Asia; AQIM; and AQAP. Human trafficking is more of a "common" pattern in the Sahel region and less in Yemen. Human traffickers and kidnappers connected with al Qaeda cells in Sahel engage in proactive recruitmentof migrants, the journey to the staging points in Senegal, Mali (Gao), and Niger, and the crossing of the Sahara Desert. In addition, this zone, moreover, has for centuries traditionally been an intense zone of passage and of informal or illegal economic exchanges. The first incident occurred in 2003, with the kidnapping of 32 tourists in the southern part of Algeria. When the

European tourists were abducted in 2003, the Malian and European governments relied on a former Tuareg rebel leader and current head of AQIM-linked Ansar Eddine, Iyad ag Ghali, and Tarkint's mayor Baba Ould Cheikh to act as intermediaries in the ransom negotiations, which shows the entanglement between state authorities, organized crime, and terrorists.[77]

Another incident was about the kidnapping of two Austrian tourists in the south of Tunisia on February 22, 2008.[78] In April 2012, these actions took the form of the kidnapping of 42 foreigners from different countries (Algeria, Tunisia, Mauritania, Niger, and Mali), who were subsequently moved to the north of the latter country. In recent years, 24 hostages have been released and 5 killed, some at the time they were captured and others during their captivity.[79] There were still seven hostages in the hands of AQIM at the start of 2013.[80]

In the same sense as AQIM in Sahel and Maghreb, AQAP takes advantage of migration routes. These routes have flourished in the Gulf of Aden for decades, and have been encouraged by Yemen's decision to grant prima facie refugee status to Somalis in 1991, following the outbreak of the civil war in Somalia.[81] Much speculation has surrounded the relationship between AQAP and the Somali jihadi group al Shabaab; however, the exact nature and the depth of this connection still remains in doubt. What is doubtful is the fact that in ungoverned spaces of Yemen, AQAP is in charge of a "migration" economy that involves arms trades, kidnappings, and possibly some connections to piracy networks. As far as kidnappings are concerned, several events demonstrate the AQAP factor. Among others, an Austrian man and a Finnish couple became in March 2012 the latest victims of abductions. A Swiss woman was also kidnapped in Hodeida, western Yemen, on March 14, 2012, besides three French aid workers near Seiyun, Hadhramaut province, in May 2011. AQAP activity in the region has expanded to places such as Hodeida, Abyan, and Shabwa. But for those kidnappings not directly attributable to al Qaeda, it has not been ascertained if kidnappers act on al Qaeda's behalf, for security purposes; nor has it been determined that the groups act on their own with the intent or purpose of handing the kidnap victims over to al Qaeda at a later date, in exchange for an agreed upon sum.[82]

Allegedly, AQAP derives these revenues by raiding public institutions, including banks, police garrisons, and government offices. Other sources include tolls charged at checkpoints for "policing" the roads.[83] AQAP is more akin to this strategy since it can take advantage of Yemen's "fragile" nature while AQIM's operational manual to date has not yet subscribed to such tactics. It is not unlikely that perhaps AQAP or smaller cells of al Qaeda in Sahel and Yemen follow a similar tactic first employed by Islamist groups during the Somali civil war and international humanitarian intervention during 1992–1995. Islamist groups raided, attacked, and in several instances penetrated foreign aid in order to self-fund their activities. In the case of Yemen, there are no official donor research initiatives, such as the

UK Department for International Development's "Drivers of Change" and the Swedish International Development Cooperation Agency's "Power Analysis"; they have been penetrated by AQAP but it is an issue that needs close monitoring.

Another much speculated source of potential revenue for an associated al Qaeda organization is piracy. Al Shabaab, the Somali al Qaeda affiliate, has reportedly been associated with piracy with links to Somali pirate groups.[84] International attention has been on the region for the number of ransoms and the estimated $53 million paid, on average, annually as late as 2013.[85] The World Bank has placed the 2005-2011 annual economic impact of piracy off the coast of Somalia at approximately $18 billion. According to the World Bank the amount is equivalent to a 1 percent tax on the vessels.[86] International efforts to contain this money generator have not been effective. For example in 2008, a transit corridor was established in the Gulf of Aden, patrolled by international naval forces. Somali pirates, however, have adapted accordingly.[87]

Al Shabaab's relationship with al Qaeda was speculated to have begun before the formal pledge of support in 2012. Al Shabaab's Mukhtar Abu al-Zubair pledged to Zawahiri to "march with you as loyal soldiers."[88] As of early 2015 that pledge had not been replaced with a pledge to ISIS.[89] Al Shabaab's association builds on a preexisting pattern of association between Somali fighters and international jihadists. Indeed, al Shabaab fighters are thought to have acquired more battlefield experience than their Yemeni counterparts during the 2006–2009 time period.[90] While there is assumed to be some training and exchange of information between the two organizations, there is currently little evidence of joint command and control or any apparent strategy for joint operations.

Other issues like interaction with the migration or commodity networks have been reviewed as well. Neither open-source material nor anecdotal information bears out the proposition that violent extremists are using migration networks to move between the two continents, or that AQAP is recruiting from among Somali nationals living in Yemen. The energies of rank-and-file al Shabaab fighters are needed to pursue the conflict inside Somalia. Somali men interviewed on Yemen's coastline in spring 2010 claimed to be fleeing forced recruitment by al Shabaab, rather than having fought for them.[91]

To the extent that there is a connection between pirates and radical Islamists, it seems to be only a business relationship. Islamists in Somalia and Yemen, and Yemeni offcials are reportedly in an informal network of a "win–win" situation: the pirates dominate Somalia's shadow economy and become squatter landlords who expropriate former government buildings and lease them to displaced families. The Somali pirates have an important income in order to finance their activities, and the Yemeni offcials have an extra surplus to their underpaid salaries.

Valuable commodities like oil, gold, and diamonds offer yet another convenient method for transmitting value across borders. Al Qaeda has been
also linked to this kind of activity.The crackdown on al Qaeda financing
may have led the group even before 9/11 to transfer a portion of its exposed
assets into untraceable precious commodities. One such commodity was
diamonds. West African diamond smuggling is said to have supported the
Revolutionary United Front (RUF) and Unino Nacional para a Independen-
cia Total de Angola (UNITA). By some accounts, al Qaeda prior to and after
9/11 was involved in transfers of gold, diamonds, tanzanite, and other precious commodities. Wadi el-Hage and Abu Ubadiah al-Banshiri were sent
by bin Laden to Tanzania, where he established Taher Limited, a gold and
diamond mining business.[92] Al Qaeda's reported association with precious
commodities was first presented in 2003 when the prosecutor for the Special Court on Sierra Leone said that Liberia's Taylor had harboured al
Qaeda members who had come to trade in diamonds from Sierra Leone.
Each person tied to the transactions admitted diamond business involvement in Sierra Leone and Congo, but they denied al Qaeda links.[93]
The FBI conducted an intensive international investigation of the conflict
diamond issue, including interviews of key witnesses with direct knowledge
of the relevant facts, but found no evidence of any substantial al Qaeda
involvement; the CIA has come to the same judgment.[94] The al Qaeda
involvement was tested again when Ahmed Ghailani in Pakistan in 2004.
Ghailani, a senior al Qaeda operative, confessed to buying conflict
diamonds. He reportedly spent a great deal of time traveling in and out of
West African conflict zones between 1999 and 2002.[95] However, Ghailani's
confession did not prove al Qaeda involvement, large-scale or small.
Al Qaeda risk aversion probably makes the involvement less likely. As far
as cells such as AQAP and AQIM are concerned, the advantages of profit-
ing from dealing in gold and diamonds particularly diamonds from African
mines is neither simple nor convenient. They need to be transported by
hand, and that always carries the risk of seizure or theft.[96]

Other criminal activities that al Qaeda cells in the Arabian Peninsula and
Sahel have been involved in include oil smuggling and secondary car thefts,
illegal trade of stolen goods, and other illegal activities such as piracy of
DVDs and counterfeiting of luxury goods. Some of the al Qaeda money
may have been coming from refined products stolen from oil refineries
and then sold on the black market. However, the volume of smuggled oil
generated as much as $200 million annually for insurgents in Anbar, Iraq.[97]
Unfortunately there is no substantial evidence and studies for both AQIM
and AQAP to show which sector contributes the most to financial revenues
for each group; thus, any attempt to do so would be only speculative.

Another relatively new source of financing terrorist activities that has
received much attention especially after the Internet's big bang in the late
1990s regards the involvement of al Qeada in cyber crime. It is the same

way that the Internet has allowed information to move across boundaries, digital technology has transformed the way money moves across borders. According to various sources and recent analyses that have been publicized, al Qaeda tried to recruit computer professors from Eastern Bloc countries, with the aim of taking them to African countries, from where they were supposed to hack into key Western targets. These included systems controlling airports and power and water supplies. Nevertheless, this concerns the cyber terrorism aspect, which is not the aim of this chapter. The main concern is how al Qaeda cells have been exploiting the Internet in order to raise funds. The most intriguing cases deal with Younes Tsouli, or Irhabi "Terrorist" 007, as he is more famously known. Tsouli started in the world of cyber terrorism at the age of 19. The son of a Moroccan diplomat, Tsouli quickly became known as the expert in hacking secure systems, defrauding banks, and credit card fraud.[98] He advised, trained, and aided many mujahideen working with Abu Musab al-Zarqawi. Irhabi created training videos, provided security tips, advised the use of proxy servers, distributed suicide vest how-to instructions, and developed and distributed the now-famous beheading video of the American Nicholas Berg. The beheading video was downloaded over 500,000 times.[99] During his three years of action, he worked under virtual anonymity.

Al Qaeda, as an organization, made no significant investment toward Irhabi's support for its cause, but the return on investment from his activities brought al Qaeda untold value. He helped create a sophisticated machine that will only advance as technology advances. When Irhabi was finally caught, law enforcement acknowledged the challenges of combating online criminal and terrorist activities. Law enforcement's capability to charge and convict Tsouli was grounded in the standards of the United Kingdom's Terrorism Act 2000, not the Computer Misuse Act of 1990. When he is released, there is no assurance he will not enter the same network again. Tsouli's capture took three years even though he functioned in a country that vehemently enforces its cyber laws and standards.

But what if he had initiated his activities in one of the Sahel states where even geographic borders have no real monitoring; the relatively small overall Internet presence has even fewer regulations and standards. The problem for those governing Sahel's cyberspace is the pace with which technology changes and the global reach of that advanced technology. Its cyber-control ministers have significant infrastructure concerns and critical cyber-control problems. AQIM also exploits its Sahel location, the region's seamless borders, the area's few security concerns, and its even fewer enforced government regulations. AQIM is now part of the fabric of the area contributing to its instability with terrorist attacks, kidnapping, drug trafficking, and weapons sales. Nigeria, third in the world for cyber crime perpetrators, offers AQIM unfettered access to perpetrators of electronic fund fraud and other Internet crimes. Nigeria is home to the Yahoo boys, a group known for their preference for Yahoo's users, its chat rooms, and email access. Nigeria exercises minimal information communications technology (ICT) oversight and has one of the most experienced cyber crime cadres in the field. The perpetrators are within AQIM's demographic and could train large numbers of recruits in the same successful practices. According to a recent descriptive study of the Yahoo boys, the young men are between 22 and 29, and are university educated, as are their parents. However, the average family monthly income is between 25,000 and 30,000 Naira, equivalent to roughly U.S.$160, and many of the perpetrators are unemployed.[100]

Looking at each component separately, we recognize that investment in this venture is minimal. Hacker software setup can be acquired for $250 to $500. Yahoo boys could assist with the crimes committed or execute them directly. In 2009 authorities estimated U.S. Internet losses at $240 million.[101] Nigeria's Muhammed Rudman, chief executive of the Nigeria Internet Exchange Point, indicated that the worldwide total was $114 billion. Many of the schemes originated in Nigeria taking various forms to increase the chance of success. According to the study, they already have tested strategies that work. For instance, the young men know how to develop a relationship with security and bank personnel. They have developed local, national, and international networks that AQIM could leverage to its own advantage. Any participant included in this activity would continue to enjoy social acceptance, as cyber crime is a highly practiced endeavor by both men and women. Finally, the expansion of virtual currencies outside virtual worlds further opens up avenues for terrorist exploitation through digital crime Digital currencies "[enable] standardized international financial transactions," which, combined with speed and anonymity, is attractive for money launderers. The return on investment can be very high. Furthermore, recent cases has shown that the development of mobile banking, or m-banking, has become attractive to these hackers. The lack of formal oversight may allow funds of any amounts to pass unnoticed. The subsidiaries of big banks such as the First Direct of HSBC with the Monilink World Wide Web or the National Bank of Dubai and the Norwegian/European mobile company LUUP could evolve into prime targets for al Qaeda-hired cyber crime experts.

Finally, through the use of m-banking possibly, groups such as AQIM or their contractors (Yahoo boys) sought to legitimize their illegal funds through a process known as "cyberlaundering." The process of cyberlaundering mirrors the traditional methods, with the launderer ordinarily loading electronic currency onto its SVC at specialized vending machines, at the bank, at compatible ATMs, through the Internet, and even over the phone.[102] There is vast availability of options of cyberlaundering. The recent example of athlete Shanthakumaran Sreesanth, who had links with the terrorist Dawood Ibrahim, shows how complex the picture of cyberlaundering is. Any individual could establish an online gambling site and transfer funds from an online bank account (established using a false identity) to the online gambling site; any proceeds of the gambling website would thus appear legitimate to authorities tracing the audit trail of the profits.[103]

HOW AL QAEDA MOVES ITS MONEY

Hawala

For its more than 25 years of existence, al Qaeda, and later its affiliates, have used various methods to transfer funds. One system that proved most effective and was leveraged quite often was the hawala system. Its lack of a paper trail permitted each user to avoid detection by the authorities. International financial institutions estimate annual hawala transfers at about $2 trillion, which represents 2 percent of international financial transactions annually.[104]

Hawala, like other informal transfer systems, is fast, with transactions happening usually within hours, perhaps taking up to a day or slightly more for transactions to the more remote regions. The main benefits of the hawala are cost-effectiveness and the lack of a paper trail. Using the hawala system, criminals and terrorists are assured of anonymity as they launder or transfer illegal funds. The most common way that a hawala operates is through connections. These connections allow for the establishment of a network for conducting the hawala transactions. There are several possible ways in which this network could have been constructed.[105]

While al Qaeda used hawalas prior to 9/11, they did not use them specifically for the 9/11 plot.[106] The hawala system proved more practical for ease and familiarity. The most well-known hawala organizations were the al-Taqwa (Piety) and al-Barakat (Blessings). The Barakat came under heavy scrutiny and was shut down by the U.S. authorities. One of the most recent examples of the effectiveness of the hawala system concerns Faisal Shahzad, who would be later known as the "Times Square bomber." Shahzad used an informal hawala network that was relatively unregistered. By using this type of transaction, there was no suggestion in any subsequent investigations that Shahzad's middleman knew the purpose for money.[107]

The Internet facilitated hawala use, increasing the speed of transactions and accuracy It is perhaps a greater threat now combined with the use of satellite communications. The various forms of satellite telecommunications are named according to the ground-based devices used to send and receive signals. VSAT is the acronym for very small-aperture terminals, devices with an antenna generally less than two meters in diameter. Using "anonymous" locations has added to the difficulty in tracking terrorists. Internet cafes are also known as cybercafes.[108]

Cash Transactions and Couriers

There are instances when the Hawala system will not work for the purpose intended. Terrorists and criminals move cash across international borders; they typically conceal it in vehicles, packages, luggage, or anything else that can hold large physical volumes of cash. One usual way of moving money is through couriers. Al Qaeda relied on couriers to move money in the 1990s and before the 9/11 attack. The investigation into the 9/11 attacks provided a good example of how al Qaeda used human couriers to move money. One of the financial backers of the attack, Khalid Sheikh Mohammed, passed a large amount of money (possibly as much as U.S.$200,000) to Abdul Aziz Ali in Dubai, who subsequently transferred it to the hijackers in the United States.[109]

The Formal Banking and Islamic Banking

Government-regulated financial institutions and other regulated financial service providers constitute the formal financial system. In the last 30 years, regulation of global capital markets has decreased as many countries have been gaining access to markets in New York, London, Tokyo, and Hong Kong. Countries that integrate into capital markets accordingly reduce their cost of capital. Al Qaeda's financial network reaches around the world. The goal of investing in these markets is to gain access to cheaper sources of financing and more stable rates of return. Thus, legitimate or illegitimate groups used in order to move and store funds.[110] As far as al Qaeda cells were concerned, due to the higher security measures taken by international banking institutions after 9/11, and especially after the "Tsouli" incidents, high-volume transactions using the formal banking system were out of question. We are still unaware of how cells operate in international bank branches located in countries with low-level enforcement. Al Qaeda reportedly used U.S banks for the $300,000 estimated to execute the 9/11 attacks. The attackers used their own identies when interacting with the banks, even executing transactions using ATMs and debit cards. At the time of the attack, the planners were proven quite accurate because all but $36,000 was gone. Other sums totalling $47,600 were deposited internationally. This included $9,600 in Saudi Arabia and $38,000 in the United Arab Emirates.[111] The 2004 Madrid and 2005 London bombings were executed similarly. However, by the London bombings, the attackers were including self-funding. Mohammed Siddique Khan reportedly paid for most of it from his own assets. His self-contained approach permitted below the radar activities that paid for and executed the attack, making the July 7, 2005, London subway attack a more difficult to track approach.[112,113]

Formal banking is usually the gateway to the world's principal interantional financial transactions. Al Qaeda has in the past used the formal financial system as a means of moving money to support its own cells and affiliated terrorist groups, financing their actions. The speed and ease with which money can be moved via the international financial system enables terrorists to move funds efficiently, unfortunately often still with relatively small risk of detection. The existence of formal banking thus gives the opportunity for cyber crimes, credit card frauds, and hacking banking accounts.

The growth of the modern "Islamic banking" from its 1963 Egyptian origins to its current expansion throughout the world provided unparalleled opportunities for followers of Islam to conduct business and adhere to the tenets of the Qur'an.[114] Al Qaeda reportedly used this avenue as well from 1995 through 1997 when it transferred up to DM3.5 million to affilates.[115] Islamic banks fulfilled Quranic guidance on interest (riba). Using Islamic banks assured observant Muslims they could comply with religious requirements and function economically.[116] Beginning in the late 1970s, Saudi Arabia and other Gulf countries settled a banking system aimed at promoting and propagating (Dawa) Islam around the world. In 1974 the OIC summit in Lahore voted to create the intergovernmental Islamic Development Bank (IDB). Based in Jeddah, it became the cornerstone of a new banking system inspired by religious principles. Moreover, the Bank of Credit and Commerce International (BCCI) in 1972 along with the the Dubai Islamic Bank—the first modern, nongovernmental Islamic bank—was opened in 1975 and symbolized a turning point for Islamic banking. In 1979 Pakistan became the first country to embark on a full Islamization of its banking sector.[117] By 2013 the international Islamic finance industry had an estimated $2 trillion worth.[118] Its projected annual growth rate is almost 20 percent until 2018.[119] The boon of Islamic banking has encouraged Islamic banking "sharia-compliant products.[120] Britain issued its first Islamic bond (sukuk) in 2014, raising $200 million pounds for the five-year instrument.[121]

Al Qaeda used both secular and Islamic banking institutions to fund its activities.[122] Bin Laden's association with formal and informal financial systems and models reflects the diversity the organization has had to utilize to continue its activities. These accounts reflect the change in funding streams from charitable to self-directed to illicit activities.[123] It demonstrates a business approach to secure steady funding streams that permit operations to continue without the need to constantly divert energy and effort to financing. Al Qaeda cells now have access to unlimited funding through illicit activities and access to Islamic compliant and noncompliant banking institutions. This broad array of options makes access to funding less organizational and more unit or al Qaeda cell focused. No longer can international antiterror funding units center on a country or charity. It has to look across the broad spectrum of countries and previously used schemes.

Current funding schemes like those used with AQIM, AQAP, and Boko Haram include robbing banks, expanding control over territory and the actvities within that territory, and extortion.[124] This is done in broad daylight with the world watching.[125] Secrecy and anonymity are no longer desired criteria. Flaunting appears to enhance the groups' image and credibility. Pursuing such a public approach to funding schemes has coffers full, with AQIM said to have over $500 million and ISIS reportedly worth almost $2 billion.[126,127]

5

---⊶⊷---

The Drive to Survive:
Marketing and Recruiting

The evolution of the relationship between media outlets and terrorist organizations' violent events reflects the transition in status or position terrorism and its perpetrators have experienced over the last 20 years. While we all recognize these events are executed for many reasons, chief among them is media attention. Terrorists sell fear. They do this through both inference and direct event execution. Whether functioning as organizations or individuals, these event perpetrators accept the obvious: the best vehicle to sell that fear is the media and its outlets.

As early as 1977, Ambassador Andrew Young recognized this phenomenon and vehemently urged that the United States restrict institutional media coverage of terrorist events to dampen the fire print and video fueled when they covered such incidents. He was sure the institutional media provided oxygen to terrorism's blaze as it sought access to its audiences through media exposure, and while this may have been true 30 years ago, institutional media no longer holds sway over terrorists' connection to its victims, supporters, and perpetrators.

At the time that Ambassador Young contended media-fueled terrorism, his terrorism postulate was actually supported by several mass media studies. The very year Ambassador Young made the statement, Bell posited that terrorists can control the media by creating events journalists and their institutions feel compelled to cover.[1] Between 1984 and 1992, analyses examined the relationship between the terrorist act and the media.[2] Scott's 1992 analysis is of note because it suggested that the more terrorist events are executed, the more diffused the coverage. According to Scott, this explosion of events and the resulting events coverage caused a loss of focus in the media and the media's audiences, and because of the message, the coverage was therefore diffused.

One of the most famous studies of the relationship between terrorists and the media was the 2006 Rohner-Frey "common interest" work.[3] In this study, Rohner and Frey surmised that a win-win relationship existed between the two entities, with one or the other modifying behavior when needed.[4]

However, by 2010, technology changed that equation because the vehicles available to terrorism's perpetrators changed as well. As Weimann has suggested, the technology of the Internet has particularly changed the equation, making global interaction with terrorism more intimate. No longer are terrorist events executed mainly for the media exposure they can elicit for terrorist constituent group's interaction. While it is true that al Qaeda's greater dependence on the Internet is a result of its loss of a safe haven for vast physical training facilities and safe houses, the reality is that this transition to the Internet has served al Qaeda well. It has expanded access to a wide audience, provided virtual training and functioned as recruiting facilities, creating outlets that help mold the viewer's to fit the specific requirements of the mission. For instance, in 2005 al Qaeda launched Sawt al-Khilafah, an online al Qaeda newscast designed to shape potential recruits' outlook on events of the day.

This newscast leveraged al Qaeda's, and actually the whole terrorist industry's, direct access to the "consumer." It also sheds light on the dwindling influence institutional media has as a primary conduit between terrorist groups and terrorist group constituents. As a matter of fact, institutional mass media has, at times, played the role of "relayer of information." For instance, the upload of a video onto an al Qaeda website is identified by avid monitors of terrorist websites or announced through press release from the organization. This information is relayed to institutional mass media. Journalists in those mass media outlets "report" this information to its audiences. Uncertainty and fear may build in those audiences, but they, too, can make use of the Internet to search for additional information at alternate information access nodes. Al Qaeda, like other organizations trying to reach their various stakeholders, recognizes that the Internet offers opportunity to pinpoint its message to the specific audience sought. It has done this over the years with various magazines, forums, chat rooms, and training material. These vehicles have served various purposes, but the basic purpose of each is marketing for recruitment. Even as each story is relayed and builds fear in the listener (or reader if online access is utilized), al Qaeda or its affiliates are assured the information is delivered unfiltered. When Jama'atu Ahlis Sunna Lidda'awati wal Jihad, also known as Boko Haram, stole the female students from their schools, an international uproar resulted. Once they captured international attention, Boko Haram used the limelight of that center stage to demonstrate their advantage in the situation. Their released YouTube video statements were carried by institutional media and retained in cyberspace for on-demand repeat play by individual viewers. Through these well-timed publicity pieces, Boko Haram taunted and played with the international community as they changed their message from one of acquiring the young girls to dangling the idea of marketing them as slaves to finally demanding release of fellow members from Nigeria's jails in exchange for those who have not converted to Islam.

Al Qaeda and its affiliates recognize that the technology of electronic communication offers opportunity to pinpoint a message to the specific audience sought, with the appropriate messaging vehicle available. This ensures no external filtering. Employing knowledge of its market's demographics, al Qaeda need only access a CNN market when necessary.

As an organization, al Qaeda only needs to communicate with this audience for event announcement or warning. Potential recruits or other stakeholders have alternate nodes of access to information tailored to that audience's needs. When Anwar al Awlaki created English messaging vehicles, he followed this same approach, expanding the al Qaeda message dissemination capability. In doing so, he expanded the reach of the organizations' recruiting, training, and resource accessibility. Before al Awlaki began his work, the Islamic male between 18 and 25 years of age, was still the target, but the materials and guidance were in Arabic. Al Awlaki removed the language barrier and added outreach that had a sense of authority centered on the individual English-speaking potential recruit. His one-to-one effort leveraged the Internet, exported the al Qaeda message to the United States in a more palatable manner, and became a topic of discussion on institutional media.

Al Awlaki's move into English propaganda offered the recruiting and marketing process a means to better control how members of the target demographic traverse several critical initial steps before even crossing the line to a final decision to join and subsequently kill: first, the decision to access information; second, acceptance of potential that the message embedded in the presented information may be correct; third, internal agreement to return for more information. Moving the potential recruits past these initial steps to regular forum visitor, cyber crime initiator or suicide bomber is critical for al Qaeda, and other groups like it, to continue functioning. To do this, al Qaeda must guide the individuals to the point they willingly cross the line into the territory of wrestling their soul on throwing the bomb.

Al Qaeda and groups like it are adept at creating an atmosphere that motivates the target to cross that line. It is the crossing of that line that is a sign of the group's successful control of the target, with the most visible result being those same targets perpetrating vicious attacks. When they are asked why, the perpetrators parrot the mantra of radicalization. For instance, during Michael Adebolajo's trial, he was asked why he killed Fusiler Rigby. Adebolajo insisted that he rammed Fusiler with a Vauxhall Tigra and cut his throat because "your people have gone to Afghanistan and raped and killed our women."[5,6] Adebolajo's speech at the trial is faintly reminiscent of one given by Ayman Zawahiri at his December 1982 trial for aiding/supporting the assassination plot of Anwar Sadat. Zawahiri, too, claimed, "[W]e are not sorry, we are not sorry for what we have done for our religion, and we have sacrificed, and we stand ready to make more sacrifices!"[7]

Adebolajo's intentional decision to perpetrate viciousness was the end result of a guided decision-making process engrained enough that it did not steer from the path directed by the al Qaeda recruiting/marketing arm. Radicalization is an external process; understanding the internal decision-making process could offer the critical counter needed. We will have to recognize that each person comes with his or her own experience base and will require and understanding, too, of those points in the decision-making process where that experience base is critical.

GENERATIONS BEFORE ADEBOLAJO

In his book *Journey of the Jihadist*, Fawaz Gerges chronicles Kamal el-Said Habib, a 1980s "warrior of God," and one of the originators of the modern jihadi movement.[8] Habib led a generation of revolutionaries through the militant arm of the Egyptian Islamic Jihad (EIJ). Among EIJs "victories" was the assassination of President Anwar Sadat.[9] They felt, after several incidents—one of which was providing refuge to the Shah of Iran, he had lost moral authority over his country. Habib, and his compatriots, were impatient for change, a change that had to comply with their interpretation of Islamic ideology. They were willing to do battle for that ideology because their whole beings were dedicated to the struggle. Since leaving prison after serving 10 years for the assassination of President Sadat, Habib has become more moderate. He still wants change; he just wants it without violence. He sees no real benefit from it.[10] But he came to the struggle on his own with no real recruitment or "maintenance" after that recruitment. He is of the generation that fought alongside Ayman al-Zawahiri, but he wants to take a different road. How do you recruit and keep that Muslim generation of under-30 that represents almost 60 percent of Islam today?[11] How do you keep them engaged, or do you go with the average and assume a running influx of disheartened idealists, an influx that should continue—as long as the enemy is clearly defined. For Ayman al-Zawahiri, technology is the platform on which his recruitment is structured. He has also taken it to a global potential market.

This new generation had zeal for using the education they possessed and a focus that exceeded the borders of their countries.[12] Mass media opened a whole new world with their coverage of successful revolutions in Iran, Afghanistan, and Sudan. As Abu-Jandal (Nasir Ahmad Nasir Abdallah al-Bahri) emphasizes in the *Journey of the Jihadist*, "We began to follow events in Afghanistan, the battles in Khost, and, after that the fall of Kabul [to the mujahideen]."[13] (They had hope that if they worked as one, they could free all Muslims from oppressive regimes.[14]) Zawahiri and bin Laden leveraged this zeal with calls-to-arms, focusing their message on 16–25-year-olds.[15]

Through the entire time, three elements remained the same for bin Laden and Zawahiri: defense of Islam from the West message, "toughest bad guy" public perception, and world reach. The defense of Islam against the West has acted as a galvanizing force when the groups approached had regional, tribal, or ethnic differences.

This message was used even in the period Kamal el-Said Habib rebelled against Egypt's government and later moved toward "modernity." With no Internet or online forum, Kamal was able to raise like-minded troops and oppose the then government of Anwar Sadat. He advocated an Islamic state; however, during Habib's tenure as a leader in jihad, the method of employing extreme violence did not bode well with the ordinary citizens of Egypt.[16] Bin Laden employed the technique of behavior modification and gradually sold the idea of martyrdom with a redefinition of noncombatant civilian. This broadened the eligible area of attack and began the process of desensitizing for the loss of young students as the image of a martyr transitioned.

This was important for al Qaeda as it repackaged the concept of Islamic governance of the land of the Two Rivers. Marketing to and recruiting from this redefined landscape offered an al Qaeda-controlled picture and response that was advantageous to future al Qaeda activities.

Initially, the call to arms came with the August 23, 1996, Declaration of War against the Americans Occupying the Land of the Two Holy Places. This was issued by bin Laden alone. But as the "Islamic newspapers and magazines" began to chronicle the Iraqi ummahs' successes, the hope of young idealism set fires of desire in others to participate.[17] These fires were burning in a young educated generation, one that had skills and capabilities. Their zeal was affected by the struggles highlighted in the world spotlight—struggles like Bosnia, Algeria, and Eritrea[18]—and the romantic idealist concept of the struggles presented in "Friday sermons, tape cassettes, the magazines and other media."[19] One imam with skills honed in recruiting during the Soviet-Afghanistan campaign, Salman al-Awdah, was especially good at instilling and fanning the hope-fires in young Muslim youth. Azzam's training camps, and later Osama bin Laden's, graduated highly skilled professionals capable of leading operations anywhere Azzam and bin Laden felt the fight should continue. But once the Afghanistan freedom fight ended, these jihadi "al-Faruq War College" trained cadre "moved to other fronts like Bosnia-Herzegovina, Chechnya, the Philippines, Eritrea, Somalia";[20] Awdah and 24 other Saudi Arabian religious leaders issued an electronic open letter in 2004, urging all Iraqis to get behind the fight. Everyone knew it would take more than an Internet letter to keep the steady flow of recruits needed to sustain battles on all these fronts. A significant recruiting and marketing campaign was required. Bin Laden has always been well aware of the importance of communicating with cadre. He contributed to Abdullah Azzam's *al-Jihad*, a free circular for the mujahideen.[21] But he was especially aware of the importance of the established media in the 1990s when he wanted to engage all of his constituent groups: investors, employees, potential recruits, Muslims in the West, Muslims in the Middle East, Other Terrorist Organizations, Opponents of Israeli Sovereignty, and Opponents of the United States. Concentrating on the Middle East at first, particularly Saudi Arabia, bin Laden sent an open letter to the Kingdom of Saudi Arabia's Chief Mufti, Abdul Aziz bin Abdullah bin Baz, after Chief Mufti issued two fatwas: the first declaring it acceptable to have U.S. troop presence within the Holy Land, and the second declaring it permissible for Muslim soldiers to fight in Operation Desert Storm. Bin Laden, then only 37, took Chief Mufti to task for what bin Laden believed was bending to the external pressure of the king in issuing the two fatwas and not adhering to the rules of the Qur'an.[22] His first statement did not receive extensive coverage in the media.

When he finally decided to address the world, after release of his 1996 Declaration of War against the Americans Occupying the Land of the Two Holy Places, bin Laden did not wait for the media to come to him. Instead he approached specific outlets, inviting each to Afghanistan for a face-to-face interview.[23,24] Bin Laden realized a successful declaration of war against the United States was contingent upon his stakeholders accepting that declaration and helping to enforce it. That included the United States as it was necessary for the United States to provide the impetus for jihad response. The United States' initial dismissal of the Declaration for bin Laden stakeholder buy-in was critical to achieving his goals.

He also recognized it was a good recruiting opportunity. Known to journalists in the Middle Eastern Arab world, he wanted to increase the West's awareness of him as well.

Bin Laden's media savviness was visible from the very start; in 1988, he established As-Sahab, which was al Qaeda's media arm and also demonstrated the continued mantra that the mujahideen were winning without technology against the United States with all of its technology. Bin Laden sought to define that bin Laden also maintained a presence in the West with the London-based Committee on Advice and Reform (ARC). Run by Khalid al Fawwaz, the ARC acted as al Qaeda's propaganda and media coordinator from 1994 to 1998. It was Fawwaz who arranged the meeting with all the print and broadcast journalists in 1996[25] and arranged for Jane Corbin of the BBC's Panorama to meet with him at his London office to explain al Qaeda's position on and the reasons for the 1998 fatwa.

At that time, the concerned constituent groups could assess the effectiveness of the group when the exploits were dramatically presented in the evening news. So they would reach out to selected members of the media from time to time to present their position. Another person who was also very technology savvy was Abu Musab al-Zarqawi, who had grown up in the jihadi movement with the slogan and dedicated himself to the cause. Aided by young technology-savvy recruits to the cause, Zarqawi distributed videos, statements, and an online magazine, *Zurwat al-Sanam*. He made video tapes as a part of his media department from the very start.[26] As-Sahab was part of that chronicling of "the underdog" winning bravely against the ogre Soviet Union. Once that war was over, the highly trained cadre did not want to stop fighting, so bin Laden took the fight elsewhere. Azzam and he differed over where that "elsewhere" should be, but after Azzam's death, and with Zawahiri's influence, a larger newer threat was forged. At the time jihadists, in general, were in dispute over the direction the struggle should take.[27] All agreed secular governments in or near the Holy Land had to go. But how to make that happen was the point of contention.[28] Zawahiri forced the issue and the direction away from the Islamic lands to the United States since that is where most Muslims believed the fault laid, when you drilled down to the root of the problem. Once the United States left Somalia in 1993, Zawahiri and bin Laden had a call to arms. The underdog had won. Fear of the United States could be managed, particularly with young fighters infused with the zeal of jihad. Soon there was an international fighting force full of the burning desire to join the excitement of defending Islam. They needed nourishment for their souls to keep the zeal high.

The media wing jumped into full swing. Everything was taped, as demonstrated by more than 1,500 audio tapes donated to the Yale Library after they were found in an abode from which bin Laden had made a hasty retreat.[29]

This audio connection to every aspect of jihad life and the database developed to track all personnel issues and concerns were cutting hedge when bin Laden introduced them. Al Qaeda remained cutting edge when Zarqawi's media team posted the video of Nicholas Berg's execution. Half a million downloads within 24 hours made all realize a new era of communication had arrived. By the next year, Zarqawi had an online magazine called *Zurwat al-Sanam*.

Marketing during periods of transition permitted al Qaeda to highlight the changes and give those making the change a chance at center stage while al Qaeda ensured the message—we are still here—was the underlying sentiment.

One such marketing point was in 2004 when al Qaeda filled a compact disk with Osama bin Laden's speeches and distributed them to all those who wanted them in Afghanistan, Pakistan, and other Middle East countries. This provided a means to reach foot soldiers who were, by U.S. assessments, cut off from their al Qaeda commanders. At initial delivery, each of the speeches was directed at different audiences: the United States, Pakistan, and Europe.[30] Repackaged, the overall theme was a grassroots campaign to inculcate al Qaeda's approach and justify its tactics. These compact disks were a lifeline for the group as adherents tried to retain the zeal from earlier periods of success. After packaging the speeches, al Qaeda launched the Pakistani youth-focused group Jundullah.[31] Jundullah was the center point of an organized effort to create a new generation of jihadis within the Pakistan-Afghanistan borders.

Al Qaeda was also adept at taking advantage of relationships to market its goal and increase access to recruits. Around the same time Jundullah was born, the Taliban leveraged participation in one skirmish into retaking control of North Waziristan.[32] The two Waziristans were under the control of Pakistani forces until jihadi fighters employed a tactic from the Iraqi conflict: improvised explosive devices (IEDs). These, along with remote-controlled bombs, were low tech enough to be easily obtained and efficient enough to be highly effective in an intensive campaign against the Pakistani forces. The result was a withdrawal of the forces and a victory for the jihadi fighters. However, the fighters had not calculated governing in their algorithm to win. Their lack of a plan left a void that was filled with roving gangs in their early twenties and late teens. The Taliban took on one of the roving groups of youngsters who had filled the leadership void. The confrontation was not hard for the Taliban.

After taking them on and winning the contest, the Taliban killed them and simply displayed their severed heads and bodies for all to see. Very soon the Taliban were in complete control of North Waziristan, and later South Waziristan. A call went out for members, and jihadis who had been idle returned in droves. Within short order over 10,000 supporters within Pakistan answered the call and supported the Taliban. This ultimately benefitted al Qaeda, who had been working with the Taliban. Al Qaeda declared the Taliban-fighter-heavy-North the Islamic State of North Waziristan and the South the Islamic State of South Waziristan. This new government configuration and the desire to fight was a draw for thousands of youth. Between the draw of al Qaeda and the Taliban-governed Islamic state, it was estimated that over 40,000 fighters became active cadres.[33]

Working with al Qaeda gave the Taliban a slingshot assistance to return to power; the Taliban became the force to consider when the future of Afghanistan was under discussion. The Taliban, a group that started as a student movement against the Afghanistan's warlords, emerged as the driving governing force for the country; after being driven out by U.S. forces, they were back.[34] The Taliban brought courts, law enforcement, and tax collection. With their return, the Taliban also brought new life to al Qaeda, giving its constituent groups another success in beating its odds against the U.S. superpower.[35]

Transition within the jihadi movement is not new. But marketing that transition requires marketing a call for zeal. Kamal el-Said Habib brought his zeal to the jihad movement after discussions with like-minded individuals at the university. There were no training camps in those days. But those young zealots executed events that captured headlines and brought the concept of jihadi demands for Islamic institutions and governments to the world stage.[36] Habib, and the others, fought within Egypt focusing on issues that called for Islamic reform. He wanted to restore "broken links between tradition and modernity" as a means to "Islamizing state and society."[37]

Osama bin Laden's recruitment to and zeal for the jihadi movement developed from his face-to-face relationship with Mohammed Qutb, Sayyid Qutb's brother, and advanced after bin Laden met, worked with, and supported Abdullah Azzam.[38] During his time in Afghanistan, he observed the impact of structured training on the success of events executed by those recruited to the cause and the ease of recruiting if the message focused on Islam and its defense. As they transitioned from Afghanistan freedom fighters to "Islam defenders" in al Qaeda's nascent 1988–1989 organization, their dedication to the cause of "Islamizing state and society" remained strong particularly as they turned their attention to the governments within the Middle East region, like Saudi Arabia, Iraq, and Afghanistan, and the perpetrators of wrongdoings—the West, particularly the United States. The United States could act as the galvanizing force for the new fight, just as the Soviet Union had acted in the fight for Afghanistan. Recruiting was labor intensive. Training was logistics dependent and marketing was limited to outlets that were controlled by external media.

However, recruitment, marketing, and exploitation of the media techniques aimed at achieving desired recruitment and marketing results have evolved over time, with the technology associated with the Internet leading the way in that evolution. By the time we see the zeal of Faisal Shahzad, accused in the attempted New York Times Square bombing; the focused determination of Nidal Malik Hasan, accused for attacking the Ft. Hood medical processing center who wounded 32 and killed 13; and the ardor of Rhonara Choudhry, the convicted assailant who stabbed Stephen Timms, British Member of Parliament, the training has moved from strictly land based to online and the logistics are left to the perpetrator. All al Qaeda has to do was continue to pump zeal into the online jihad community through focused attention on the West and its "anti-Islam" behavior. Shahzad, Hasan, and Choudhry all triggered their acts of Islam defense after hours of listening to Anwar al Awlaki and his online advocacy of anti-American attacks. Nidal Hasan exchanged emails with Anwar before embarking on his attack. It should be noted, though, that Awlaki focused on the same single message in his face-to-face mentoring as in his online guidance. These sessions were powerful and very effective. Said Kouachi reportedly met with al Awlaki in 2011, more than three years before the Charlie Hebdo attack.[39]

The Internet's impact on the jihadi recruitment process is significant. The recruitment, training, and marketing processes between 1988 and today are vastly different, in part due to al Qaeda's ability to aggressively pursue young people with an intertwined propaganda message that the West has always targeted and persecuted Islam. However, the newly configured media-terrorist event relationship may actually represent some problems that could have al Qaeda trying to find its footing.

One very important problem is control. In its drive to survive within the digital age, al Qaeda has relinquished a significant amount of control of distribution of its message. There are central sites for release of official information, but online training of attack perpetrators incorporates an acceptance of the limit of control over the use of that training. This online training brings another potential concern: self-recruiting. Self-recruiting carries several assumptions. The most significant of those assumptions is trust. Internet users' trust has a connotation for both sides. That connotation says that if you took the chance to connect to "us" (jihad movement) and we have vetted you sufficiently to continue in the group, then you are worth the trust and risk needed to extend the tie for additional bonding. That trust must extend to both organizational and personal interactions. Familial preferences may not be known with an online self-recruit. This could present an additional problem if negative familial preference limits or hampers mission dedication. However, if the forum or online community is the social network node to which familial preference has been transferred, then mission dedication will be reinforced.

Virtual training sessions have no associated verifiable tracking that can be initiated to determine, for instance, who is or how many are in a room when the online training is conducted, or ascertain how many attacks or attempted attacks are executed based on the training.

One perpetrator with friends (recruitment tool as well?) can leverage that training session so that more than one attack can occur. In such sessions fear of law enforcement is not a risk for al Qaeda leaders or its trainers. If law enforcement even entered the room during training, only the individuals at hand would be detained. Capture of the trainers is more difficult, a matter that is frustrating for law enforcement as the trainers are connectors to al Qaeda "perpetuity." This online training is also a recruitment tool because for those who cannot or do not choose to go to Pakistan for training, a meaningful connection with those who represent the jihadi cause is no less profound. Done in the privacy of a virtual encounter, the event offers a means to live out a dream, and if action is taken, there is the ability to move from being a "forum-hideen" to infamy.[40] The martyr will have his name reverently listed among those who went before him. As each of these forum-hideen move to violent action, they raise the stakes for those left behind. Humam al-Balawi was a pediatrician, a jihadi website administrator, and adherent. But he wanted to do more, contribute the way the heroes had. On December 30, 2009, Balawi set off a blast that killed seven, wounded six, and earned him a martyr's reception at the forum. He was praised in the forum by Abu Kandahar az-Zarqawi.[41] Using Balawi's cyberspace nom-de-plume (Abu Dujanah al-Khorasani), az-Zarqawi praised his friend, letting everyone know Balawi's most sought-after level—martyrdom—was achieved. After years of seeking the top level, he won. Shortly afterward, an online jihadi named "Raheeg, extended the same honor to az-Zarqawi that az-Zarqawi had extended to Balawi. Kandahar honored az-Zarqawi with his own praise death notice."[42]

Al Qaeda's members are technology savvy. Sheikh Omar Bakri Muhammad is reported to have said that "thousands of bin Laden supporters [are] currently studying computer science as a way to support the cause" and as such they have created an environment that leverages the rate of change online technology is experiencing and incorporating any and all aspects of that change into the jihadi experience.[43]

In addition, the transition of control of message from established media to al Qaeda-controlled entities means any event, whether a successful attack or captured trainees, will have an anti-West spin in the forums of Shumoukh al-Islam or the Fallujah Islamic Network.

MECHANISMS

When al Qaeda markets its wares through the Internet, it leverages vehicles such as the *Inspire* magazine for the propaganda, marketing, and recruiting value it brings with the one communication-technology instrument. We have to recognize that any communication vehicle al Qaeda uses must be considered for its propaganda quotient. That influence value is derived from a communication vehicle. The influence of interest is that which is focused on the largest number of al Qaeda constituent groups. While Abdullah Azzam encouraged the use of technology to advance the goals of al Qaeda, for him the aim was to capture data for initial management of member information. But the advancements in communication technology have leveled the playing field such that anyone who can wield the tools effectively can function equal to any nation-state or organized international group. Al Qaeda members have exploited the level playing field the Internet provides with targeted tactics that are successful in the struggle for the young men and women who make up most of al Qaeda's market. When compared to other entities such as nation-states, jihadi web cyberspace residents function as though they are equal to any state entity.

Prior to the Internet, recruitment and marketing of the jihadi cause was more direct with recruiting occurring through direct one-to-one relationships. It was an outgrowth of the recruiting for the Afghanistan freedom fight. Exploiting those same access nodes seemed natural. Allegiance and commitment to oath was easily assessed, as was mission knowledge. Those who influenced could quickly make their preference known. Over the years the Internet tools jihadists have had to employ to achieve some of these same objectives are the chat rooms and forums. Beginning with the early Yahoo! groups, the email lists that were generated from the groups functioned as distribution of information.[44] Transition from this listing beginning through email lists to disseminate information to leveraging the vulnerabilities like the concept of spam emails to send messages demonstrated the comfort and ease that was arising. Blanket messages appearing to contain pornographic information or sports requests were blasted to a wide audience. Most of the recipients just hit delete. But the intended recipient knew a next step was imminent. This simple change in cyber use signaled an increase in jihad appreciation for the tool at its disposal. Whether this meant more computer savvy members were joining or the current members were expanding their capabilities (and imaginative use of the tool), the introduction of the use of spam email traffic as another cryptic courier of jihad information transmission was one of the earlier signals that the technology was going to provide the means to organizationally respond to external pressures like attacks on training camps. Whatever the motivation, the connection to the individuals who are critical to the movement's continuance appears to remain the primary goal. The critical nature of this connectivity is demonstrated in the propaganda message that pervades all external communication: We are not afraid. We are taking action. We are taking back our land. The message must remain angry or "martyr" fighters will cease to step forward. However, anger (hate as well) takes significant energy, and sustaining it is difficult. Fanning the fire of anger is one thing. Feeding the fire with additional examples of "oppression" is something else. Constant reiteration of the message stokes the embers of dissatisfaction. The external message must, therefore, continue to find current examples of Western ongoing "oppression," or support from constituent groups will fade. So the propaganda that pervades all communication outlets contains these elements.

External access to global media exposure is no longer a high priority, but retaining control over connectivity is very much so. Connectivity is the key, even during periods when the Internet was not the main recruiting tool. The market is still the same: a Muslim for whom the historical rancor of Western intervention in Middle Eastern affairs is a sore point. This audience has the potential to be susceptible to messages for support, financial aid, vital information, or volunteer to mission jihad.

Al Qaeda's first website "maalemaljihad.com" came online in February 2000, and content was usually limited to leadership statements, news, a "gallery of 'martyrs,'" and theological support for the use of suicide missions.[45] Regional al Qaeda entities managed their own cyber presence.[46]

Yusef al-Ayyiri had "al-Battar" in Saudi Arabia, and Zarqawi had "thurwat al-sinam" in Iraq. In the early days, bin Laden or Zawahiri would have their speeches copied onto a computer disk and then someone else would secretly upload the information to cyberspace using an Internet café's connection to the cyber world. But now al Qaeda (and the entire jihad community) has its own connection to the cyber community with GIMF's ability to disseminate information to the network of forums that connect to the individual cyber supporter.[47]

Using the Internet, we have experienced the phenomenon of "self-recruitment," the process of reading, studying, and internalizing jihadi materials only through self-guided online sessions. These self-recruits have usually also self-radicalized; one such self-radicalized self-recruited attacker is Arid Uka. Uka killed two American airmen and severely wounded another as they boarded a bus at Frankfurt Airport in Germany.[48] Uka had apparently watched a YouTube video that depicted several Islamic women raped by American soldiers. Taking the video at face value, Uka secured a weapon one day in advance of the attack on the airmen. Two weeks before the attack, Uka posted a Facebook message that read: "My weapon is ready at all times." Drawing on guidance from Facebook "friends," they were able to leverage important relationship nodes like Sheikh Abdellatif, a Moroccan preacher who was a member of the Dawaffm network.[49]

Guido Steinberg divides the jihadi relationship with the Internet for marketing and recruiting (to include propaganda distribution) into three phases: Early stage, up to 2003, where most of the activity comes in the form of a sprinkling of this recruitment outside the Internet. The second phase was the period 2003–2008. During this period, according to Steinberg, videos supplemented "conventional" approaches like essays, letters, magazines, and books. However, by 2008, the Internet was the preferred method of communication for the young, with YouTube at the top of their list for quick communication of thought, visual, and one-to-one attention getter.[50]

By 2008, there was more comfort with the Internet from the standpoint of al Qaeda leadership and calls for "individual Jihad" to go out on the Internet. This reaching out to the individual, making the message personal, was a departure from preaching a controlled message. This "trust" in the receiver of the message expanded the roles of potential attackers exponentially. There was a trust that the message was received and that a certain percentage would execute the mission as closely as possible to the prescribed methods offered in the electronic training materials. The probability that this approach offered success increased when considered from the perspective that any attempt would garner media attention and successful attempts would garner significant media attention. Hedging this bet has paid off tremendously with events like the Boston Marathon bombing.[51]

Now all forms of social media are employed on jihadi sites. Everything from Facebook to Twitter to Pinterest is used to convey messages to the broadest audience possible. This includes delivering in-progress attack messages. Al Shabaab issued a Twitter message to the Kenyan government during the 2013 attack on the Nairobi Westgate shopping mall.[52] They also leveraged Twitter as a resource by discarding one account and quickly accessing another to provide updates on the progress of their assault.[53]

Organizations have also turned to YouTube, often establishing official YouTube pages, replete with sophisticated video presentations, music background, and only successful results to battle encounters. Advantages of electronic locations like YouTube, or Vimeo, are low cost, immediate update, and fast turnaround. Battle Footage shot in the morning can be on the Internet before lunch. It is easily accessible and, again, available to the individual anywhere in the world. Any recruitment message seems to speak directly to the viewer, no one else. The onus is now placed on the viewer to determine if he/she has what it takes to participate, to be a doer and fight.

Lethality and gruesomeness are relative to the organization developing the message. For Jabhat al-Nusra, the Syrian element of al Qaeda, the YouTube channel provides an avenue to effectively display its latest violent attack or killings. Videos contain killings of 1–50 people. Blood and bodies are carefully filmed and uploaded. Extensive photography capability is unnecessary and anyone can upload a video.

Zarqawi was often aided by media outlets like Al-Rai TV, a Syrian-based television station that focused most of its broadcasts on Sunni attacks against U.S. troops and the Iraqi security force.[54] The station ran from 2004 to 2011, to oppose U.S. intervention in the Middle East, and ceased only when the U.S. troop's withdrawal in Iraq was on a glide path to zero. Station owner Mishan al-Jabouri said the station did what he wanted "and there was no longer a need."[55]

Zarqawi's aggressive media use is continued in the Islamic State of Iraq and Syria (ISIS) high-technology approach to its target audience, young Western teenagers. Social media is incorporated and it is suspected that some of the recruiters are Westerners as well.[56] The current approach includes scheduled releases of beheading videos, a series of elaborate propaganda films featuring the hostage British journalist John Cantlie functioning as a war correspondent, and a "Grand Theft Auto" style video game with the tag line that ISIS fighters "do the things you do in games in real life on the battlefield."[57]

While much of the current analysis of terrorists' command of electronic communication tools could lead one to conclude that al Qaeda-ISIS-et al. have the upper hand communicating with their target market compared to counter messages from other sources, the truth may be less certain. Command of the technology and control of the message may be two separate things. Both ISIS's al-Baghdadi and al Qaeda central's Zawahiri want to continue to create a war of the young, one that permits an opportunity for them to create an atmosphere of excitement and a sense of duty and history. The young would only have to bring the fuel of fervor for the cause.[58]

This sense of adventure and commitment to a cause from a sense of duty can be seen with brothers Dzhokar and Tamerlan Tsarnaev, and Said and Cherif Kouachi. Private Lee Rigby's killers Michael Adebolajo and Michael Adebowale definitively present the sense of duty in the post-attack rant.[59] In all three cases, the young people defined each attack; they were in charge. They controlled the violence and executed it within their determined purview.

POTENTIAL RESPONSE

The Internet permits personal connection to establish a sense of adventure and commitment to the al Qaeda cause. Vulnerability for this recruitment must come from the Western young themselves. If they are willing to provide insight into points of opportunity that could be exploited, tactics to counter the sophisticated media campaign have a chance to succeed.

On the other hand, there are those recruiters for whom a strong, reliable Internet connection is not in the recruiter's tool kit. Once electronic communications is not an option for continued message bombardment, other tactics for marketing are employed. The North Africa recruitment region, and parts of the Middle East, have a target audience that does not have a stable, trusted connection. Boko Haram has developed several recruiting techniques to surmount that problem. One of the most chronicled techniques Boko Haram uses is kidnapping young new recruits from the local communities it devastates. By the moment the young recruits are kidnapped, Boko Haram has already instilled fear into them with the atrocities of mass killings and the group's reputation for cruelty and viciousness. These recruits come not from a commitment to the caliphate (one declared in 2009) but from fear and the need for money. Another method is conscription.[60] A third, less-publicized avenue used is that of reaching out to tap the unemployed members of gangs in the border towns of Niger.[61] As one gang member from Diffa, Niger, said, "We have no jobs; some of us are still at high school but we need money. Violence has become a form of work for us."[62] A final avenue used is that of leveraging ethnic relationships. This one simply exploits the loyalty of the Kanuri since that is the ethnic group to which Boko Haram's current leader, Abubuakar Shekau, belongs. Other areas of northern Nigeria and nearby Cameroon also offer opportunity to exploit the link of similar culture and backgrounds and have been the grounds for inducing young men from those regions to join. Boko Haram follows the al Qaeda training protocol of all the potential jihadists introduced to the Qur'an and the concept of defending their faith in training camps. These young impressionable recruits are often taken to their military training by a cleric associated with Boko Haram.[63]

The recruiting and marketing continue the imperative issued almost immediately after the Afghanistan conflict, that is, to create an atmosphere where the West remained the opponent and a hypocrite. That representation permitted the framers of the "Islam defenders" argument and media message to function as truth tellers. It put the "hypocrites" on the defensive and allowed the "Islam defenders" message framers to claim the position of holder of values. The West was then easily cast as a usurper of universal values, leaving the defenders to quickly claim the media battleground for executed media attacks that very often resulted in "Islam defenders" media success. The underlying message was fear for religion, fear for a way of life. The message was still fear.

All of these concepts signal one important reality: the relationship between marketing and recruitment and the terrorism event differs vastly from that of 10 years ago. Much of that is due to the evolution of communication tools, but some of it is also due to the marketing of fear on both sides of the conflict. Both have their market-responding corps of "subject matter experts" that have arisen. Both have their entrenched conservatives who refuse to believe anything positive about the other side, and both have a number of outlets available to their audiences to create a diffused environment; because of these points, the message transmission success rate on both sides should be compared to that of the pre-technology era to determine effectiveness. New studies need to assess the changed equilibrium and identify all of its component parts to determine any vulnerabilities this diffused environment may create. We also need to know how successful the West could be at exploiting al Qaeda-ISIS-et al. rivalry problems. However, the most significant assessment needed is one that would identify a new approach that recognizes the capabilities of the target audience and the factors the West can leverage in order for members of that target audience to help solve this difficult problem. All of our children are the targets and potential victims of these carefully crafted strategies and tactics. For their sake alone we need to find answers.

6

—∞∞∞—

The Internet: The Personalization of Terrorism

On March 11, 2004, Abu Musab al-Zarqawi cut off Nicolas E. Berg.[1] By that evening, the video of the beheading was available for viewing to anyone connected to the Internet.[2] Most who watched it were stunned. All major media outlets decried the viciousness of the deed, refusing to air the actual video. But the video was available to each Internet-connected viewer, in the privacy of that person's home. At that moment Zarqawi personalized terrorism's viciousness, making it available whenever the viewer wanted to "take one more look." The Internet became a staple in the arsenal of terrorist groups. Each watcher could make the fight his/her own. The more young people visited the sites, the more they became a part of a transition process of acceptance—acceptance of the acts perpetrated and, for some, a desire to participate.

Very quickly, visitors to jihadi websites began to find manuals for developing weapons, videos regaling the successes of the terrorist fighters, and advise on avoiding identification by Western intelligence. This was no longer a world of just propaganda, recruitment, and attack instructions. It now had drama, and while Zarqawi added drama, a young 20-year-old added capabilities that swiftly helped carry the jihadi movement into the twenty-first century.

That 20-year-old, named Younes Tsouli (aka Irhabi 007), provided lists of servers the jihadists could use to upload and share information.[3] He brought his self-funded talent, time, and knowledge to an organization willing to let him help even if he was young. He returned the trust with guidance on identifying and exploiting security flaws so that third-party organizations would unwittingly host the jihad data.[4] He is also reported to have uploaded videos provided by Syed Haris Ahmed and Ehsanul Islam Sadequee, two Americans convicted of casing the U.S. Capitol, the World Bank, and a Masonic Temple for attack.[5] Before his conviction and 16-year prison sentence, Irhabi 007 changed the way al Qaeda operated.

With his technical skills and Zarqawi's media savviness, al Qaeda has leveraged the Web for its maximum capability to influence the behavior of its constituent groups, modifying constituent use of this tool as constituent groups incorporated technology changes into their ordinary lives. It is a unifying force for the ummah; the young keep joining, and keep ensuring that al Qaeda, and its associated organizations, stay ahead of the electronic trend curve, remaining capable of leveraging any new technique that will reach out to all al Qaeda stakeholders.

JUST A GENERATION AGO

Al Qaeda's use of the Internet is central to its advancement from a group of four in Afghanistan, as the Soviet conflict ended, to the worldwide organization of today.

As early as 1988 Osama bin Laden maintained a database with personnel, activities, family information, and financial resource identification data.[6] These data provided families with specifics on loved ones in the Soviet-Afghanistan conflict and then became the basis for an initial repository of personnel records for al Qaeda as it began to function as an employer of individuals deployed worldwide. The equipment, and its capability, logically moved to other aspects of the organization as time moved on. When Ramzi Yousef executed the 1993 World Trade Center bombing, he followed the organizational model of using computer support for coordinating, monitoring, and controlling the entire event.[7] This proved expeditious for Yousef, but it also exposed the vulnerability of keeping critical data on a drive and/or removable storage that is discoverable by non-al Qaeda personnel. When Yosef was captured, he left behind the data, which exposed command and control information to investigating authorities and became evidence for subsequent prosecutions. That vulnerability would wait many years before cloud computing offered an alternative.

In those early years, though, bin Laden recognized the value this resource offered him for communicating with the foot soldiers. That is why, in 1996, he created a communication vehicle directed toward the foot soldiers. Working through his London representative, bin Laden authorized a website for jihadi news and world information.[8] Babar Ahmad broke new ground with www.azzam.com. He tapped a new vehicle to deliver the same message bin laden had touted in mosque speeches. Relying on those speeches, bin Laden had limited reach. Moving to the Internet expanded that reach tremendously. Other groups soon followed suit. By 1999 there were at least 30 groups with a Web presence. Since then every other terrorist organization has had at least one Web-based vehicle for constituency jihadi news and world information. That 30 grew to approximately 5,000 five years ago and an estimated tens of thousands today.[9] In *Terror on the Internet*, Weismann portrayed these sites as a skeleton for structured communication from terrorism leadership to terrorism stakeholders, but they are more than that. They are active instruments created and configured so that they help control constituent behavior.

JUST A WORKPLACE ASSET

Before September 11, 2001, computer use in the workplace was approximately 50 percent for professional and administrative staff.[10] By November 2001, al Qaeda was close to that rate. According to bin Laden's biographer Hamid Mir, personal computer use was so imbedded for al Qaeda that when members moved to safety after the collapse of the Taliban that year, he saw "every second al Qaeda member" with a laptop.[11]

Over the next few years, al Qaeda expanded its Web presence by creating a "cyber training facility" that ostensibly reached more than the 20,000 recruits trained at al Qaeda's Afghanistan training camps between 1996 and 2001.[12] While there was no control or confirmation that concepts were successfully transmitted, the number of attacks that "on-liners" initiated demonstrates that data dissemination occurred. This cyber training and other cyber presence also permitted reaching out to non-Arabic-speaking constituent groups, offering a fast-growing new audience bomb-making and chemical weapons training.

As these transitions occurred, nation-state cyber security entities have tried to eliminate al Qaeda from the Web. One tactic entailed inhibiting Web service to the al Qaeda websites. Government authorities hoped to turn al Qaeda's need for Internet connectivity into a vulnerability.[13,14] Working with Internet Service Providers (ISP), authorities found ways to either interrupt the service supporting the websites or shut the site down completely. The interruptions ranged in length from a few hours to several days. However, that tactic was challenged in the U.S. courts and government authorities lost.[15] This defeat sent counter cyber threat planners back to the drawing board. The result was a discreetly developed cyber security plan and an associated proposal entitled "The National Strategy to Secure Cyberspace." The proposal sought to create an "Internet-wide monitoring center to detect and respond to attacks on vital information systems and key e-commerce sites."[16,17] Since then government tactics have included infiltration by intelligence personnel actively monitoring and observing message traffic for hints of future action.

A March 2012 connection interruption for al Qaeda's al-Fajr media center showed how al Qaeda had grown. The blackout lasted almost 12 days, and when the service finally returned, members were introduced to al Qaeda's new al-Fajr, equipped with Twitter account. This Twitter account was one of the first social media forays for al-Fajr; it catapulted al Qaeda to a much more strategic communication capability with its market and the terrorism industry. Al Qaeda has since become quite proficient at using the tool as an alternative service for official material release.[18,19]

CYBER GENERATION

Given the demographic of al Qaeda's target market and the group's penchant for Internet presence, al Qaeda observers should have anticipated a migration toward "all things cyber." The cyber community offers anonymity and virtual geography. Al Qaeda has often transitioned to newly introduced technology. The organization has long since expanded social media to such outlets as Facebook and Vimeo. Members of al Shabaab, al Qaeda's affiliate in Somalia, notified the world by means of a "tweet" that they were the perpetrators of the attack on the Westgate Premier Shopping Mall in Nairobi, Kenya.[20]

RELATIONSHIP DESTROYER

One of bin Laden's unstated, but most observed, uses for Internet outlets has been to establish and destroy relationships. From the very beginning bin Laden crafted relationship-destroying messages when he sought to demonize the West and everything and everyone associated with it. The message defines the one choosing al Qaeda as the stronger, loftier, and more idealistic—the one true to Islam; it followed that those who did not choose or were opposed to the decision were not true. It ultimately drives a wedge that severs relationships. This forced decisions like the ones made by New York City accountant Sabirhan Hasanoff. Feeling guilty for his well-to-do lifestyle, Hasanoff provided "an advanced remote control for explosives attacks" and basic New York Stock Exchange functioning information to al Qaeda. At his sentencing, Hasanoff said he regretted his choices that he had only wanted to get closer to Islam.[21]

Initially al Qaeda established firm control over contact with each constituent group. As technology advanced and al Qaeda changed, its leadership recognized a coordinator of message products was needed in order to maintain a modicum of control. This brought many positives, particularly in relation to the release of message content to the ummah. The most immediate positive was an avenue to disseminate bin Laden's recordings without relying on conventional outlets to the general public. This increased al Qaeda's message-shaping control significantly.

As al Qaeda propaganda proliferated, it succeeded in increasing tension between the West, Middle East allies, and the people of the Middle East. Al Qaeda's call to remove all infidels from the Holy Land rallied al Qaeda's constituency and established a direct confrontational relationship between "the infidels" and all followers of Islam. Al Qaeda framed the "argument" and defined all categories of participants in the framework.

Once this framework was established, it was Zarqawi who modified it so that it fit into the laptop (and eventually cell phone) cyber world.[22] This was the world of his target audience. He made the jihad a one-to-one discourse between him and the viewer. He knew the visuals spoke volumes to the right audiences. Opponents responded with fear and anger, while potential recruits and supporters exuded pride. Target regimes displayed frustration. Others just showed curiosity; it was this "other" group that offered significant potential. Zarqawi exploited the "one-to-one" capability by providing products that could build a relationship with not only the adherents but this "other" group as well. He maintained an "information" wing that pushed the communication tool envelope. He began the practice of global dissemination of jihad news, with "an average of nine online statements" a day.[23] He spread videos (even offering download versions to accommodate different Internet connections). This sometimes put him at odds with al Qaeda leadership. But he responded by working in the open, on the very visible Internet, when coming to terms with that leadership.

The killings, blasts, and carefully crafted messages made Zarqawi's force into superheroes. These superheroes even had a cheering section. Compiled lists of suicide bombers were made available to forum members who could congratulate family members on the bomber's martyrdom. When one particularly prolific forum member, with the Web name Zaman al-Hawan, crossed the "divide" and moved from forum cheerleader to suicide bomber, we could see the advantage of disseminating the list to forum members, the ripest candidates for recruitment as suicide bombers.[24,25] This may have been one of the earliest jihadi uses of "Gamification." The response of other members was more of hailing Hawan as a hero.[26] Sites actually started moving to a point system for postings, increasing the similarity to gamification tactics.[27]

We had an inkling of al Qaeda's use of the technology as a command and control tool in November 2008 with the 12 coordinated Mumbai attacks. Al Qaeda trained LeT members in the fine art of an electronic command center. At the time of the attack the West did not have solid evidence of the technology used by al Qaeda.

The new knowledge framed a transition from propaganda, media, networking, data mining, online reference materials, online training modules, planning and coordinating, strategy, and, of course, fund raising. In its early days these uses provided a means for the computer to support networking and data repository. Networking and planning usually occurred in a rather static environment, that is, one in which data were entered, maybe sorted, but usually just accessed for reference or information sharing. But as Western allies curtailed the physical territory on which al Qaeda could function and targeted the leadership, attack planners, and spiritual guiders for removal from the network, al Qaeda turned to the one tool it had available that could connect it to its decentralized membership. Migrating to the Internet al Qaeda became the first guerilla movement to form physical space in cyberspace.[28] Al Qaeda recognized that its membership was more than willing to accept the responsibility for planning, executing, and even funding the events without central leadership input. Guidance on goals and focus remained in the hands of al Qaeda central to ensure the message was not corrupted as it passed from one cell to the next. But as technology became more interactive, this concern for message control eased. Focus moved to interactive capabilities, harnessing the power in this new cyber world, and conquering its geography so that it best supported al Qaeda needs. While not all of those objectives were achieved to the same degree of success, message control stayed constant during the early period, with emphasis zeroed in on demonizing the West to all of its constituent groups remaining central.

Demonizing the West is based in Abdullah Azzam and bin Laden's influence from Sayyid Qutb. Qutb's anti-Western sentiment pervades bin Laden's work and his judgment of the governments in the Middle East.[29] This sentiment was particularly evident in the two fatwas bin Laden released, the 1996 Declaration of War against the Americans Occupying the Land of the Two Holy Places and the 1998 Declaration of the World Islamic Front for Jihad against the Jews and the Crusaders.[30,31]

For bin Laden, Westerners walking on the holy grounds of Mecca and Medina was insufferable. This, compounded with the U.S. support of Israel and the West's sanctions against Iraq, made the declaration of war mandatory, in bin Laden's mind. This fatwa was released before al Qaeda had its own magazine-style website so Osama bin Laden had to rely on conventional external media communication channels to distribute its angry threat. These channels were not as responsive as they are today and did not disseminate bin Laden's message as he would have liked. The threat was, therefore, not known to a large percentage of Americans and was not taken seriously by the U.S. government. Release of fatwas today is managed via the cyber highway, and every issuance by al Qaeda, fatwa or not, is assessed for its threat potential to Western national security by the media and federal government.

SITE CATEGORIES

Each individual navigates an intimate decision-making process before accessing an al Qaeda site the first time. This includes weighing the pros and cons of that decision: Is this a path I really want to take? Does it hurt to look just once? Why can't I see for myself? Al Qaeda's recruitment face, that is, its public interaction face, creates an excitement for the "do it" result for that process. To facilitate that process, al Qaeda, and other terrorist groups, use three categories of Internet sites: official sites, chat rooms, forums and blogs, and distributor sites.[32] Each contributes to the aura of camaraderie needed to ensure subsequent visits occur.

The official sites offer jihadi leaders an avenue to constituents to access authorized information.[33] This authorized information is not always considered legal by external nation-state entities, but it is authorized communication the believers can accept as appropriate material that supports, in the case of al Qaeda, its philosophy, strategy, training, tactics, and techniques. These sites are frequently the work of ideologues who provide Islamic history, Sharia law interpretation, and jihadi literature.[34] Mustafa Setmarian Nasar (aka Abu Musab al Suri) was one such ideologue. He developed two of the most influential documents, both of which were warmly embraced by hardliners: *The Call for Global Islamic Resistance* and *The Syrian Islamic Jihadist Revolution: Pains and Hopes*. With these treatises, al Suri created a strategy and guide-on for the future. Greatly influenced by Shaykh Abd al-Qadir bin Abd al-Aziz, al Suri outlined a future jihadi movement that favored a decentralized organizational approach that trusted the mujahideen to accomplish the task without a governing body to oversee.

Anwar al Awlaki, American-born cleric based in Yemen, maintained an English version electronic presence, with statements justifying killing for jihad. Al Awlaki created a stir and major concern within the Western nation-states because his site was the first in English. The concern appears to have been justified as subsequent to al Awlaki's introduction of an English/Western culture-focused platform, several attackers have specifically named him as a significant factor in the decision to go through with the attack. Among those who have professed a connection to al Awlaki are Major Nidal Malik Hasan, Umar Farouk Abdulmatallab, Jesse Curtis Morton, and Zachary Chessar. Chessar started a radical blog, threatened the creators of the television show "South Park," and contributed to al Awlaki's blog.[35,36] He was captured trying to go into Somalia to join al Shabaab.[37]

The second group of websites is the chat room and the forum. Chat rooms, while not always as organized as forums, offer members an informal virtual "living room." The discussion may not always stay on topic, but the structure is one that may be good for the first timers to "try it on for size." Forums easily achieve two goals: communicate public messages and promote camaraderie.

These, along with blogs, are the main areas for individuals to have their say. They are more public than email, but they offer a speedy avenue to reach a large number of "members" or similar-minded people.[38] In these forums, members can keep discussions general or go to subdirectories and discuss specific topics like politics, or the Qu'ran. Some forums members become quite renowned. One who did was Humam al-Balawi, a Jordanian physician who was known as Abu Kujanah al-Korasani in the forum. Balawi, who also administered the Al-Hesbah forum, a "top tier al Qaida social networking forum," and participated in discussions, gave an interview in September 2009 to *Vanguards of Khorasan*, an al Qaeda publication.[39]

There he lamented encouraging others to take the step and act on their beliefs but not doing it himself. Balawi finally joined the action when he detonated a bomb strapped to his body, killing eight people, seven from the Central Intelligence Agency employees and one from Jordanian intelligence.[40] He was lauded in the forum after his death.

Chat rooms have proven to be quite versatile. They do not have to adhere to the *comment-to-a-comment* format. In 2007 Abu Adam al-Maqdisi, a member of the Islamic State of Iraq, participated in a live interview, answering questions proposed to him directly from members.[41]

Al Qaeda's internal and external constituent groups (or its markets) extend from trainees to financiers, with each critically assessing every communication effort al Qaeda uses to transmit whatever concept is needed for the targeted audience. Chief among the requirements is to reflect Sharia orthodoxy to fulfill the expectations of its core market.[42] Each effort of communication should interlace the basic tenets of Islamic economics: (1) distributional equity, (2) tawhid/brotherhood (i.e., the oneness concept that all are from the Creator), and (3) work and productivity act as a common ground for the reader to connect to all other followers of Islam and to al Qaeda.[43] Transmitting this focus was initially limited to the chat forums used.

Blogs are a more recent addition to the jihad Internet communication arsenal. They offer a versatility that chat rooms do not. In his study of jihadi sites, Rohan noted that blogs were sometimes used to facilitate links to other jihadi websites.[44]

The third category of sites, distributor sites, can also act as middlemen to other websites, link to lists of jihadi websites, or act as tribute sites for a cause or group. For instance, "Voice of the Jihad" focused only on al Qaeda in Iraq.[45]

One group of sites classified as distributor sites is the media group. These are the sites that carry message material for constituencies, often disseminating publications that ensure an organizational response to Western media news stories. This group of sites has significantly changed since the launch of www.azzam.com in 1996. Named after Abdullah Azzam, azzam.com offered daily news on Chechnya jihadi events, serving the same purpose as information organs like Manba'a El-Jihad. An early magazine that encouraged and reinforced the mujahideen of Khost, Manba'a, *El-Jihad*, was developed by the Haqqani Network during the Afghanistan battles.[46] Bin Laden never forgot the support the magazine provided and made sure to include something similar as he formed al Qaeda.

INTERNET FROM THE START

Hamid Mir, Osama bin Laden's biographer, related a story about bin Laden's headquarters staff as they were evacuating Afghanistan. After the collapse of the Taliban (around November 2001), Mir watched the staff hurriedly depart, grabbing essentials as they did. According to Mir, "every second al Qaeda member" had a laptop.[47] Bin Laden used the technology for organizational purposes, but his "people" understood the tool had potential.

Babar Ahmad was one of the first to start a website, www.azzam.com, in 1996. It connected al Qaeda's constituent groups until 2002. According to Evan Kohlmann, the Ahmad site "taught an entire generation about jihad."[48] He is purported to have run the site from the college network at Imperial College, London, United Kingdom.[49] The site offered a jihadi video library, photo library, stories, and news. Ahmad functioned from the United Kingdom but created an environment that jihadists all over the world used as a source for jihadi movement information. In its six years of existence, the site had to function amid frequent service interruptions because of attempts by authorities to disrupt the message dissemination and product distribution conducted by its operators.

However, by the time the United States finally indicted Ahmad, and his fellow www.azzam.com operator Syed Talha Ahsan, the larger jihadi community had recognized the control and reach this vital communication lifeline provided to target constituent groups and sites began to proliferate. To the jihadists the Internet's reach into the privacy of the individual computers brought freedom from conventional print magazines and broadcast media.[50] This freedom also brought the added bonus of message control, a critical asset at any time.[51]

Over the next few years, al Qaeda communicators embraced the technology and introduced concepts like a "cyber training facility" that ostensibly reached many more than the 20,000 trained in Afghanistan training camps between 1996 and 2001.[52] While there was no control over the quality of the transmission of concepts, data dissemination occurred. The cyber presence also permitted reaching out to non-Arabic-speaking constituent groups. As al Awlaki's English-speaking outreach demonstrated, adding languages took advantage of the tremendous opportunity the Internet offered to touch new audiences. Through the Internet al Qaeda could teach bomb-making and chemical weapons training worldwide.

POST-BABAR AHMAD

Just as Ahmad's Internet present ceased, a new figure came along, Abu Musab al-Zarqawi. Zarqawi was an avid Web user long before he was associated with al Qaeda.[53] Al-Zarqawi's use of the Internet began in 2004 with the Ansar forum. Zarqawi would have his al Qaeda spokesperson articulate a message and a link of interest, and the conventional media would then disseminate it. The site really became a point of interest by all external media after the beheading of Nick Berg was carried on Ansar. Aided by "Irhabi 007," al-Zarqawi provided a platform for other terrorist organizations to establish a Web presence.

Zarqawi leveraged the magnitude of the Internet's ability to influence when he aired the Berg beheading or the caging and killing of Ken Bigley. External media would replay the tape and remark on the violence.[54] Zarqawi made his speeches available, distributed his concept of the Islamic State of Iraq, and communicated directly with ummah.[55]

Al Qaeda's online magazine *Muaskar al-Battar* took advantage of this higher profile and began advocating that its readership use the Internet to train "in your home."[56] With *Muaskar al-Battar*, al Qaeda could provide an electronic alternate to young men boarding planes to travel thousands of miles to attend training.[57] Al Qaeda built an extensive "online library of training materials" and guided readers through the creation of ricin poison and bomb making. Other instructions included killing U.S. soldiers and biological weapons information presentation.[58] Ideologues like Mustafa Setmarian Nasar used the Web to publish and disseminate their missives. A prolific writer, he published his massive tome the Global Islamic Resistance Call, and his little 15-page guide to biological weapons.[59,60] Both called for significant action against the West. The small booklet was of particular interest because it drew on the Japanese Unit 731 activities to encourage dissemination of plague or use of carrier agents to act as incubators for the agent. The agent can then be dried for later aerial distribution.[61]

The modern communication technologies that use the Internet as the medium to "exchange between" and "connect to" al Qaeda's constituent groups have supplanted the umbilical cord of conventional media as the conduit to the terrorist community. Now conventional media receives jihad videos only after the videos have been released to the jihadi community. Al Qaeda's control over dissemination of its own messages is considered one reason for the increased danger al Qaeda represents.[62] As early as 2006, Brachman advocated more focus on al Qaeda and its shift toward leveraging the boundlessness of the cyber world to "transform itself into an organic social movement."[63] Once al Qaeda controlled production of, dissemination of, and access to its message, it became empowered to wage war with its own brand of cyber explosive devices. Al Qaeda harnessed cyber technologies as they evolved. It was the harnessing of cyber technologies that permitted al Qaeda to do what other large organizations have done: transfer many of its operations to the Internet. This reduces the resources needed to execute attacks because training and training materials can be made available directly to the individual planning the attack. Even if it were assumed there would be a statistical average number of attacks that are not executed correctly, there would still be a sufficient number of successful ones for exploitation and conventional media coverage. Al Qaeda entities still receiving direction for al Qaeda central leadership need only concern themselves with select strategic targets.

For this "statistical average-strategic target" approach to work, al Qaeda must have reliable Internet connectivity. Its connectivity is more dependable now because of current technology capability. However, al Qaeda had to develop this connectivity self-sufficiency because Western authorities found ways to interrupt the service supporting the websites Internet Service Providers (ISP) that al Qaeda had a website on their service and the ISP would shut down the site. The interruptions were not for short periods or a few hours, either. Sometimes they lasted for days. Between 2006 and 2012 service disruption of more than 24 hours occurred six times. But with current technology support, al Qaeda has branched so that it has a presence on many social media platforms like Facebook, Twitter, and Vimeo. These platforms have been particularly useful in making recruiting and marketing easier. According to Gabriel Weimann, about 90 percent of terrorist recruitment occurs on the Internet.[64]

Al Qaeda achieved this control with development of entities like the al-Fajr media center, the primary distributor of al Qaeda's materials online, and partnerships between al-Fajr and the Global Islamic Media Front (GIMF). Both offer a seamless movement from idea development to creation to production and then distribution. Now organizations from al Qaeda in the Islamic Maghreb to al Qaeda in the Arabian Peninsula to As-Sahab Media Foundation have a process to assure quality media products on their time frame.[65] These two tools alone have solidified the independence of all participating jihadi organizations from conventional media. As technology advances, these entities appear to do the same.

INTERNET AS A WEAPON

Daniel Clark once stated, "Cyber attacks would not have the same dramatic and political effect that terrorists seek. A cyber attack which might not even be noticed by its victims or attributed to continue delays or outages has proven that even if delayed discovery occurs, the response is so very dramatic that will not be the preferred weapon of terrorist groups."[66] But if the Ghostnet cyber attack taught us anything, it taught us that these attacks could be "attention getting" and world dominating in focus. Using September 11, 2001, as a gage, it is easy to see that al Qaeda would secure the technical skills needed to strike a jugular blow.[67]

The Internet facilitated framing the response of all constituent groups and increased interest in other organizations wanting to form alliances with al Qaeda. Its control of message and resources to successfully execute missions positioned al Qaeda as the leader in Internet use for terrorist training, messaging, and recruiting. Within al Qaeda, one of the best users of the Internet was Zarqawi.[68] He maintained his own "information" wing that pushed the communication tool envelope for usage.[69] He modified al Qaeda's mantra so that it graphically grabbed the viewer using just the laptop (and eventually cell phone) to access the cyber world. He worked in the open when coming to terms with Osama bin Laden. He spread videos (even offering download versions to accommodate different Internet connections).

He made training materials like "All Religion Will Be for Allah" available to anyone even if one had only a cell phone to view it.[70] Supported by 20-somethings who were very comfortable with the Internet's cyber landscape, Zarqawi leveraged his online support system, to carry his specific interpretation of al Qaeda's message to their counterparts throughout the high-tech highway. Zarqawi transitioned al Qaeda into the high-speed Internet world. Bin Laden was in his 20s when he first joined Abdullah Azzam. He transitioned al Qaeda into the computer world recognizing that the computer was the best tool at the time to organize the far-flung membership. Without having to touch each and every one he knew how to manage them all and their information with his computer's database. Zarqawi's Internet team exploited the just blossoming high-speed connectivity Iraq's Internet offered.[71]

Beheading Nicholas Berg brought Zarqawi to the attention of the world, but his use of the Internet to leverage that attention made him a jihad household name. Other groups imitated his tactics, including posting beheadings of their own.[72] The harshness of the actual beheadings took on a more depraved tone when the acts were described using terminology associated with butchering of an animal. Describing the acts in this manner removed Zarqawi's victims from the human race. He used this tactic well. One month later, Zarqawi released a "full-length propaganda" film.[73] It coupled suicide bombers names with their attacks, praising each effort as a win against the enemy. The film was released as chapters because the technology available to his organization at the time did not accommodate such a large file. While it was seen as "hardly ideal" at the time, in reality it was an opportunity to serialize the event for repeat message dissemination.[74] It offered his audience something to anticipate, a reason to continue to anxiously access the site. Releasing information directly to the Internet bypassed the "established media" and its censorship, a censorship that prevented airing Daniel Pearl's death tape.[75] It increased control over his message, a control that ensured his constituent groups saw and heard exactly what he wanted them to see and hear. He even shaped their reception of the message with audio releases that insisted his tactics were correct and anyone who disagreed was a politically incorrect "slave."[76]

The killings, blasts, and carefully crafted messages made Zarqawi's force into superheroes. So much so that those who followed onto the site or in associated forums wanted to participate. This superhero syndrome may have been part of the push for Zaman Hawan to participate in a Zarqawi feat after his 178 posts. He got what he wanted. He, too, was hailed a hero.[77]

VICIOUSNESS NOW A STAPLE

Viciousness is now a staple in the videos that are almost universally disseminated through the al Qaeda-controlled services of As-Sahab media. Control is the transition term that is most significant. Bin Laden and Zawahiri released their tapes through Arab satellite television.[78] They were usually prepared messages delivered in such a way that the camera remained trained on the speaker. Conventional Western media did not always publicize these releases, so the constituent groups within the confines of conventional Western media did not always see or hear the tapes.

The direct-to-Internet release of the materials fanned the fire of desire to join the jihad and branded vicious jihad with al Qaeda. This new image of al Qaeda increased even more interest in alliances from those organizations that wanted to associate with the well-known al Qaeda or felt an affinity for the approach the increased viciousness offered. They also found that the only response the West had to the websites was to temporarily halt them. With each removal of a website, the mystique of being a member of an anti-establishment group grew and its appeal seemed to grow as well. Again al Qaeda went to the root of its problem and determined that since ISPs were being forced to remove its websites or the piggybacked hidden ones were identified and closed inconveniently for the jihad message, the only solution was to find an alternate. Reportedly around 2008 al Qaeda created and implemented an Intranet-like service that was "hidden" in plain sight of infrastructure of al-Fajr.[79] It was created to circumvent email providers.[80] This is the very same al-Fajr media center that, combined with the Global Islamic Media Foundation, offers all serviced organizations a high-quality total communications support package.

In its early days al Qaeda enlisted the help of young people relying on them to carry out all levels of technology duties. During that period, the al Qaeda leadership did not overly manage technical Internet access tools because they had little experience with them. When Younes Tsouli assisted Zarqawi, he did so using his own resources. He came fully trained, using that training to share his knowledge with other members, not only Zarqawi's followers but others as well. Tsouli was taken seriously and used as a viable asset. His actions had such an impact on the jihad world and Western world powers, they are still being felt today. He influenced others, teaching them so they could replicate that same impact. For someone in his early 20s, that was not bad. Would the West have permitted him the same opportunity, for their mission and objectives? Probably not. Should they? It merits serious discussion. Facebook, Twitter, and Apple were all started by 20-somethings.

Security grew, too, with experience. As nations increased denial of service and website closure tactics, security became a major concern. Chat rooms, email, and Web postings became vulnerable and they reached out to find ways to counter. Members helped each other maneuver these early impediments.[81]

They moved to exploiting cell phone Internet capability, especially as a means to transmit audio, video, and text data. With this capability, last-minute modifications to event execution became possible. For instance in 2008 al Hesbash posted guidance on using a cell phone's global positioning system (GPS) to monitor and exploit an area or a "target."[82] The same year the Mumbai attackers used GPS for their simultaneous attacks. Discussion forums proposed and detailed using mobile Internet technology to observe, monitor, and film target activities and operations. There was also discussion on using the equipment to integrate into a missile head to film the target as it was attacked.[83] One technical supervisor at Ansar al Jihad suggested[84] "voice changing software for making VOIP telephone calls" for both Skype and Vonage.[85] Microblogging, using Twitter for quick group interaction, keeps members in discussion with almost conversation-style response.[86] All of these had to remain operational for efficiency and effectiveness considerations.

This does not mean electronic forums have been abandoned. In 2011 the al Mojahden English Network offered news, commentary, and speeches from Anwar al Awlaki.[87] It was these English focused sites that incited individuals like Nidal Malik Hasan at Ft. Hood, Texas, and Umar Farouk Abdulmutallab, the so-called "Underwear Bomber from Nigeria."[88] At these sites visitors checked for the latest news, suggestions, and information on "using AK-47s, making bombs, getting fit for jihad and evading FBI informants."[89]

These English-speaking forums were quickly followed by sites in Urdu, Hindi, Bangla, Pashtu, and Persian or threads in French, Turkish, German, and Hebrew.[90] The focus remains on youth, for example, the 17-year-old General Muhammad Bin Qasim Al-Thaqafi, whose exploits won territory that is a significant part of modern India. His conquest of the Sind and Punjab regions is touted as an example of great deeds young dedicated warriors full of zeal can accomplish.[91] There is usually no indication of the daily communication the young general kept with his mentor and uncle, Al-Hajjaj ibn Yusuf.[92] The communication provided guidance for each action, ensuring the young gifted commander would attain success.

The Internet has facilitated development of more sophisticated media products and materials. The al Qadisiyyah Media has created materials as part of a concerted effort to improve the offerings recruits can access. One who has shaped the philosophy and strategy for today's jihadi media is al Qaeda's Abu Sa'd al-Amili. With a directive entitled "The Reality and the Role of the Jihadist Media" published in September 2010, Amili pushes all jihadi media to act boldly and to use their "media pulpits" in support of the mujahideen. In this edict, which was translated into English, he equates the work of the jihadi media to that of the front-line foot soldiers, cajoling them to remain single-minded in delivering their message to the members.[93] He continually refers to the tools used as "pulpits," insisting "[w]e have seen-praise be to Allah-the extent of the abilities of the Jihadist media pulpits" and "[t]hese blessed Jihadist pulpits are a boon from Allah Almighty to his Mujahideen servants and also their supporters."[94] He differentiates between the "pulpits" and websites, but urges aligning the two in order to better serve the cause and the mujahideen in the field. He addresses the vehicles that are readily available on the Internet, demanding that a goal should be to own a video channel. He outlines programming and audience goals, emphasizing the need for control by insisting on taking an offensive approach in support of jihad, "the sharpest weapon for the community of Muslims."[95]

This is in stark contrast to the RAND report of December 6, 2011, that criticized the online al Qaeda community and its Internet strategy. Citing lack of successful attacks when he testified before the U.S. House of Representative's Committee on Homeland Security Subcommittee on Counterterrorism and Intelligence, Brian Michael Jenkins declared that the strategy was a failure and its implementation lacking.[96] Jenkins indicated the lack of violent events is a direct result of the vigilance of U.S. intelligence efforts and indicates American Muslims have rebuffed al Qaeda's overtures to follow its ideology.[97] According to Jenkins, the Internet offers inspiration and some instruction for people like Michael Finton and Major Nidal Hasan, or shift to Internet solutions for training, and attack preparation demonstrates a change in strategy and signals a significant weakness in current impact on the American Muslim community.[98]

Within a week, jihadi forum community respondents spoke out, using the Internet to disagree with Jenkins. Most sought to discredit Jenkins in the eyes of other forum members. One respondent named "Abuhamza" insisted Jenkins did not understand the virtual jihadist.[99] Another, Abu Hafs As-Sunni, structured a response that divided the report into four parts and addressed each of those four parts.[100] As-Sunni is well known in the jihadi forum community, and his analysis would carry weight in the minds of those al Qaeda constituents who might also read the report. It would also frame the reaction to the report if the "onliners" read his analysis first and then seek out Jenkins's testimony.

Addressing the response as an indicator of the thinking of onliners, the consensus was that their role was just as important as the violent acts that cause physical destruction.[101] The themes presented in the counter-arguments followed the guidance offered by Amili.

The Internet is also a place for those among the mujahideen who want to go directly to all other mujahideen. When Omar Hammari of Somalia's al Shabaab decided to capture his place in jihadi history by writing his autobi-ography, he developed a version and then he made it available as a portable document format (pdf) file on the Internet. Saying he wanted to follow the advice of Abu Muscab as-Suuril, Hammari posted what he deemed Part 1 of his life in jihad. A major reason for the narrative appearing on the Inter-net was the ease of bringing his manuscript to this medium for quick shar-ing of his fast-moving life's events. He used the same approach later when he disagreed with the strategy of al Shabaab's Mukhtar Abu Zubeyr. He publicly voiced to his Internet audience what he considered intolerable wrongs.[102] When abu Zubeyr's people killed Hammari, it was carried on the Internet as well.

SUMMARY

In 1998 bin Laden used audio tapes. He still used them up to the time of his death in 2011. In 2004/2005 Zarqawi posted on the Internet. In 2010 Anwar al Awlaki posted messages to YouTube, counseled via the Internet, and inspired "forum-hideen" to action. Abu Mus'ab Abdel Wadud posted an audio tape to a jihadi forum in 2008, but in May 2012, AQIM's Wadud issued a call on the Internet for al Qaeda rebels to support the Mali rebels.

In June 2011, Yaman Mukhaddab used Shumoukh Al-Islam to call for the creation of the Center for Electronic Terrorism (CET), an entity he pro-posed would focus on destroying the infrastructure of the United States, the United Kingdom, and France. The proposal contained background infor-mation so that readers could immediately act on the idea, and he urged those who could participate to join in to this electronic jihad.[103]

The center's purpose is simple: attack Western sites, particularly the United States, the United Kingdom, and France. In June and August 2012, in the same forum, AQAP placed several online advertisements for "a few good terrorists." AQAP wanted "lovers of martyrdom" to consider online training for attacks against "personalities [individual] who fight Islam and Muslims; economic targets, military targets, media targets." Those chosen were promised direct access "to al Qaeda leadership and their media committees" to develop the respondents video will. The advertisements emphasized that there is no need for passports or visas "to confront the enemy and kill them"; the training can occur in the security of the respondents' own home and they can serve in their own neighborhood. This is particularly interesting because the advertisement posters know that the intelligence community watches and reports on the forum's activities. Placing these advertisements in this manner leverages all of its internal and external audiences. Supporters and members are aware that the need has grown. Those who may have an interest in participating but have "never ventured forth," for whatever reason, can now "do it." Young people are willing to create their own virtual world in the privacy of their room. This permits access to information, ideologues, training, and immortality. They will be forever remembered for doing something big. For young people richly gifted with a desire to right what they perceive to be an unprovoked wrong, it can't get any better.

In the first two weeks after the advertisements ran, there were 3,500 responses; that's 3,500 individuals who may be in Germany, the United Kingdom, the United States, or France who are ready to launch a self-initiated attack with AQAP not having to provide any support other than online training and an online meeting with al Qaeda leadership. AQAP also has the post-attack luxury of either acknowledging the attack or not, depending on whether they want to accept credit (or blame). There are no additional costs other than personnel for online training, an online meeting, and the digital video will development and management. The business model is tremendous.

In July 2011 al Qaeda in Iraq again looked to the Internet for financial support when the administrator of al Qaeda in Iraq's online forum Seif Saad called on online website followers to submit suggestions for fundraising.[104]

Past avenues are not as prolific as they used to be. For instance in 2003, Internet scams run by Tariq al-Daour, Waseem Mughal, and Younes Tsouli enticed unwitting email respondents to "verify" personal financial information. This "verified" information went directly to the three 21–23-year-olds who were using the data to fund al Qaeda attacks, by going directly to online stores to purchase needed items,[105] such as "night-vision goggles, global positioning satellite devices, telephones, and survival knives and tents."[106] They racked up U.S.$3.5 million in total charges to support, travel, and guide jihad attackers. They also tallied a number of thousand-dollar transactions in online gambling to launder monies from the compromised credit cards. Winnings were deposited in the three young men's bank accounts. Tsouli also uploaded detailed instructions on computer hacking and bomb making.[107] His instructions on hacking sites very likely offered the basis for Abu Musab al-Suri's proponents attaching his work to an unwitting host site, www.fsboa.[108]

On January 10, 2012, Abu Hafs As-Sunni detailed a strategy for disseminating al Qaeda's message to the United States, and one of the tools he suggested was hacking, a skill introduced years ago by Tsouli.[109] This should not be a surprise and we should only expect more encouragement to use this tool, especially since online attacks have been sanctioned by *fatwa* since October 2008. At that time the Islamist Egyptian Muslim Brotherhood published a ruling from Egypt's Al-Azhar University of Cairo, which declared: "This Jihad is no different from the armed one. In fact, it might be more important if you consider the global dimension of the Internet."[110]

Al Qaeda supporters and sympathizers submit hundreds of documents each day to the Internet. Eliminating its use is a nonstarter.

To counter this dynamic Internet activity, a proactive response is needed. The International Center for Political Violence and Terrorism Research has started to develop a tool that harnesses all of the terrorist-generated data and groups for Asia and assesses the data so that selective data can be identified and extracted. They are seeking to develop a viable analysis tool that may fill current information gaps.

The Internet is a skeleton to a steady stream of contact with all of al Qaeda's constituent groups. The number of bones in this skeleton is so numerous that to remove one or two is no longer effective.

In the universe of cyberspace, al Qaeda is equivalent to a nation-state. It can communicate with its constituent groups, issue orders to its defensive forces, develop and disseminate strategy, and execute major attacks against any nation-state it chooses. Its lack of geographic borders eliminates the vulnerability of retaliation to specific physical structures or territories. Adversaries are confined to eliminating individuals.

In the not-to-distant future, we can expect the Internet to become a cyber territory analogous to a current sovereign nation-state with defined borders. Within that new cyber territory, there will be no fear of a Sykes-Picot Agreement, Balfour Declaration, Faisal-Weizmann Agreement, or a McMahon-Hussein agreement. But these same communication vehicles will continue to be used to incite fear, anger, and distrust.

Cyber territory is, to date, relatively negotiable whether you are a nation-state, terrorist group, or unaffiliated observer. There are sufficient means for hackers to circumvent established governances from nation-states, and the one in control determines use of the cyber terrain. If al Qaeda creates an environment in which its "citizens" function under al Qaeda domain and regulations/guidelines, current nation states will have to consider the possibility of negotiating with the group from a position of equals. Recognition as a nation-state would change the playing field forever. They have money, time, personnel, and expertise. It is no assumption the terrorist industry will remain ahead of the cyber power curve. We must identify ways to make that strength into a vulnerability, so that it is as negligible as our status of "superpower" when combatting them.

7

⚬⚬⚬

Yemen and al Qaeda in the Arabian Peninsula

Yemen, home to al Qaeda in the Arabian Peninsula (AQAP), is a bolus of contradictions. Its 168 tribes, 85 percent of the population, rely on that structure for resolution of almost all problems.[1] Yemen is home to Tawakkol Karman, winner of the Nobel Peace Prize, yet it is a country with at least four fighting factions and a "radical jihad" faction that is expanding at a phenomenal rate.

Yemen's strategic maritime location makes it a prime candidate for foreign investment and international relation development. However, it is the near-draught condition that is most critical for the nation.[2] It is home to the seaport city of Aden, a major port of the critical shipping route connecting the Gulf of Aden, the Red Sea, and the Mediterranean Sea. Vessels en route to and from China, Europe, and southern Africa transport goods for trading partners. The United States has a military base on the Socotra Islands, and the United Nations has deemed the wildlife reserve on the islands a World Heritage Site.[3]

Yet Yemen has no water. The scarcity of water is such that Sana'a may become the first national capital to run dry.[4] One of the poorest nations in the world, Yemen, and its economy, are victims of the government's lack of control and volatile environment. So many forces are in play that it is almost too hard to keep score. There are mixtures combining al Qaeda, the Houthis, the southern Yemen separatists, and the government leveraging one group against another.[5] There is abject poverty and political disarray. There is even a caste system, with a "lowest of the low" known as the Akham.[6] They too are followers of Islam, but are shunned and legally discriminated. The Qu'ran's demand to relegate race, language, and other "human made distinction" is moot because all under Islam are equal does not hold true.[7] Together, these confluences have made the people and land of Yemen fodder for al Qaeda and its affiliates.[8] To understand how and why Yemen has been surrendered to al Qaeda, it is critical to understand the political lay of the land.

POLITICAL LAY OF THE LAND

Yemen has four major forces competing for control of the country: the Muslim Brotherhood, the Houthis, the Salafist, and Ansar al Sharia.[9] The Brotherhood initially allied with President Ali Abdullah Saleh, establishing its Al-Islah party in 1990 with Saleh's blessing.[10] But by 2011 the relationship had soured, and the Yemeni Reform Movement made the Brotherhood Saleh's greatest opponent.[11,12] The Houthi demand for their own separate region with no control from the Saleh government has led to a "north-south divide" that is in addition to the problems that evolved with the 1990 unification of the northern Yemen Arab Republic (YAR) and the southern People's Democratic Republic of Yemen (PDRY).[13] The Houthis also control their own seasoned military, a powerful force with which the Yemen government must reckon. That is not to say the Houthis are the only pressure on the fragile Yemen unification. There is cronyism (a charge that emanated from the Saleh regime and has carried over to the Hadi government), the military in the south, and disputes over oil.[14] The Houthi military is a powerful force. Backed by their military, the Houthis control all of Sa'ada province and sections of Jawf, Amran, and Jajjah.[15] They have waged six wars between 2004 and 2013 and have begun to issue releases against the United States and Israel.[16] There is also concern that Iran may have begun supporting the Shi'a Houthi as Iran seeks to broaden its reach in the area.[17] Saleh used to counter the Houthi attacks using terrorism funding from the United States.[18] There is no verification the Hadi government continued that practice.

Houthis have a long history in the northern mountainous region of Yemen. Their Zaydi imams were arbitrators for tribe disputes as early as the ninth century. Even when the Ottomans controlled the area, it was strongest in the urban areas. The mountains of north Yemen remained the enclave of the imams. The imamate remained until 1962.[19] Under their control and even sometime after, Zaydi Shi'a and Shafa'I Sunni coexisted without great discord. That was until around 1980. At that time the region began to welcome back its fighters from Afghanistan. They brought with them a vigilance for Sunni interpretation of the Qur'an that conflicted with the peaceful coexistence. There was a growing call to move away from tolerance. The Zaydi recognized this call as a growing threat against them. This was particularly difficult because the president of the newly unified country, Saleh, was himself a Zaydi. There had been tremendous upheaval because of the unification, one of which was the resistance mounted by the Houthis. This came to a head in 2004 when the Zaydi leader Hussein Badr Eddin al-Houthi spearheaded an attack against the Yemen government.[20] Houthis felt the reunification of 1990 had left them with no real voice, even though President Saleh was himself a Zaydi. After months of battle, al-Houthi was killed, but the struggle did not diminish. The clash between Houthi separatists and the government of Yemen continued, claiming the lives of thousands. Each side accused the other of human rights abuses, a charge President Hadi assured the world he was investigating through "an independent commission."[21] The Human Rights Watch 2013 report took issue with both sides when it accused both of using children to patrol streets and stand guard at checkpoints.[22]

The third major force competing for control of Yemen is the Salafists. Ordinary citizens in the West often misunderstand Salafists, fearing them more than they do the Muslim Brotherhood.[23] That may be because the Brotherhood appears to work through the democratic political system in Egypt, espousing equal treatment for all religious groups.[24] While that perception may or may not be true, the reality is that the espoused position of the Salafists is one of following the example set by Prophet Muhammad exactly, with no modern deviations. That adherence to no modern deviations is often open to interpretation because the Salafists are not an organized group, per se. Rather they are a growing movement with a number of adherents who demonize religious "innovation."[25] To them it runs contrary to traditional religious Yemeni tribal governance. This movement, often equated to the "Wahhabi" or Saudi Arabian version of Islam, is a major force because of the way it is administered by al Qaeda in the Islamic Maghreb or Ansar al Sharia in lands they govern.

Salafism is especially evident in Yemen's northern region, where it has caused strife between the Salafists and the Zaydi Houthis. In the south, Ansar al Sharia-controlled areas have pitted the al Qaeda affiliate against the people of the region who do not espouse Salafism.[26]

Salafi adherents do not always participate in politics, but the potential political reach they can achieve can be seen in Egypt's 2012 election of 33 representatives from the al-Nour political party to the Egypt's parliament. Their election made many Western governments uncomfortable.[27] The general consensus in the West was that such elections would move a proven ally away from Western ties.[28] Apparently there were reservations within Egypt as well because efforts were exerted to marginalize the conservative groups. The efforts peaked when the military abruptly removed elected president Mohamed Morsi, and replaced him with an interim government. That abrupt replacement triggered both an outcry from Morsi's supporters and an international quagmire for those nations that were relieved that more secular decision makers were in charge but were concerned with the manner in which those decision makers were put in place.[29]

Under Saleh the Salafi were not as much of an "irritant" as seen in Egypt. When pressed, they often chose Saleh.[30] Under President Abdo Rabbo Mansour Hadi, there appears to be an effort to continue to work with government. Hadi brokered a truce between the Houthis and the Salafis; both sides indicate a tempered adherence. But charges of foul play were levied on both sides. The Houthi fighters insist the Salafists used their Dammaj terrain for training terrorists.[31] The Salafists decry violent attacks they insist the Houthis have executed against them.[32] Both sides demanded justice. After consideration, Hadi's settlement required the Salafis to leave Dammaj.[33] The Salafis yelled "foul." They felt betrayed.[34] Hadi may have sided with the Houthis because of the violence they can wage. His central government must choose its battles carefully and a battle with the Houthis may not feel wise.

Yemen is also home to the controversial U.S. drone strikes. Yemen has the dubious honor of being the site of the first drone strike to kill an individual outside of Afghanistan and the location of the first drone strike to kill an American citizen.[35,36]

As individual Yemeni citizens, particularly potential recruits for al Qaeda's Ansar al Sharia, try to function, in spite of the government's inability to provide basic infrastructure services, they have the opportunity to compare the lives of those who prospered under Saleh and those who did not. Those who prospered included Sheikh Hamid al Ahmar, a billionaire, thanks to mobile phone investments. Al Ahmar's father was one of the most powerful men in Yemen. Contrast this with the reality that more than 40 percent of the population is poor, with inadequate health-care services and safe drinking water.[37] Against this backdrop, young demonstrators voiced their outrage at conditions and demanded a change from the Saleh government. But while the Saleh government is no longer in power, al Ahmar continues his family's control over Al-Tajammu Al-Yamani li-l-Islah, more popularly known as al-Islah.[38,39] Al-Islah is Yemen's Muslim Brotherhood. Al-Islah snatched the very vocal movement for change that erupted in the streets of Sana'a from the Yemeni young demonstrators, after joining together tribal leaders and Islamic ideology. The young people were given their change in government and Yemeni powerbrokers remained in charge. Both achieved their goal, but only one is happy.

Against this backdrop the people of Yemen must still look to their central government for support services, including developing a strong economy and providing infrastructure requirements. Instead, Yemenis endured 15.8 percent of its population below the poverty line in 2001 and then watched that level balloon into 45.2 percent by 2003.[40,41] That steep poverty level increase resulted from a consistently decreasing national economic real growth that dropped from 2.8 percent in 2003 to 0.1 percent in 2012.[42] Unemployment in 2003 was reported at 35 percent.[43] It has remained at that point ever since. In 2005 the Yemen Central Statistics Office (CSO) reported that the unemployment rate dropped to 16 percent,[44] but was back up to 29 percent by December 2011.[45] The greatest segment of the population (63 percent) caught in the quagmire of such high unemployment is the 24 and below age group, al Qaeda's prime marketing target.[46] From a national perspective, there are several avenues to climb out of this dilemma, including investments and crude oil production, but from an individual Yemeni citizen's outlook, there is one approach that is not being utilized: the government shifting its emphasis toward delivering consistent services to both North and South Yemen on an equal basis. In an interview with the *New York Times*, one Sana'a resident said, "Our national crisis is the biggest problem. There is no water, electricity, everything from the government stopped."[47] One major complaint the Houthis had against the Saleh regime was a lack of support from the government. The Houthis charged discrimination when Saleh allocated resources needed for everyday community security. Saleh continued to cast the Houthis in a negative light and sent soldiers to squelch the continued uprising. He began to forgo the promised fight against AQAP to pursue Houthi strongholds.[48] Saleh justified his dogged effort against the Houthis by insisting the Houthis represented an Iranian threat against the United States.[49]

When those services stop, the need remains. The tribesmen react by taking matters into their own hands with violent attacks against the government, protesting lack of jobs and infrastructure support. Tribesmen blew up the main pipeline several times.[50] They decided they can do a better job themselves. As described by Sheikh Sadiq Bin Abdullah Bin Hussein Al-Ahmar, sheikh of Hashed tribe, "the tribesmen want to control their own political and social change to create a civil state."[51] Al Qaeda used the chaos of events like the barrage of attacks on the pipeline to ensure the state does not get a good footing. Al Qaeda even attacked the pipeline like the tribes.[52] It increasingly plays the situation to its own advantage. This has, at times, put the tribes in conflict with al Qaeda.[53] The people of Yemen have a tenuous relationship with al Qaeda, one that is strongly connected to the economy.

A 2011 survey of Yemeni adults (individuals 15 and above) found that 35 percent of the general population saw overall security as the leading issue of concern, even with its dire national economic picture. It scored twice that of the next closest issues, other economic issues (17 percent) and other political issues (16 percent).[54] There are many contributors to this nation's security nightmare, chief among which is sectarian conflict. When these same issues were examined by sectarian affiliation, stark differences were exposed. Imami Shi'a and Zaydi Shi'a saw the concern of security as most urgent, and the Ismaili Shi'a and Sunni respondents indicated economic concerns were paramount. The reality is that al Qaeda exploits the differences between the fighting factions as it flourishes throughout the country. Ending the economic turmoil is heavily dependent on resolving the political instability and removing al Qaeda's exploitation leverage point.

YEMEN POLITICALLY SPEAKING

If we take a look at the political instability in Yemen from the top-down, we have to acknowledge that President Hadi is at a disadvantage. He has "no substantial political base and cannot stabilize the country on his own."[55] But before jumping the gun and delineating what he "should" do, we must first recognize that, politically speaking, Yemen has been in turmoil since its beginning. Like Afghanistan, Yemen is a country over which many external powers have tried to exert control. As early as the Roman Empire to the Himyarite Era, Yemen's strategic geographic location has made it the target of external governments.[56] The Ottoman Empire annexed it and the British Empire created Arabia Protectorates in what is now South Yemen. Egypt's Gamal Abdel Nasser tried to insinuate his will on the Yemen government, as did Abd al-Aziz al-Saud of Saudi Arabia.[57] While South Yemen has suffered the most from these external government operations, attempts to include North Yemen have been much less successful.[58]

In 1990, Yemen achieved a tenuous unification of the former Arabia Protectorates in the South and the tribal-controlled areas of the North; however, all parties have not accepted that unification. One of the major reasons for that lack of acceptance is the disparity of resources made available to the North and South under Saleh. There has always been a "North Yemen" and "South Yemen" and conflict between the two after the ousting of the Ottoman Empire from South Yemen magnified it. Since the ousting of the Ottoman Empire, Yemen has struggled against the British and Egyptian governments as they executed attempts to control Yemen.[59] The British usually sought control of the ports, and Egypt, particularly President Gamal Abdel Nasser, sought control over the government. Yemen has long been the home of the northern Houthi liberationists and the South Yemen secessionists. After the Afghanistan-Russian conflict, fighters from these areas returned to Yemen and complicated the political scene with their determination to escalate their struggle at home so that it resulted in a government that followed Sharia law, at least Sharia law as they defined it. Ever since then, al Qaeda has built its stronghold within the nation.[60] From this base, al Qaeda has been able to launch attacks against the United States and many of its allies. Yemen did not cast out al Qaeda like Sudan, Saudi Arabia, and Pakistan had. Instead this draught-stricken nation became a refuge for al Qaeda fighters fleeing these other nations and an asset for the Yemen government.

President Ali Abullah Saleh was an ally of the United States for two decades, and he became adept at manipulating the U.S. military aid system to his advantage.[61] Saleh used the presence of al Qaeda to secure weapons and military support from the United States. He then used the resources against the internal resistance exerted by the Houthis in the North and the secessionists in the west. Al Qaeda freely roamed the South, a portion of the country the government and Yemeni military offered no real protection.[62] Even when they were sent to oppose the al Qaeda fighters, the Yemen military proved poorly equipped and lacking support. The military turned out to be no real threat to al Qaeda in South Yemen. Functioning under the title Ansar al Sharia, al Qaeda controls significant portions of the region, finding greater resistance from the intermittent towns and villages that do fight because they recognize they are on their own.[63]

Whether they resist or not, the people are in the middle. This forces their tribal leaders to craft a path of survival for their people. As the economy declines, the relationship between al Qaeda and the tribal leaders strengthens.[64] That relationship is tested when al Qaeda enforces its brand of Sharia law. When al Qaeda controlled the Abyan region of Yemen, there were reports of floggings, crucifixions, beheadings, and limb amputations, which were punishments enforced for infractions against al Qaeda law.[65] Functioning under the moniker Ansar al Sharia in Yemen, AQAP claims that it brings order to the regions it governs. It does not detail the cost of that order.

It does not address the individual stresses these "competing pressures" place on the people as a whole, and the young in particular. They must function every day. At times they respond to al Qaeda's system of justice and fear mongering with strong resistance. That resistance is not always directly head-on confrontation. Once, after al Qaeda was ousted from Ja'ar, a suspected al Qaeda member was found dead, apparently tortured after being arrested by the People's Committees. These were locals who fight against al Qaeda.[66] The People's Committees admitted they attacked al Qaeda but insisted the dead suspect had been arrested and provided proper surveillance. His disappearance was deemed a mystery.

Other towns have also taken up arms against al Qaeda elements, sometimes in conjunction with the Yemen army, but many times alone.[67,68]

However, most of the time al Qaeda's fighters are reportedly much better equipped than the Yemen army and the people.[69] So much so that in May 2012 al Qaeda struck and killed 90 soldiers in Yemen's capital city of Sana'a and in September 2013 it struck at the Hadhramaut region's port city of al Mukalla, driving out an army headquarters unit. The Yemeni Special Forces retook the city several hours later, but the ability of al Qaeda to achieve the win in the first place speaks to its ability to function against nation-state forces in the region.[70]

Now al Qaeda/Ansar al Sharia functions throughout the southern part of the country. The stronghold al Qaeda has on the country has been attributed to several factors: bin Laden's Yemeni heritage, the al Qaeda fighters returning from Afghanistan, the unstable economy, and al Qaeda's affiliation with Tariq bin Nasser bin Abdullah al-Fadhli, son of the last sultan of the al-Fadhli sultanate.[71]

The al-Fadhli sultanate was one of 16 former British sheikhdoms of South Yemen.[72] Zinjibar, one of the towns captured by Ansar al Sharia, is actually located in the area of the al-Fadhli sultanate. The sultanate, as a form of rule, began in 1700 and continued through the establishment of the British protectorate.[73] Al-Fadhli and the other British sheikhdoms in the Aden Federation were, in part, in existence because of the Sykes-Picot Agreement.

These protectorate governances were the regions that emerged as South Yemen in 1967 when the National Liberation Front (NLF) took over all of the area previously managed by the British. The NLF was a Marxist armed organization that had declared an anticolonial war on the Royalists, seeking to remove all presence of the United Kingdom from Yemen.[74]

The terror campaign it unleashed reached such a peak that the United Nations tried to broker a settlement that would remove British governance and introduce a "caretaker government" representative of all segments of the populace.[75] The NLF rebuffed the United Nations, defiantly maintaining that a political settlement would not be entertained.[76] They simply continued violent and, at times, vicious attacks, heightening tension at the United Nations and in the United Kingdom. When direct negotiations were finally conducted between the British and the NLF, there was no semblance of representation by the different people and factions.[77] The negotiations proceeded under an NLF-defined Yemen delegation. In the end the British withdrew. The terror campaign had worked. The NLF leader, Qahtan as-Shaabi, was declared president and prime minister of the People's Republic of South Yemen. NLF leaders became the new government and South and North Yemen united.

When they did, the validity of long-held beliefs about differences between the North and the South became starkly apparent. The South had gardens, schools, parks, and drivable roads.[78] The North did not. Both the British and the Marxist advocated education for all.[79] The supporters of secession flew the old South Yemen flag in defiance of unification.[80]

UNDERLYING NEED

Tariq al-Fadhli, who has described himself as a "tribesman, heir to the Abyan sultanate and crusader of Islam," declares that he joined the secessionist movement.[81,82]

The region that contains al-Fadhli's ancestral sultanate is part of the area with a strong AQAP/Ansar al Sharia presence. Yemen fighters have been part of the al Qaeda movement from the beginning. According to Camille Tawil's *Brothers in Arms*, Osama bin Laden had targeted South Yemen's Marxist government for overthrow, even while he was still fighting in Afghanistan. Fadhli and he are both considered to have been behind the 1992 attack on the Movenpick and Mohur Hotels in Aden. While the real targets were U.S. soldiers, the actual victims were a hotel worker and a tourist. Reunification in 1994, along with the ouster of the Marxist sympathizers, halted bin Laden's plan to transition to Yemen immediately.[83]

But some al Qaeda fighters still made their way to Yemen. A few, like al-Fadhli, returned home invigorated by the Soviet defeat. Other Afghanistan alumni came to Yemen as refugees because of difficulties in their own homeports.[84] Included in this category are alumni like Abd al-Aziz al-Jamal, Jamal al-Nahdi, members of Ayman al-Zawahiri's Egyptian Islamic Jihad, and Abd al-Rahim al-Nashiri.[85,86]

But the Yemen that al-Fadhli returned to in order to reclaim his father's sultanate had changed. The new Yemen achieved goals Fadhli initiated upon returning from Afghanistan. He was central to a movement that fought to oust Western presence. But his turn may be ending and a younger, fresher outlook may be in place. When Ansar al Sharia chose its Emir for the Emirate of Abyan, it was not one of the older more experienced sheikhs. Rather it was the under 30 Jalal al-Bal'ayidi al-Zinjubari, also known as Abu Hamza. Zinjubari is from an even older, longer heritage family from the same area as al-Fadhli. His tribe, al-Maraqasha, extends back to "ancient rule," which would trump al-Fadhli's claim. It seems to have exerted more strength than al-Fadhli.[87] Western experts questioned the reason for that surge of strength. A close examination of al Qaeda and its training might identify if AQAP is the source of that new strength. It would follow the al Qaeda's mode of operation is moving out the old and bringing in the new.[88]

Yemen is in a unique position to function as a bridge to the Sahel of North Africa, particularly if Ansar al Sharia gains control of its ports and waterways. Combined with Somalia's al Shabaab, its waterways and the Sahel represent two of al Qaeda's most critical regions. Yemen is home to AQAP, and Sahel represents the fertile failed state locations AQIM freely traverses. Each has leveraged the fragility of the region to its advantage and expanded a correlating sphere of control to more than half of the political borders. Using Yemen as a guinea pig, al Qaeda tested governance by becoming Yemen's Taliban. Acting through Ansar al Sharia, AQAP tried governing the townships Ja'ar and Zinjibar. These areas functioned as test tube experiments for al Qaeda's identification of a way forward with governing a region. Since then Ansar al Sharia has moved toward creating a fear that controls larger swaths of area.

YEMEN TRIBES

In Yemen one's tribe is critical.[89] Yemen tribes are said to originate from two major groups of people: the Qahtani, considered descendants of Noah, and the Adnani, descendants of Ismael, son of Abraham.[90] This lineage also holds heritage for the people of Iraq and the Wahabbis of Saudi Arabia.[91] One trait all fighters from Yemeni tribes have long been regarded for is that of being one of the toughest. These are the same fighters who helped defeat the Rashidun Caliph, found the second Umayyad dynasty, and withstood the overshadowing of Islam as the distinctive identifier for Yemen.[92] Tribal affinity and ideology have outlasted any other critical factor for connectivity as a people.

One misconception is that Islam binds all of Yemen, but within the geographical borders of the nation, there is a division between the northern Zaydi Houthi tribe and the southern Salifi tribe on Islam.[93] This, according to Prentiss, is in contrast to the efforts of the Qu'ran, which sought to discredit tribal connection and replace it with Islam. The Qu'ran was positioned to bring the Islamic community together, as one, when they had many opponents to their religion and no state to call home.[94] It is this oneness on which bin Laden relied when he issued his calls of jihad. It has not held true though, with tribal community entities remaining strong.[95]

These tribal community relations have had an impact on Yemen-Saudi relations. Saudi Arabia and Yemen have long had a tense relationship. Some of that relationship dates back to the 1960s when Saudi Arabia subsidized tribal groups, and sometimes political leaders, who resided along the common border.[96] Yemen considered this interference and retaliated by distributing cash grants to the Houthi tribal constituents right on the border of the Kingdom of Saudi Arabia.[97] This support to the Houthis helped Saleh maintain control for over 30 years and Saudi Arabian support of tribal communities kept Saleh dissidents engaged.[98] The Yemen-Saudi Arabia border is also important for the expatriate Saudi Arabians who influence Yemeni-Saudi Arabia relations. Saudi Arabia is deeply concerned that this group is significantly influenced by anti-royalists who have transferred their operations from Saudi Arabia to Yemen.

ANSAR AL SHARIA

Al Qaeda functions as Ansar al Sharia within the borders of many countries including Libya, Tunisia, and Yemen. In Yemen, Ansar al Sharia controls a large portion of South Yemen. By early 2014 it had had strong presence in areas near Mallah, Ja'ar Azzam, Rawdah, and a significant part of the Hadhramaut governorate. Ansar al Sharia is AQAP local. It leveraged the upheaval during the protest demonstrations started against the Saleh regime. It commandeered the uprising and used the unrest to implement its takeover of vulnerable locations. Members included Yemeni fighters who returned from the Afghan war as well as fighters from Saudi Arabia, Somalia, and other countries. Among the leaders of Ansar al Sharia (AQAP local) was Khaled Abdulnabi, Sheikh al-Fadhli's second in command. As the organization strengthened, it negotiated with AQAP for protection while providing it the Yemen logistic access needed for AQAP to execute operations.[99] The two groups that were exploited were the original AAS and the Aden-Abyan Islamic Army. They were soon molded into al Qaeda.

Al Qaeda's active presence in Yemen dates back before 1992, long before the well-publicized joining of al Qaeda of Saudi Arabia with al Qaeda of Yemen to create al Qaeda of the Arabian Peninsula (AQAP) or the unveiling of Ansar al Sharia and its heavy-handed treatment of the tribal areas of South Yemen.[100] Yemeni veterans of the Afghanistan conflict, including Tariq bin Nasser bin Abdullah al-Fadhli, had returned to Yemen by 1992. Al-Fadhli, who was a warlord at the time, reportedly created Yemen's first jihadi group. He lost no time implementing Osama bin Laden's plan to target the United States and is believed to have planned and executed the Gold Mohur hotel attack that targeted U.S. military members.[101] While no U.S. military personnel were harmed, the attack created an environment of cooperation between Yemen-al Qaeda contacts and al Qaeda central's Osama bin Laden. The Port of Aden became center stage for Yemen's al Qaeda with the failed attack on the *USS Sullivans*, the successful attack on the *USS Cole*, and the repeat of a suicide attack on the French tanker *The Limburg*.[102] Whether the Yemen government had direct or indirect knowledge of the network's activities is difficult to ascertain. But one point is certain. Most of the al Qaeda activities were conducted outside the region where the capital is located, the only area where the Saleh government had control. Yemen was also home to the Islamic Front, a training support and funding effort for Yemeni volunteers who were willing to export their efforts to conflicts in "North Africa, Kashmir, Chechnya, China, Bosnia and the Philippines."[103]

AQAP IS A COMBINED EFFORT OF NASSER ABDUL KARIM AL-WUHAYSHI

Yemen leaders in al Qaeda and Nasser Abdul Karim al-Wuhayshi, from the Yemeni governorate of al-Baida, fought in Afghanistan in the late 1990s. He once acted as Osama bin Laden's secretary.

Barrett suggests Saleh was aware of the AQAP development, but he (Saleh) did not consider al Qaeda a greater threat than the call for secession in the South and the Houthi rebels in the North. To Saleh, and his advisors, al Qaeda set a goal to diminish the United States and therefore was the U.S. problem, not Yemen's.[104] However, at the same time al Qaeda realized it had the ideal replacement for Afghanistan as its operation base. There was no real central government exerting control on regions outside the capital, and al Qaeda employed negotiations with local leaders, which created an environment in which al Qaeda could live. This approach proved successful enough for al Qaeda to start using Yemen as a base for logistic preparations. Once set up, al Qaeda was able to make a home in the southern areas, leaving the capital pretty much unscathed.

Yemen became the logistics lynchpin because it offered the perfect geographic and political environment to create what became the most efficient (read this as remote and unsecured) road possible for securely transporting weapons and other requirements. That logistics network strengthened over time, offering al Qaeda the framework for a seemingly impenetrable structure against the Royal House of the Kingdom of Saudi Arabia. The Saudi Arabia-based al Qaeda honed a support network offering ammunition and a safe haven. One of the first to help establish and later benefit from this network was Abd al-Rahim al-Nashiri, who planned events as early as 1997 but is best known for the attack on the USS Cole.

Al Qaeda leaders who are part of the Yemen government include Tariq al-Fadhli, another former Afghanistan fighter. Al-Fadhli "wept when he heard that Osama bin Laden had been killed."[105] He readily admits he fought with bin Laden against Russia and then returned home to continue that jihad in Yemen.[106] While he insists he is not part of al Qaeda now, he also acknowledges that one of the reasons for his support of the jihad was to fight those who had forced his father out of his sultanate.[107] He was an angry young man. He established the Islamic Jihad, a group that became known as the "Afghan Yemenis."[108] He fought against the socialist party in the war between the North and the South. He supported President Ali Abdullah Saleh in exchange for weapons, cash, and half of the office the socialists had occupied in the South.[109] Once unification became a reality, al-Fadhli used a different tactic. He worked very closely with Saleh and in return he received significant state support. His name was synonymous with a direct government connection. When he spoke, the government listened.[110] He used that power to his advantage. He forcibly took lands in and around the area of his father's sultanate. In return, though, he became a part of Saleh's "establishment" functioning within the Shura and General Committee, that is, until he felt the establishment had abandoned him.[111] His relationship with Saleh seesawed so much that no one was sure of his position on any given day. He even figures into the Houthi conflict because his wife is the sister of Ali bin Muhsin al-Ahmar, the commander of forces against the Houthi uprising. One thing appeared to have continued; there is a strong indication that during this entire time period he had not relinquished his contacts with al Qaeda.[112] He was known to have provided connections when relationships were critical.[113] AQAP leverages all exploitable relationships, and Tariq al-Fadhli was crucial in the Abyan governorate region.[114] Given the assignment of the emirate, al-Fadhli's usefulness may have expired. But he does not appear to be ready to just disappear.

AL QAEDA: FINANCIAL BENEFIT TO YEMEN

The one question to ask is why Yemen leadership did not do more to really stop al Qaeda. Saleh is reported to have finessed the international community so that al Qaeda's presence in Yemen worked to his advantage. Saleh must have appreciated the U.S. military and other financial aid boon al Qaeda became for his government. It was easy for Saleh to play one against the other. We also have to remember that Saleh was well aware that al Qaeda was a major employer; it provided jobs in regions that had the worst unemployment rates.[115] The regions under al Qaeda control have begun to reflect a "good governance" that appears stronger than the Saleh or Hadi central government ever displayed for the region. That is, they have begun to administer a consistent judicial system, instituted law enforcement, and identified infrastructure services required.[116]

Saleh really did nothing because it was the U.S. problem, and he had limited resources to respond to the Houthi uprising, which was, in his mind, a greater threat to him and his regime. It was a strategic business management decision. He also recognized that continuing the U.S. relationship placed Yemen on an international stage, in a limelight not otherwise enjoyed. Once in that limelight, though, Saleh had to suffer its judgment glare when the 2011 prison break occurred. He acknowledged his nephew ran the prisons and the guards offered no resistance to the escapees.[117] In short order, 15 suspected terrorists escaped a Central Security prison in Manssora, Aden, an area within the sultanate of Tariq al-Fadhli.[118] Public scrutiny and judgment followed.[119] The event received worldwide coverage.

Yemen's AQAP is not closely aligned with al Qaeda central.[120] Rather it, like other al Qaeda affiliates, is run by rules that work best with its local leadership and environmental conditions. It interacts with al Qaeda central but is not run by al Qaeda central. AQAP had a beginning in the local unrest that existed in Yemen and Saudi Arabia. The government of Saudi Arabia came down hard on anti-government elements that used violence as its anti-government response tool. Yemen's government responded similarly but did not have the capability to vigorously deliver that response, like Saudi Arabia. Both Yemen and Saudi Arabia anti-government factions that defied the established government authority realized they had to identify a different solution. They realized acting individually would not produce a successful result. They therefore combined their strengths and leveraged their individual capabilities to ensure the end result would keep the movement viable within both countries. The result was an entity that would work in both countries. Headquartered in Yemen, AQAP is considered one of the most dangerous of the al Qaeda affiliates.[121] It is also one that leverages an opportunity. AQAP has learned to leverage the West's susceptibility to bowing to pressure to save hostages and thus will pay ransom fees.[122] According to Nasser Abdul Karim al-Wuhayshi, AQAP's leader, over $20 million has been extracted from Western sources and used to fund activities in Yemen.[123] In 2013 AQAP produced a video in which Dominik Neubauer, a 26-year-old Austrian student, pleaded for his life. Neubauer makes his case for paying a ransom, under the watchful eye of an AK-47 armed guard.[124] Neubauer was finally released after the intervention of the government of Oman. AQAP is a fast learner. It has worked with AQIM, obtaining training and logistics support from them, learning the value of self-sufficiency.[125] AQAP has made Yemen one of its goals. But with Ansar al Sharia, its implementer Yemen is the main sufferer. It has seen more than 10,000 people displaced by the conflicts with Ansar al Sharia. With no significant natural resources and the highest unemployment rate, the region has no real avenue to pursue revenue streams like tourism.

The international focus is on AQAP, AQAP benefits to AQC, and AQAP's relationship to AQIM, while AQAP appears to have adopted a stance of Ansar al Sharia acting locally and AQAP conducting international incidents. The international community has to ask what is the definition of success for Yemen. This is a country that provided Zawahiri refuge when al-Turabi ousted Zawahiri for shooting two boys who had been coerced into acting as spies for the Egyptian intelligence.[126] It is a place where a UN Brokered Peace is exploited by al Qaeda as a negative. We have to ask as we monitor Yemen (and Syria and Iraq) what locations are we leaving to flourish on their own. Should we monitor Thailand and the Philippines more closely, not only for their individual activities but for the impact they can have on Yemen and the Sahel region as well?

Of Yemen's 25 million population, more than 63 percent is aged 24 or below, with an average age of 18. That young, future workforce already has over 13.9 million mobile phone subscribers, 2.3 million Internet subscribers, and 33,206 Internet hosts.[127,128] All of these communication statistics will significantly increase by the time the population is expected to double in 2030.[129] The current unemployment rate of 35 percent is a major area of concern because that plus the limited central governance outside the urban areas results in Yemen being one of the poorest countries in the world. There are exploitable opportunities for the international community within the data, opportunities that permit opponents of al Qaeda to chip away at its stronghold.

8

———∞∞∞———

Iraq and Syria: The Evolution of al Qaeda in the Land of the Two Rivers

Al Qaeda refuses to disappear when it comes to Iraq and Syria. The two countries share cultural and historical bonds but for al Qaeda. From Zarqawi's invasion in early 2002 to the present, al Qaeda has become an ever-returning menace. The only greater display of tenacity and resilience has been that demonstrated by the focused and driven Iraqi people and their ever-constant fight against the harnesses placed on them by al Qaeda, the Ottoman Empire, British rule, or corrupt leadership. Underlying that greater tenacity is the drive of individuals. Each individual within the borders of the state makes a conscious choice on how to respond to the ever-changing power controllers. As battles occur, participants make choices, choices that vehemently resist the externally imposed controls of these outside entities.

This resistance has a human cost, one that is felt at the individual level, in areas like limited or nonexistent health care, displacement, trauma, and death. The continued clashes are an indication that individuals on all sides have come to their own personal conclusion that violence is the only response. Al Qaeda has recognized that the decisions are individual from its inception. As an organization it has always focused on reiterating an organization-defined "logic" that exploits this very individual-driven decision process. If we want to achieve any modicum of success countering this well-oiled machine, we must turn our attention to emulating al Qaeda. During the sixteenth century, external efforts to control the region pitted Shi'a against Sunni as the Shi'a Persian Safavid Empire fought the Ottoman Empire for control of the region now called Iraq. By the seventeenth century, it was apparent that the external control wasn't where the real power was, which lay with the local tribal confederations,[1] and Fallujah was one of the critical natural hubs for communicating with that authority.

Fallujah's physical location positions it as a natural strategic center between two critical external points (Syria and Jordan) and two internal nodes (Baghdad and Ramadi).[2] In 1914 the British enhanced this natural strategic layout with easier accessibility when they built a road through Fallujah to the city of Baghdad. Its location near the Euphrates has also been key.

But while location is one of the city's most attractive characteristics, Fallujah has a fierce reputation for resistance against any occupying force. The people seemed to have experienced an especially keen chafing to the presence of Western forces. Before the August 1920 Treaty of Sevres ending Ottoman Empire was signed,[3] a Fallujah uprising erupted; it was quelled only after 10,000 Iraqis and 1,000 British soldiers were killed.[4]

Pockets of resistance continued intermittently. There was the 1941 uprising, the 1959 revolution against the monarchy—with Fallujah, Baghdad, and Ramadi center stage at critical points, and, of course, the 2003–2004 resistance to U.S. troops. The battles that started around 2011 saw al Qaeda target some of its favorite locations in Iraq: Fallujah, Ramadi, and Baghdad. U.S. troop withdrawals were in full swing and control of these critical nodes was at stake. The 2011 uptick in attacks was said to have sparked from Maliki's charge on the sit-ins at Ramadi.[5] Maliki insisted he was routing al Qaeda in Iraq (AQI). His critics say he was expunging his rivals.[6] However, the surge of 2011 started, the origin can be traced to those 2003–2004 battles.

It was those battles that found the United States targeting Zarqawi as he built his network across Iraq, augmenting the one he had earlier built in Kurdish Iraq.[7] He successfully established the network by employing a crafted, strategically deployed intentional chaos—a calculated chaos, if you will.[8] Quite simply, he wanted to keep everyone else off-balance while he expanded his sphere of influence. To achieve this he chose targets/individuals against whom he could achieve the greatest tactical media exposure. Using his organization Tawhid wal Jihad (ISIS precursor) as a backdrop, Zarqawi declared the United States (and its allies) invaders and thus legitimate targets for death. Zarqawi then went on to list all groups he deemed associated with the invaders, declaring them targets as well. Among the other targets were supporters of the invaders, Shiites, or religious and political figures who would illicit resentment in the media. His focus was the media impact his tactics would have, and he knew timing was key. He had watched the 2001 attacks on U.S. icons and realized he had to leverage that type of timing in order to make it an effective element of his approach.

The focus was on ensuring that his acts of violence were more than just a modicum of success.

At around this same time period, Zarqawi's violence-focused approach was affirmed by an Egyptian Sunni cleric named Sheikh Yuffef al-Qardawi. Qardawi supported Zarqawi's concept of resisting the "aggressors" to protect Islam, equating suicide missions to the "new human bomb weapon worthy to be called religious martyrdom."[9] For al-Qardawi, this martyrdom was "the noblest form of war."[10] Qardawi was also one of the first religious leaders to declare the killing and abducting of Americans appropriate action for the ultimate goal of eliminating the United States.[11]

Today the Islamic State of Iraq and Syria (ISIS) carries on the same ferocious practices initiated by Zarqawi. The more extreme the brutality, the more intent ISIS is on ensuring the media carries those brutal examples, often in their entirety.

As Syria devolves into planned disarray and Iraq erupts into a series of calculated, strategically executed attacks, we are made keenly aware that ISIS is successfully executing Zarqawi's philosophy of intentional strategic chaos. To ISIS, Syria and Iraq are seamlessly connected, a fact that became painfully evident as ISIS executed simultaneous precision attacks in Fallujah, Ramadi, and Aleppo. The attack's strategic execution treated the land as one entity, disregarding the political boundaries defining Syria and Iraq.

This seamless entity approach is an ISIS tool used to demonstrate reach, control, and power. It acts as an intimidation and portent of a future where Syria, Iraq, Jordan, and Turkey cease independent government structures and all fall under one Sharia rule. That Sharia rule would, of course, be ISIS defined and enforced. ISIS is also aware that any movement it makes toward removing Sykes-Picot boundaries will be seen as rightfully redressing an egregious historical wrong by its own ISIS members or potential recruits, and be taken as an affront to the current delicate political balance by the West and its allies. The accompanying Western media frenzy would act as fodder to promote the new world map.

As it spreads its seamless web, ISIS uses its controlled chaos strategy to impose rules on local towns. It introduces division within the towns choosing to create a desire to survive in the inhabitants so each family (and even each person within families) assumes an air of survival. One such town in which this strategy was used is Raqqa, whose residents battled ISIS and lost. When ISIS emerged the winner, it imposed a "tribute" on the Christian inhabitants. This pitted the neighbors in this formerly tolerant, even friendly to all, town against each other.[12] Now Raqqa's Christian townspeople could have no representation of their faith visible to the public. There could be no drawing of a cross outside a church, and Raqqa's Christian citizens had to adhere to an ISIS-defined decency dress code.[13] As each such proclamation was issued, ISIS imposed a tiered system on the Christian and Muslim residents. As each proclamation was enforced, Muslim residents became secondary implementers of ISIS's Sharia process. Even if they disapproved of the new rules and regulations, these former neighbors, friends, and family have more incentive to do nothing in support of their friend, family, or neighbor. In so doing they can be deemed to tacitly approve the new way of interacting. Whether conscious or unconscious, each Muslim resident assumed a survival persona, one that recognized that any outwardly displayed hints of disapproval of ISIS edicts would (not could) evoke the wrath of ISIS, thus redirecting attention away from "the other person" to "me and mine."

These Muslim neighbors, friends, and family exhibit a natural aversion to the swift, harsh, temporary chaos that would follow. At the same time, these same residents evolve to survive within the new ISIS norm. This survival mode adjusts to the new rules a little more each day, accepting the two-tiered approach to justice as a necessary evil for surviving in the imposed world order.

When local fighters observed this phenomenon in captured cities and towns, they often felt compelled to expand their fight from just the Syrian government to a fight against the Syrian government and ISIS. This became a significant drain on the rebel's limited resources. This access to limited resources worked against the rebels in two ways. First, when they fought ISIS and ISIS won, ISIS-imposed rules could become retaliatory. However, if they fought al Qaeda and they won, the Syrian government could then engage its larger stores of warfighting resources to lay siege on the fighters' neighbors, friends, and families, telling the fighters the locals receive food when the fighters surrender.[14,15] After watching children lose hair and teeth from lack of food, surrender seems a bitter pill to swallow to end the siege.[16]

Ultimately as Assad's troops lay siege, starve fighters, and put down resistance, ISIS wins.[17] This, however, may fit into Assad's plan. If, as reported, ISIS struck a deal with Assad so that ISIS could flourish within the borders of Syria, Syria benefits from the West's continued influx of resources to fight the "al Qaeda" problem and ISIS has a base of operations to train British and European recruits before sending them back to their homelands to wreak havoc.[18] Again, controlled chaos is out and about.[19]

Creating such a cozy relationship between the governing authority of Syria and the leadership of the unrecognized state of "One Iraq and Syria" resulted in a win-win for both sides. It permitted Syria to leverage all external influences to its advantage and it offered ISIS an opportunity to expand its control to even large portions of Syria. It did complement the already growing ISIS sphere of control in Iraq. But as ISIS solidifies its "statehood-ness," the governments of Turkey, Jordan, and Lebanon feel pressure to increase their own border protection measures. Turkey started defending its borders near northern Syria as ISIS's attacks began to creep closer to Turkish territory.[20] The Syrian government, on the other hand, is in an even better position than ISIS. Syria enjoyed Russian cover as this Security Council permanent member blocked UN actions against Syria. Turkey fought al Qaeda on Syria's north border. Local rebels fought ISIS and the al Qaeda drained rebel resources. Watching from the outside, the West is frustrated and portrayed as an impotent opponent to the situation.

HOW WE GOT HERE

Syria is the hub of an unstable region bound by Turkey, Iraq, Jordan, Israel, and Lebanon. Its own internal "uprising" began in the small town of Dana'a when 15 teenage boys decided to repeat a protest move they had seen carried out in other Arab Spring remonstrations. Armed with contagious enthusiasm for change, the young demonstrators "graffitied" the phrase "freedom, freedom and freedom only" on a school in town.[21] They were later arrested and tortured. All but one were finally released. That one was never seen again. The close-knit community protested the boys' treatment. The state response was swift and heavy handed.

Initially, when citizens demonstrated to protest the heavy-handed response to their outcry, the Western media started speculating how long Assad would remain in power. The underlying assumption was that Assad would succumb to the pressure of public opinion and citizen displeasure. But no one anticipated Bashar al-Assad would respond the same way his father's regime did in 1982 when President Hafez al-Assad's troops perpetrated the Hama massacre.[22] Speculation has alternated blame for the 20,000 deaths between Assad and his brother, General Rifaatal al-Assad, who actually directed the killings; whoever ordered the deaths, the fact remains that the killings occurred under Assad's rule.[23] They kept him in power and the world community did not depose him. He retained his close relationship with Russia and created a Syria that, at his death in 2000, was a critical lynchpin in a region that would soon start to lose its post-World War I European definition and start to reshape itself in its own image and likeness.[24]

Even with this history, the Syrian demonstrators had high hopes that Assad's son would respond differently when faced with peaceful opposition.[25] They were sure he would respond peacefully. They did not expect him to emulate his father and destroy his own citizens to squelch resistance and remain in power.[26]

Many Western Middle East speculators assumed Syria (Assad) would capitulate like Egypt, Yemen, and Libya.[27] But three years after the teens' demonstration, arrest, and disappearance, more than 150,000 Syrian deaths are estimated to be directly attributable to the "uprising." Aided by logistics and UN Security Council support from Russia, Syria has navigated unpleasant media coverage, dismissed internal pressures, and invoked Sykes-Picot to weather the storm. It appears to be counting on the international community's inability to do more than express its displeasure through verbal espousals on Syria's internal affairs. No international military interference is expected. All the international community can do is scold, rebuke, and castigate.

Syria's leaders and fighters know this. They also know that the U.S. Congress is war weary as are the American people. The U.S. Congress also recognizes that any response must juggle the fact that the region is a hotbed of anti-American sentiment and one U.S. military boot on the soil of any Middle East sovereign state that once functioned as a colony under "the West" would serve as the fuse for explosive anti-American activities and recruitment fodder for al Qaeda and its affiliates. There is every likelihood that after thousands of deaths, hundreds of bombings, and many traded accusations of human rights abuses, President Assad will remain in power. ISIS will grow in strength and the West and the United Nations will have diminished in influence because of inaction. Everyone is tired now, especially the Syrian ill-equipped rebels.

When we look at Iraq, we see the same battle weariness. Iraq's citizens are just as tired of war as the Syrian people; they are especially angry that their initial demonstrations of dissatisfaction with government corruption have been usurped by ISIS, to its own good, not theirs.

Iraq's Fallujah, and its sister city Ramadi, were the site of some of the 2003–2010 war's most fierce and casualty-filled fighting. More than a third of the reported U.S. military deaths occurred in Anbar, the province in which Fallujah, Ramadi, and Baghdad are located. Fallujah was also home to some of the most controversial events of the war. One of the most heavily media-covered events was the insurgent ambush of a convoy carrying four U.S. contractors, their killing and mutilation, and the burning and hanging of their bodies by an angry mob of Iraqi citizens.[28] Another was the U.S. Marines Firepower surges used to pursue Abu Musab al-Zarqawi.[29] Zarqawi was an Afghanistan-Russia conflict veteran who had an entrenched al Qaeda network. He publicly pursued establishing the original Islamic State of Iraq. Anti-U.S. sentiment rose during the surges, particularly when U.S. officials responded to casualty counts that included women and children by calling these deaths "collateral damage." This led to increased anti-American demonstrations and incidents of reprisal. The winners in all of the exchanges were al Qaeda and Abu al-Zarqawi.

Zarqawi knew how to derive the most from the core fighters he trusted to support his violent pursuit of jihad.[30] This pursuit often put Zarqawi at odds with Ayman al-Zawahiri, not unlike ISIS's Abu Bakr al-Baghdadi. Zawahiri's lack of control over Zarqawi may have been a foreshadowing of his troubles with Abu Bakr al-Baghdadi. Zarqawi refused to reduce the violence associated with his force. Al-Baghdadi refused to submit to Zawahiri's prohibition to merge with the Jabhat al-Nusra. In addition he expanded his areas of control within the Syria-Iraq border areas, creating a means to a seamless sphere of influence in the future, one that rivals the central government for both countries. The future looks at the concerns that will influence Bahrain with the Shi'a attacks and Saudi Arabia with its support of the rebel forces. Saudi Arabia, which has previously expressed displeasure with the Assad regime (and its benefactor Iran), would have significantly more opposition to any al Qaeda-enforced governance.

HOW IT STARTED

Most Westerners were unaware of Fallujah before March 2004, and they may never have come to know the name if four Blackwater contractors had not stopped overnight after getting confused looking for the Al Taqaddam Air Base, just west of Fallujah. The contractors were escorting three flatbed trucks belonging to ESS Support Services Worldwide (subcontractor to Kellogg, Brown, and Root). Ignoring advice to avoid the downtown area, the team decided it would be faster going through the city's downtown area. Heading toward the area without Marines escort, the contractors and the flatbed trucks were caught in traffic. It was around this time that insurgents focused on the Blackwater team and opened fire on the escort vehicles. The flatbed trucks and their drivers escaped unharmed. But the Blackwater team was shot, burned, dismembered, and then dragged through downtown. At some point two of the bodies were hung from a bridge that crossed part of the Euphrates River.[31] The event was videotaped and broadcast across the world on the evening news. Initially there was international outrage. The Marines first proposed surgical attacks on strategic targets, a response that sought to downplay any appearance of revenge. Washington's civilian leadership felt a stronger reaction was needed.[32] The final response design had objectives of capturing Zarqawi and ending Fallujah resistance.[33] The events of that day and the subsequent attacks over the months that followed were costly in lives and credibility for the United States. Commentary on what went wrong has been presented in almost every format, from an opera to soldiers' memoirs, to films like *The Grand Wars of Civilization*.[34,35,36] Chief among the comments is the strong resistance that Zarqawi's fighters presented when clashes occurred. The operation, named Vigilant Resolve, ended with public opinion going against the United States, insurgent activity against coalition forces increasing throughout Iraq, and Zarqawi slipping away.[37]

Zarqawi had a reputation that ranged from "gangster" to "freedom fighter."[38] He waged war on the Shiites, beheaded Nick Berg, and created a whole new approach to terrorism with his prolific use of the Internet. Fallujah was the ground floor or foundation of his and al Qaeda in Iraq's reputation with al Qaeda central and the rest of the world. Fallujah was a city whose residents were caught between the U.S. forces and Zarqawi's so-called freedom fighters. Zarqawi and his followers (later renamed Tawhid wal Jihad by Zarqawi) killed Shiites and foreign visitors alike.[39] Fallujah residents were uncertain whom to support, but they knew Zarqawi's fierceness and feared that more; they were also aware of the effects of resisting his advance into and overtaking of the city.[40] Zarqawi was strategic about his viciousness as well. He executed fewer attacks than other groups, but his ferocity demanded attention and his attacks were the ones followed by the world.[41] He knew he could force the balance of power his way by forging a path of terror, much the same way ISIS does with current fighting.

Zarqawi is known to have entered Iraq as early as 2002. He came through the northern region that was controlled by independent Iraqi Kurdistan.[42] Under Zarqawi, Fallujah became home to torture chambers that were immortalized in videos Zarqawi uploaded onto the Internet. Zarqawi advocated controlled chaos. On the surface this approach could appear to be an undisciplined program. But under Zarqawi, it was used to strategically select areas and circumstances of attack for "frenzied events," effects they could evoke. This approach made a name for Zarqawi and provided the environment for him to slip out of Fallujah during the United States' first Fallujah attack; it also created an environment for Fallujah to become a rallying cry that solidified anti-U.S. fervor. All of this worked in Zarqawi's favor.

The United States never really recovered from what became the greatest public relations disaster of the entire conflict. Fallujah, meanwhile, achieved the reputation of the most dangerous city in all of Iraq.[43] Ultimately, it was al Qaeda's first city-state.[44] Fallujah was al Qaeda's open door to the rest of the country.

A second, better-coordinated coalition forces attack strategy several months later did result in taking Fallujah back from Zarqawi's fighters.[45] But the region remained a hotbed of resistance, so much so that as the 2014 U.S. drawdown became real, Fallujah again sat front and center in the crosshairs of conflict.

Ten years after the first two struggles for the control of the cities, Fallujah and Ramadi were again at stake. Before the uprising, the United States had even hinted that it had control and the area was on the road to democracy. Then fierce fighting broke out between the Maliki government forces and protestors. But the protestors were augmented (whether they wanted it or not) by the current perpetrators of Zarqawi's vicious violence fighting under the banner of ISIS. ISIS proved worthy of the Zarqawi legacy. They caused significant bloodshed in Fallujah, Beirut, and Syria, all at the same time.[46] The Syrian freedom fighters were battling both the government forces and members of ISIS.[47] Maliki, a Shiite, struggled to maintain control of his country as the United States prepared to leave, and while Maliki worried about the entire country, ISIS chipped away at northern Iraq, securing its hold on tribal areas.

Maliki has broadened al Qaeda's base for recruiting with executed security crackdowns and mass arrests of Sunnis. Whether fighters are joining in the fray because of sectarian issues is only one of many concerns. The dissent expressed by citizens in the areas illustrates their dissatisfaction with the current central government.[48] There are cries of corruption and affiliation of local Shiite leaders with Hezbollah that has gone unpunished.[49] Even as Maliki tried to respond to these allegations with crackdowns on Shiite leaders, ISIS continued to expand its control in Syria, Lebanon, and northern Iraq.[50] The strong control ISIS demonstrated as it executed attacks against Ramadi and Fallujah resulted in the government ceding control of the two cities to ISIS more than once as ISIS set fire to police stations, freed jailed prisoners, and took over mosques.[51] Families began to flee Fallujah, and Anbar Province as a whole, at rates that hinted soon none would remain.[52] As they left, they reflected on how the situation at the time was a repeat of 10 years ago.[53] The cities where ISIS was in charge showed signs of the group's continued commitment to extreme violence as the means to control.[54] Yes, their brutality echoed ISIS's Zarqawi legacy. But the capability of ISIS to simultaneously conduct attacks in Syria, Iraq, and Beirut, Lebanon, spoke volumes about its growing strength.[55]

The Islamic State of Iraq and al-Sham's is an outgrowth of Zarqawi's Jama'at al-Tawhid wal-Jihad.[56] Zarqawi was a proponent of brute force rather than keen strategy to achieve his goals.[57] His efforts were deemed successful, though, as he pummeled his way through Iraq. He executed attacks but never wavered from his ultimate goal of removing Jordan's leadership and eliminating Israel as a nation. Zarqawi controlled a loose coalition of groups that included Ansar al-Islam, Ansar al-Sunna, Jaysh Mohammed, Al-Jamma Salafiya, Takfir wal Hijra, and Jund al-Sham.[58]

Zarqawi aligned himself and his group with al Qaeda, but did not agree with al Qaeda leadership, particularly Zawahiri, on not killing Shi'a and avoiding civilian deaths. Zawahiri was haunted by the death of Shayma Abdel-Halim, a 12-year-old little girl who died when Zawahiri attempted to assassinate Egypt's then prime minister Atef Sedki.[59] Sedki survived but Shayma died when a door unhinged by the blast crushed her. Her funeral was the scene of outrage against Zawahiri's group, as the perpetrators. Her grandmother's devastation and the city's outrage were exploited by the government and caused significant backlash against Zawahiri.[60] Zawahiri knew the negative impact civilian deaths could have on the public's response. He was willing to use that backlash against the United States for any civilian women and children it killed. He wanted to minimize his organization's contributions to those deaths. Zarqawi felt otherwise. He had no bad memories haunting him. He only knew the media attention that could come from graphic deaths and was not afraid to use that attention. In his writings, he justified the viciousness of his acts with the Qur'an.[61] His viciousness was part of the impetus for the United States to advance during the First Battle of Fallujah.[62,63]

Looking back, the tactic most in play during the clashes between the United States and the insurgents was the effort the insurgents made to make the United States fight as hard as it could for every inch. This played badly in the press for the United States. The Marines found 2,000 hardened fighters and 200 foreign fighters.[64] But as the Marines fought for each inch, they did so neighborhood by neighborhood.[65,66] Zarqawi's fighters were coordinated, effective, and relentless. With no real support from the promised Iraqi soldier backup, and no real political will, "the Marines were ordered to withdraw."[67] But the insurgents would not discontinue the fight. A planned effort to transition a stabilizing force using former Iraqi soldiers failed as well since most of the stabilizing force joined the insurgents, taking U.S.-supplied weapons with them.[68]

In the end, 36 Marines were killed, along with 200 insurgents. But the biggest loss was of 600 civilians. The fallout from that result is still at play.[69] At first the negatives were the loss of credibility because there was no real "Iraqi" face on the mission. There was no real stability in the city. Insurgents tried to reinforce the positions they held and even expand their sphere of influence when possible.[70]

Zarqawi is also a bridge, a connection if you will, to Syria because he lived in Syria from May to September 2002. He used a Syrian passport to pass between Jordan and Iraq as he planned the assassination of Laurence Foley, and Syria was Zarqawi's rear base. Jordan was an area to secure a strong foundation.[71] Syria was critical for safe haven routing of fighters. It was home to his training and the source of recruits for his European cells. During this period President Assad publicly questioned the existence of al Qaeda, suggesting that the group ended after the Afghanistan-Soviet conflict.[72] Evidence introduced at the Hamburg Cell Trial implicated Syria's intelligence service for its knowledge of Zarqawi and the service's tacit approval of his activities. If true, this provided cover for Zarqawi to safely continue to function within Syria.

Given this history, and the influence Zarqawi had on ISIS current leadership, we can expect no less as ISIS advances on the Sykes-Picot line and the remnants of Western influence on the economy.

Syria and the Assad regimes have functioned under U.S. sanctions since 1979. So when the international community suggested sanctions against Syria to force it to stop attacking its people, Assad responded as if this was no real threat. Continuing to function under these restrictions would not be a venture into the unknown; it instead offers fodder for those who want to foster the belief that the West will never come to Syrian rebels' aid. In addition, the delay for outside help has fostered an insurgent geographical landscape that supports over 1,000 insurgent groups, including the Islamic State in Iraq and the Levant, Jabhat al-Nusra, Harakat Ahrar al-Sham al-Islamiyya, Suqoral-Sham, Liwa al-Islam, Liwa al-Tawhid, Jabhat al-Asala wal Tanimia, Aiwia Ahfad al-Rasoul, Katibat Shuhada al-Yarmouk, and Yekineyen Parastina Gel (YPG).[73]

Given the limited geography, but strategic positioning of Syria, the insurgents found themselves scrapping, turning on each other trying to mark territory. None wanted to acquiesce to any other group. Without the "boogey man West" focal point, the resultant infighting has tallied a death toll over 3,000 with 500 in January 2014 alone.[74] This infighting led to wins for Syrian government and territory for the ISIS. Recognizing that they must do something or perish as a footnote to ISIS versus the government, 13 organizations combined efforts to force ISIS out of the picture.[75]

The citizens are caught in the middle and suffer the consequences when the Assad regime, for instance, isolates a town forcing its residents to slowly starve.[76] Since the Assad regime has begun responding to antigovernment demonstrations, attacks on civilians have been risen significantly. Both the regime and countering forces have contributed to a mounting death toll.

As a whole, Iraq was the center of much speculation with the removal of the first U.S. troops in 2011. Two years later, al Qaeda had begun to stretch its muscles, reminding everyone it would still be there, long after the United States left.[77] Al Qaeda focused on areas that had been insurgent strongholds before—the cities in Anbar Province, especially Fallujah and Ramadi.[78] The perpetrators of the fight in Anbar Province were also the hard liners in Syria and Beirut. ISIS had the resources to conduct attacks on several fronts and win them all. It had the resolve, the equipment, and the personnel.[79] Civilian casualties began to mount on all fronts as well. As ISIS continued to conduct its attacks to expand its sphere of influence, the people of Iraq began to demonstrate against policies and treatment they felt were anti-Sunni.

In Fallujah and Ramadi, Prime Minister Maliki's government troops were unable to quell the growing outcry against the treatment meted out to Sunni citizens. Encampments went up and Maliki ordered them removed. When his security troops tried to enforce Maliki's orders, a battle ensued leaving 108 dead. One thing became apparent—the security forces were not as well equipped for battle as ISIS. Even as the government tried to encourage tribal leaders to side with them to combat ISIS, the tribal leaders have to hedge their bet trying to determine which of the two is the lesser evil.[80]

The international community began to wring its hands trying to determine a solution to the civil unrest al Qaeda's invasion caused. ISIS itself began to encounter and acknowledge opposition from other al Qaeda terrorist factions. ISIS response has been one that is consistent with its already easily defined mode of operation. ISIS and Jabhat al-Nusra were an announced merger by Abu Bakr al-Baghdadi. But defections and displeasure with the announced move caused Zawahiri to speak out against it. Al-Baghdadi said he would move forward with the merger. However, after a period, Jabhat al-Nusra objected and confrontations and outright battles resulted in over 3,000 deaths.[81] Most of the fighting occurred in northern Syria. Al-Nusra's leader Abu Mohammed al-Golani has suggested arbitration to settle the matter. But ISIS continued to pursue a ferocious violence that would determine outcome. Following a path set by Zarqawi, al-Baghdadi has continued his onslaught in the northern Syrian area, advancing his area of control and diminishing that of the rival groups.[82]

The exact number is not known. But ISIS ranks grew significantly after it masterminded and executed a July 22, 2013, prison break at both Abu Ghraib and Taji prisons. The result was at least 500 inmates escaped, with estimates between 500 and 1,000.[83] No prisoners escaped from Taji; all were from Abu Ghraib. The prison break occurred only three months after factions of Syrian Jabhat al-Nusra had merged with al-Baghdadi's group.[84]

Most of those freed joined ISIS ranks. Obtaining fighters from the prisons permitted al-Baghdadi a tremendous opportunity to acquire trained, seasoned personnel without investing in that training. The fighters are ready to go and vicious acts of harm performed on or against another human being are not foreign to them. Young people following on Twitter have taken up the "excitement" and announced on their Twitter account they are joining the fight in Syria under ISIS.

ISIS is considered the strongest influence in all of northern Iraq and is growing in controlled areas in Syria. Lebanon is considered next on its list. Life under ISIS has been described as so restrictive that civilians say they have no music, pictures, or the Qur'an on tape. Women are forced to wear the veil or face execution. People are seized right off the street. Appearances before the Sharia court result in rulings that include electric shock, beheadings, floggings, and dismemberment. Amnesty International has documented many cases of abuse, one in which a boy of 12 receives over 100 lashes.[85] The war and the ISIS approach seemed to have a broad appeal, with fighters coming from Chechnya, Morocco, and Saudi Arabia. No matter their origin, the fighters implement Sharia law mercilessly.[86]

9

---✦✦✦---

North Africa and al Qaeda in the Islamic Maghreb

When the Islamic State of Iraq and Syria (ISIS) initially declared a caliphate, al Qaeda in the Islamic Maghreb (AQIM) issued a statement of support and urged other jihad organizations to do the same. But not even a month later both AQIM and al Qaeda in the Arabian Peninsula (AQAP) issued a joint statement denouncing the caliphate.[1] AQIM insisted ISIS had not followed the appropriate process.[2] AQIM reiterated its allegiance to Sheikh Ayman al-Zawahiri. This change of heart for the newly declared caliphate and renewed support for al Qaeda central caused AQIM problems. A rift began, with individual members taking sides. Some felt the caliphate had to have their support and others were not convinced of that certainty and remained faithful to AQIM's leader Abdelmalek Droukdel (aka Abu Musab Abdel Wadud).[3] Those were the ones who would pledge allegiance to al-Zawahiri.[4] In the end some defected from AQIM and moved to declare allegiance to ISIS's Abu Bakr al-Baghdadi.[5] The ISIS rift forced individual members all the way to the al Qaeda Council of Elders to take sides, with some going with Zawahiri and others declaring for the new caliphate. But how did this happen to one of the most focused of the al Qaeda affiliates?

AQIM was, up to that point, one of al Qaeda's most financially successful operational entities, controlling swaths of the Sahel across nation-state borders. AQIM reportedly even established the "Islamic State of Azawad" in northern Mali in April 2012, along with representatives from the Movement for Unity and Jihad in West Africa (MUJWA), Ansar al-Din and Boko

Haram.[6] Even though government troops forced their departure less than a year later, the fact that the state was established is significant. Formed during the Tuareg uprising of 2012, it offered a look at the solidarity that could occur if all of the dissident groups within the Sahel and Sahara collaborate. Very quickly squashed by the French, the declaration offered the Tuareg a period of union for its disparate families and clansmen. It also offered a means for AQIM to support the Tuareg in return for the continued support the Tuareg offer AQIM, support like hiding hostages for years so that governments do not know when and how to access their citizens. AQIM has become very adept at functioning in the harsh desert to continue its operations. The Tuareg may be one of the reasons why.

AQIM has functioned in Northern Africa since approximately 2003.[7] The Tuareg have for generations maneuvered the Sahara, their ancestral land. The land they call home is a region that covers portions of Mali, Algeria, Niger, Libya, and Burkina Faso.[8] It is also the region AQIM uses for kidnapping and trafficking illicit goods.

AQIM came to the region in 2003 and became part of the community. From the beginning AQIM members interacted with the Tuaregs, often intermarrying. This community interaction increased AQIM acceptance, so much so that in areas where Tuaregs are prominently visible, so are members of AQIM.[9] The Tuaregs have a common history of desire for freedom from Western influence with the original members of AQIM. However, their attempts in 1962, 1990 and 2007 to secure that freedom never bore fruit. The 2012 attempt for their own nation saw AQIM fight along side them.

Of course there are economic reasons why the group cannot negotiate a deal that would result in a Tuareg nation. The five nations across whose borders their ancestral land stretches have not found it to their own advantage to permit the Tuareg that governance.[10] That is because the region is rich in uranium and energy deposits that surpass those anywhere else in Africa. Instead the Tuareg must find other ways to survive. Some have found farming. They have forsaken the nomadic life of their ancestors and pit themselves against the drought and the wildlife to eek out a living. The land is harsh and unforgiving. The drought makes access to water a life-threatening ordeal. The lack of utility infrastructure means access to phones, electric, and hospitals to take the sick are nonexistent. Some aligned themselves with AQIM supporting the illicit trade of AQIM. Others made a way for their families by fighting in the mercenary army of Muammar Gaddafi.

Gaddafi armed them well, and when Gaddafi was overthrown, the Tuareg took their Libyan purchased weapons and returned home with their families. It is estimated that an exodus of almost a quarter of a million took place.[11] A segment of the returning forces decided to take action and rebel against the Malian government. They formed the Azawad National

Liberation Movement (MNLA). Another Tuareg group who had previously belonged to AQIM formed Ansar Dine. These former members of AQIM had initially pledged support to AQIM but also joined with MNLA for the fight to establish a homeland. MNLA, Ansar al Dine, and sympathetic recruits took over key areas of the Mali mountainous desert and the capital city, Bamako.[12] It took French intervention, but the rebellion was put down.[13] After the rebellion ended, MNLA was pushed out because of its secular nature and Ansar Dine and AQIM continued together. Together they influence pockets of territory, protecting it with their own Islamic police.

BACKGROUND

AQIM's beginnings are found in the French Front de Liberation Nationale (FLN). The FLN, led by Ben Bella, was an Algerian revolution organization that wanted freedom from France and French colonial control over its destiny. The FLN's military entity was to lead the effort for freedom. The FLN tried to convince the Algerian people they should support independence, and great efforts were made to incorporate labor unions, professionals, women's organizations, and students.[14]

As the efforts continued there was also a move to use violence to achieve independence; this move was supported by a leading Martinique psychiatrist named Frantz Fanon, who provided a very well-defined rationalization for incorporating violence into the tools used.[15] Violence was incorporated, and it soon reached a peak that caused the people to push back from this harsh tool.[16] The FLN started with "Islamic overtones" but was secular in nature. This secularism began to grate on the militant faction and they formed a newer organization called the Mouvenment Islamique Armeee (MIA). MIA focused its objectives in Islam.[17] As the movements continued, the Algerian government permitted multiparty elections. When it became apparent the Front Islamique du Salut (FIS), Algeria's Islamic political party, would win, a military junta ceased power and prevented FIS from governing. Militant factions within FIS vowed to reclaim this victory through violence.[18] This occurred at a time when the militant faction found support in returning mujahideen who had fought against the Soviets in Afghanistan.[19] While their actual combat experience was often limited, these Afghan veterans were sure they could repeat the victory of Afghanistan. They decided an Islamic state was the answer.

The rebelling Islamist groups took up arms and soon were pitted against government security forces. By 1992 a new group called the Groupe Islamique Arme (GIA) had decided they could bring victory and Islamic rule.[20] They waged a campaign of violence, sometimes killing civilians, especially foreigners, journalists, and intellectuals.[21] The GIA's terrorism challenged the government, and often polarized the people as they reacted to the group's attacks.[22] The year 1997 had the bloodiest death toll of all; toll reportedly reached 150,000, with a majority identified as GIA actions.[23]

By 1998 members of GIA's leadership tired of the attacks on civilians; they formed a new organization, Groupe Salafiste pour la Predication et le Combat (GSPC). The new group declared it would focus on government forces not civilians. Al Qaeda and Osama bin Laden even extended their blessings on the new group. By 2000 GSPC "verbally embraced Al-Qa'ida's ideology of global jihad."[24]

But just as GSPC accepted the al Qaeda ideology, the larger Algerian Islamist effort had begun to accept the political process as a means to achieve their goals. They even acquiesced to Western pressure and allowed women to participate in the electoral process.[25] GSPC did not accept these changes nor did they accept the amnesty that had been offered by the government. They recognized that accepting the amnesty required accepting the changes. GSPC focused its attacks on the Algerian military, particularly its convoys and bases.[26] These increased attacks were met with a government crackdown on the group. The group retaliated with even more attacks. During this period the group was undergoing internal disputes that rested mostly in the idea of remaining national or expanding to an international perspective.[27] An internal coup was initiated and the internationalists won. They began to extend GSPC beyond Algeria's borders and into the Sahelian countryside.[28] As GSPC extended itself into Sahel's countries, al Qaeda welcomed the group's pledge to avoid attacking civilians. It also recognized it could benefit from the European network the GSPC members could tap.[29]

The GSPC expanded its activities to include regional smuggling and trafficking.[30] The national versus international debate also coincided with the U.S. entry into Iraq.[31] The internationalists welcomed the recruiting benefit they received from the U.S. presence in Iraq and the alignment with al Qaeda it offered.[32] As GSPC links to al Qaeda strengthened, GSPC expansion activities increased as well.[33] GSPC began to aid fighters going through northern Africa to get to Iraq. It also began to extend its Sahel country attacks with offensives that killed personnel in Mauritania. These Mauritania attacks received enthusiastic approval on al Qaeda websites.[34]

On September 11, 2006, Zawahiri announced the merger of GSPC and al Qaeda. This merger reflected al Qaeda's approval of GSPC's rejection of national reconciliation, attacks on individuals from Western powers, and its operations in Mali and Mauritania.[35] By the time Droukdel pledged to bin Laden, the group had announced it would hit Western targets and it had a multinational footprint. It had also acquired a transnational reach that expanded it to Mali, Mauritania, Morocco, and Sudan.[36]

Droukdel, who has been leader of AQIM since 2004, strategically outlined the process he would use in a 2008 *New York Times* article. In that interview he methodically identified the expansion plan he expected to use and the personnel he would target.[37] Droukdel specifically defined intentions to expand across the Maghreb to the African coast.[38] He recognized he needed continuous support and personnel to accomplish this, so he said he would target Muslim youth who would "sacrifice themselves and their money for the sake of supporting Islam. We consider this as one of our greatest achievements. Among our greatest achievements is that we realized unity with our brothers as an important step towards the adult succession."[39] This harnessing youthful drive and inexperienced decision-making processes on the way to adulthood is critical to AQIM's success.[40]

ORGANIZATION

AQIM is autonomous from al Qaeda central. According to Tawill, AQIM has a four-zone regional division: central, eastern, western, and southern. The central region is reportedly the strongest and is the area where the national *amir* is located.[41] The southern zone is especially well known for its attacks against Westerners.[42] Its management organization is a "formal tiered hierarchical structure."[43] The Emir heads the organization with support from "committees and media; regional units and brigades-sized units."[44]

AQIM activity is especially prevalent in countries like Mauritania, Libya, Tunisia, Morocco, and more recently Nigeria with Boko Haram. In Mauritania AQIM has created a web of activities that include kidnappings, suicide bombings, and attacks on the Israeli embassy. These crimes became more prevalent after December 2007 when AQIM killed a French family. The next year AQIM personnel fired on the Israeli embassy. By 2009 AQIM had attacked an American who lived and worked in Mauritania, and they had kidnapped three Spanish aid workers.[45] Libya's activities have included kidnappings and other attacks.[46] In 2012 AQIM was able to increase its cache of heavy and light weaponry with equipment secured from Libya.[47] In Tunisia the AQIM cell encountered a government that reached out to moderate Islamists, opening dialogue and encouraging their speaking up.[48] Moroccan authorities too have been less of an example to oppose as they have met with Islamic Jihadists who were in the Moroccan jails. AQIM has tried to counter these efforts by continuing its message that the Moroccan government is considered apostate by AQIM.[49]

In Nigeria AQIM forged a relationship with Boko Haram (Jama'atu Ahlis Sunna Lidda'awati wal-Jihad) leveraging two of its core competencies: training and support. Through Boko Haram, AQIM is emerging in a role similar to al Qaeda central's association with its affiliates. That is, AQIM was the means to an organization (Boko Haram) securing the right to "hang the al Qaeda certification sign" in exchange for a multinational attack presence and public commitment to the establishment of a caliphate. Boko Haram's association with al Qaeda was suspected as early as 2010 when it drastically changed attack tactics. The tie to al Qaeda was suspected even more after Boko Haram bombed the UN building in Abuja.[50] The group fulfilled its multination presence as part of the deal with attacks in northern Mali and support to attacks in Mali and Cameroon. Droukdel's public statements on the AQIM-Boko Haram relationship demonstrate, too, the investment AQIM is willing to commit to in order to ensure the group's success. In that same statement, Droukdel even declared his group was "ready to train your sons [Boko Haram] on how to handle weapons and will give them all the help they need—men, weapons, ammunition, and equipment—to enable them to defend our people and push back the Crusaders."[51] AQIM managed the advancement of Boko Haram through training, attack guidance, and funding.[52,53] It is even suspected that members of Boko Haram fought in Mali in 2012 and 2013 alongside other al Qaeda groups.[54] If information like the preliminary Kimble study is substantiated by future studies, then a more complete AQIM picture may be possible and events like Boko Haram's transfer of allegiance to ISIS may be predictable.[55]

This is because changes in AQIM affiliate attack statistics could signal affiliates' network satisfaction, affiliate-to-affiliate harmony or disharmony, or even affiliate-to-AQIM in-fighting that may periodically occur. Shifts in attack data may also identify exploitable opportunities for combatting the group.

ORGANIZED FOR CRIME

AQIM headquarters in remote northern African territories offer AQIM significant interest in weapons smuggling and narcotics transportation. It has modeled itself after the FARC and leveraged its vast network to profit from it through activities like smuggling cigarettes, counterfeit goods, and stolen merchandise.[56] The Sahel is comprised of the poorest per capita income states, but the same nations are also ones with some of the richest natural resources. However, the region is suffering from draught and terrorism's destruction of the little tourist trade that had existed.[57] It did not help that Mali's President Amadou Tamani Touré from 2002 to 2012 did not earnestly respond to the threat AQIM represented. He was sure he could manage it with agreements like permitting AQIM to function in the north without government interference if AQIM contained its operations only in that region.[58] The Sahel and Saharan regions offer very little licit work for those who would pursue alternatives to AQIM as an employer. AQIM and the Sahel also benefitted from the crackdown on other funding avenues to terrorist organizations. When governments closed access to funding resources through organizations willing to act as external fund-raising outlets, the funds were still needed. There was never an option or consideration *not* to continue the terrorist attacks and propaganda.[59] Activities such as drug trafficking have significant influence on the economic livelihood in the region. Countries like Mauritania have vast pockets of land that would be designated "uninhabited desert."[60] Within that vast land live 3.2 million people who are trying to survive an underfunded government, no monitoring of the vast desert, and armed groups' insurgency.[61] For those willing to leverage its vastness and lack of government supervision, there is great profit to be had. Drug traffickers from Latin America, who no longer find it cost-effective to use the Caribbean route to move their product line to the lucrative European markets, can avail themselves of the security and transportation services AQIM offers.[62]

Visitors to the land are also subject to its harshness. Embassies have been attacked and foreign visitors have been kidnapped or assassinated, and then there is the competing local extremist group Ansar Allah al-Murabitun fi Bilad al-Shinqit (the Murabitun Partisans of God in the Country of Shinqit) that attacks as well as the international extremist group (AQIM).[63] Then there is the problem of local officials (or their families) who leverage these factors to take advantage of and benefit from the illicit economic trade opportunities that are rampant.[64]

These are just a few of the influencing factors that offer sufficient reason to contradict any suggestion that the solution to the country (or even the region) is simply one that government and its military are the alternative to the violence perpetrated by terrorist groups.[65] But the area's citizens must also navigate the complexities of their own caste and clan systems, periodic clashes that can make ethnic minorities victims of killings that can reach the hundreds and local politics that makes state and nonstate actors equally disconcerting.[66]

It will be interesting to see if there are fewer leadership appointees who are Algerian born and if more leaders are chosen from members who hail from countries of the Sahel, African coast, or Nigeria. Color has caused problems in the past both within the Tuareg society and within AQIM.[67,68] The AQIM splinter group MOJWA is the result of such dispute; MOWA makes every effort to distinguish itself from al Qaeda, even going to the point of citing those ideological references it feels are more aligned with a new organization, founder of the 1809 Sokoto Caliphate Ousman Dan Fodio, Senegalese scholar El Hadj Omar Tall, and founder of the Fula Empire Amadou Cheikhou.[69]

OPERATIONS AND TACTICS

AQIM targets both civilians and security personnel. Those security personnel can be either police or the military.[70] Using guerrilla tactics, AQIM has attacked with vehicle-borne improvised explosive devices and suicide vehicle-borne improvised explosive devices.[71] AQIM attacks that targeted civilians usually focused on residents of Western nations.[72]

The attacks were usually designed to leave a message with the leaders of the nationals. Most often targeted were nations who either had a colonial relationship in northern Africa or had supported Western efforts to thwart al Qaeda's jihad attacks. This was exemplified in the 2013 killing of journalists Ghislaine Dupont and Claude Verion. The two had just interviewed an official from Mali's town of Kidal.[73] Almost immediately they were killed by AQIM, in retaliation for French support of the Mali government's put-down of insurgents.[74] Mass killings that involve civilians is used less often by AQIM because they have adopted the Zawahiri practice of minimizing harm to noncombatants. Zawahiri learned this the hard way in 1993 after he targeted an Egyptian prime minister for assassination using an explosive strapped to the minister's car.[75] The problem arose when a little girl, Shayma Abdel-Halim, was pinned by the car door after it separated from the vehicle during the explosion. The Egyptian people took to the streets protesting terrorists and the attacks that had killed almost 240 people to that point.[76] AQIM went to the extraordinary step of issuing a statement in 2007 after a SVBIED attack. According to the statement: "We reiterate that the majority of those killed in this operation were from the police and security forces . . . and that our brother did not target innocent people as reported by the media."[77]

The tactics used on these operations usually fall in the ambush, area attack, or kidnapping categories. The "ambush" is not new. It is often used in guerrilla warfare. Algerian independence fighters used it in 1952; the fighters in Mali used in 2013.[78]

The area attack is utilized more when a vehicle-borne improvised explosive device or suicide vehicle-borne improvised explosive device is employed.[79] Al Qaeda employs this tactic especially during simultaneous detonations.[80] It was also one of the signs used by observers to begin to suggest that GSPC was associated with al Qaeda.[81]

Kidnapping for ransom has proven to be a highly successful tactic for instilling fear and increasing group funding.[82] Sources have placed the number at $360 million.[83] Their usual targets are Westerners in countries like Mauritania, Tunisia, Mali, and Algeria. This lucrative practice has provided a means to articulate opposition to country policies and increase their coffers. This is one avenue where AQIM differs from AQI, later ISIS. AQIM relies on kidnapping to extract a bounty and then they usually return the target. That has not been Iraq-based group's mode of operation.[84]

The AQIM drug trafficking is actually a beneficiary of the increased monitoring, surveillance, and prosecution of maritime and water trade in cocaine from South America to Europe. The cartels had to find a new way to move product to its intended market and the Sahel proved a perfect alternative. Moving the drugs to the less-regulated middle of the desert provided the drug traffickers with that alternative and created a difficult problem for the United States and Europe to stem the tide of drugs as it made its way through the unregulated African regions.[85]

AQIM revenue streams have benefitted from the taxes levied by AQIM on local contraband when it travels through AQIM-controlled territory. That contraband can be drugs, tobacco, or human beings. Often AQIM has moved undocumented workers through the regions of the African Savanna to the Saharan region.[86] From this region the workers can find their way through Tripoli to Europe. For those workers who desired to remain in Africa, the undocumented workers' destinations were often Libya, Algeria, and Morocco. Libya was the most desired location because it offered the workers the highest per capita wage. Some of these workers came from Cameroon, the Democratic Republic of Congo, Egypt, and Somalia.[87]

AQIM's drug, kidnapping, and human trafficking have resulted in coffers that provided members to obtain AK-series rifles, landmines, explosives, and heavy-machine mounted trucks.[88] Once obtained, these tradecraft tools were used for attacks that targeted police, military outposts, and French and Spanish citizens in the regions that comprise their sphere of control. AQIM made sure to execute attacks that spanned several nations. These attacks have occurred in Algeria, Mauritania, Mali, and Morocco.[89]

AQIM AND THE TUAREG TRIBES

When Larémont listed AQIM objectives, he identified two objectives that most other terror analysts include: first, to overthrow the Algerian government and, second, to kidnap French and Spanish nationals for ransom and bombings. But Larémont also included the objective of creating "a safe haven among the Tuareg tribes of Mali, Niger and Mauritania wherein it can obtain refuge and where it can also encourage rebellion against central state."[90] Whether it is an organizational goal or a means to achieving its other goals, Larémont brings an interesting point to the forefront. For AQIM to succeed in the harsh environs of the desserts of the Sahel and the Sahara, it is mandatory that AQIM acknowledge the critical role the Tuareg people must play. As a matter of fact, the Tuareg are so important to any organization succeeding in that region that Belmokhtar married into four Tuareg and Berabiche families and clans.[91] He reportedly became very effective at establishing an operations network in the region. When Belmokhtar left the AQIM fold to become a competitor with his own group al-Mulathameen Brigade, he very soon merged with another AQIM breakaway group, Movement for Unity and Jihad in West Africa (MUJAO) with Tuareg pedigree to create a new, stronger organization called al-Murabitoon Brigade. This new group pledged allegiance to Zawahiri.[92]

AQIM links with the Tuareg have benefitted the terrorist group's transportation services for illicit products. The Tuareg have resided in the area for centuries, running salt caravans.[93] As a people they are scattered across several nations: Libya, Mali, Niger, Algeria, Burkina Faso, and

Nigeria. They know how to survive in the land even when there is no rain. They may have taught this survivor skill to AQIM personnel. If so, it will make the group more difficult to pursue. However, they desperately want their own autonomous land. Their attempt at establishing Azawad sent a signal to the nations under which the Tuareg live that they will not stop until their goal is achieved. AQIM has found it to its benefit (for now) to work with the Tuareg to achieve that goal.

As nations seek to identify a means to halt the AQIM approach to terrorism, they have to recognize that issues such as food, water, medical, and personal security are uppermost in the minds of the citizens who may support the individual members of AQIM. AQIM is also, for some, the only employer of note, and family security is a high priority for a region that holds family, ethnicity, and clan in high regard.

FUTURE WITH AQIM

AQIM has created a solid base for itself in the Sahel and Sahara as far as land-based businesses are concerned. But it has not expanded to the realm of cyber threat to any great significance. This may not last for long.

AQIM and its media arm al-Andalus Media have already created "Africa Muslima," a twitter blog that calls for jihad within the African continent. The funding available to AQIM (and ISIS for that matter) makes development of tools to compromise facilities, businesses, and individuals in the region very easy. Moving to the targets of their land campaign, Western governments and their representatives, would not be hard.

Depending on whether they want to achieve an "effects-based" or "intent-based" result, AQIM, or their proxy, could disrupt to "generate fear comparable to a traditional act of terrorism."[94] Or they could execute a computer attack that seeks to intimidate or coerce nations such as France, Spain, Algeria, or the United States. Such attacks also put law enforcement in the sticky position of proving that the grave harm or economic damage achieved was actually perpetrated by whomever they charge. Perpetrators understand that difficulty and may intentionally perpetrate technological harm knowing the chance of successful prosecution is low. But there may be some who seek to "martyr" themselves to extensive jail time in order to achieve significant critical infrastructure damage to attain the goal of harm that is claimed by AQIM.[95] The perpetrators may then post a blog or video claiming credit for the action.

Determining an alternative to the current organizations like AQIM requires that we acknowledge that its complexity is such that we have to understand the logic at work as the interacting elements apply their force. The relationships are not linear. This means we must look at more than the organization itself. It is imperative that the analysis assume there is some distributed control across elements such as perpetrator, tool used for violence, target, victims, location of event, and constituent group response. Each element imposes some force on the end result. That is not to say each element cannot be analyzed separately to determine the specific contribution of that element's internal components. When these forces are identified by element, then they can be organized by ascending or descending order. This will permit a complexity scale that can determine independent and dependent variables within each internal component and on each element within the complex system. This does not mean that a mathematical formula is the only thing that stands between the West and AQIM as AQIM pursues its agenda. What the identification of elements will do is increase the objectivity brought to solutions considered for the immediate and long-range future.

10

⁂

Conclusions: A Look Forward

To decide where we go from here, we must identify the most immediate threat at present. The threat posed by AQIM, AQAP, ISIS, al Shabaab, and other al Qaeda central affiliates, as well as new entrants to the terrorism industry, represents the new "Jihad of choice," that is, the jihad of vicious violence. An analysis of the violence executed by ISIS, AQAP, and AQIM as organizations affiliated, or previously affiliated, with al Qaeda central displays changed patterns of attack clusters and efficiency that reveal the impact affiliation has had on each of the groups and the countries in which the violence occurs. Western focus on the expressed threat of violence and the declared intention to eliminate the West can overshadow an objective assessment of the benefits the organizations receive from association with al Qaeda central. Whether calculated or indiscriminate, this viciousness is seen in Iraq, Yemen, Syria, and Northern Africa, which demonstrates a wide use of violent jihad. It is not certain if this wide use is strategic, part of the plan. Whether it is or it isn't, the results are an increase in the noncombatant casualties and increased discord within the jihad community. While the first result is one that must be contained, the second is one that could be exploited. In addition, this new approach is a window to the transition from a Zawahiri-led al Qaeda to a new post-al Qaeda central era. This could mean an AQIM era of violence led by Abu Musab Abdel Wadoud (Abdelmalek Droukdel) or an AQAP period of violence under Nasser Abdul Karim al-Wuhayshi (Abu Basir). It could also mean a struggle between

AQIM or AQAP and ISIS. For just as al Qaeda was functioning with Zawahiri in charge while Osama bin Laden was in the shadows, giving a sense of post-bin Laden al Qaeda, the current activities of al Qaeda central and its affiliated groups give a sense of al Qaeda post Zawahiri. Before bin Laden's death, Zawahiri issued video statements, gave interviews, and controlled affiliate admission. Bin Laden had been marginalized. Current activities of al Qaeda and its affiliates demonstrate Zawahiri's lack of control. Zawahiri faced insubordination from ISIS, indiscriminate killing from Boko Haram, an al Qaeda wannabe, and lack of control in areas of insurrection like Syria and Egypt.

Zawahiri also has critics within the jihad ideologue community. There is former Egyptian Islamic Jihad leader Nabil Naeem. Naeem dismisses Zawahiri as the leader of al Qaeda.[1] To Naeem, Zawahiri is all talk, lacking the charisma necessary to lead peoples of varied backgrounds and cultures, on the torturous journey needed.[2] Then there is al-Sayyid Imam Abdul-Aziz al-Sharif. Known as Dr. Fadl, al-Sharif fought with Zawahiri twice, once with Zawahiri's Egyptian al-Jihad (EIJ) and a second time in Afghanistan during the Soviet ouster battles. Zawahiri's relationship with al-Sharif is tainted by the dishonor Zawahiri suffered when he succumbed to Egyptian police torture tactics and revealed information on his accomplices; later he ceded the leadership of EIJ to al-Sharif because of that dishonor.[3,4] Al-Sharif has written extensively on the theological underpinnings of jihad, commenting extensively on the harm violence does to the cause the jihadists purport to advance.[5] Dr. Fadl has written extensively on the theological underpinnings of jihad. His controversial writings have even taken Zawahiri to task countering Zawahiri's argument for jihad, calling one piece "Unveiling the Great Deception in al-Zawahiri's 'Exoneration of the Nation.'" It counters each of the arguments Zawahiri has made for jihad and constructs a strong argument to silence critics who dismiss objections to Zawahiri.[6] Finding a way to leverage the message of these, and similar, writings is imperative for the international community to effectively respond to the again-morphing al Qaeda terrorist threat. There are also AQIM and AQAP, as well as ISIS and al Shabaab, to negotiate their territory and the future of the terrorism industry; we have to utilize as many tools as possible to mitigate the violence they represent. We know that post the U.S. presence, Afghanistan will include the Taliban and have a high probability of not only al Qaeda but also other extremist groups entering fray battling for control of the finite space and populations these countries offer. Iraq is a good example of the scenario that could result.[7] The weak governments of Iraq, Yemen, and Somalia offer great options for al Qaeda. They offer opportunity to weave fear, leverage organizational strength, and growth area with opportunity to function under the umbrella of organized crime and terror for jihad.

When Zawahiri disagreed with Zarqawi in 2004, taking him to task for murders of the Shia civilians, these differences were touted in the Western press, but we did not employ tactics that exploited the act of Zawahiri's admonition. Even now Yemen and Iraq civilians suffer because al Qaeda-associated organizations execute attacks using tactics that do not follow Zawahiri's advice to protect noncombatants, particularly women and children. Strong-arm extortions reminiscent of organized crime reflect badly as well, but we have no ability to leverage these actions so that we aid the victims and/or benefit international policies. Creating a mechanism to present the data matter-of-factly, like an exchange presenting all information on each organization, as a member of the terrorism industry is an option. This exchange or Terrorism Venture Index would offer objective assessment of active and emerging terror industry members' statistics and economic institution contribution.[8] The index would create industry member reviews, permitting consideration of factors like functioning within a failed state or failing state environment. Commentators and industry analysts could assess individual organizations and compare that to an industry standard to examine both tangibles and intangibles. Intangibles can include mission functionality, where that functionality considers the Islamic business value of the mission, quality of the mission, and the quality of the mission's functionality to jihad.[9] Tangibles can include cost and time for attack planning. Violence factor would identify strategic violence and/or indiscriminate violence.

This function, along with attack efficiency and frequency, would offer structured approaches to assess mission effects on al Qaeda's target audience and associated stakeholders. The return on investment for al Qaeda would compare to the return on intrusion into the target audiences' sphere of habitation.

INTERNATIONAL ASSESSMENT

There are 57 individual Muslim countries, which extend beyond al Qaeda strongholds. Cognizant of this the al Qaeda message of jihad for all leverages the anticolonial fervor that continues to simmer within the former Ottoman Empire region.[10] The fact that many of the peoples within that empire smarted under the weight of heavy tax levies, corruption, and economic decline demonstrate that all the conquered peoples under that empire's rule were chaffing for relief. Dissatisfaction with these conditions led several kingdoms under the empire to break away from the proffered Ottoman Empire alignment with Germany to seek separate agreements with the British and French for World War I. Among those agreements were the McMahon-Hussein correspondence, the Faisal-Weizmann Agreement, and the Balfour Declaration.[11,12] The hope was the kingdoms would wield their own governing power after the war ended. Everyone agrees the Western allies never fulfilled the agreements, and the Arab allies did not achieve their goal.[13] Instead the allied Sykes–Picot Agreement governed the lands division, and that along with the Treaty of Sevres, determined the establishment of British and French protectorates.[14] These protectorates never knew protest-free governing. Jihad and anti-occupation force resistance existed from the very beginning.[15]

Given that these events occurred within the last century, it is evident how easy it is for al Qaeda to whip up the distaste that exists because of these occurrences. It helps al Qaeda to bypass the individuality of the 57 nation-states and perpetuate the colonialism stigma whenever it needs to pit nation-states against each other. This permits al Qaeda to play followers of Islam against each other, individuals against the West, and nation-states against each other. This exploitable circumstance has the additional complication of the international nation-state community requirement to develop policies that counter the crimes committed under the guise of Islamic Jihad. These policies apply to all of the hundreds of groups classified as terrorist and are therefore, by necessity, vague.[16] But this vagueness is also exploitable by al Qaeda as it continues to create a defensive atmosphere. Current tactics appear to include the requirement that al Qaeda not find itself on the defensive. Al Qaeda and its associated organizations continue to expand the theater of operations and redefine the target so that they control action and escalate fear. This appears to cause a problem when affiliate groups seem intent on embarking on their own path.[17] Striking the West, particularly the United States, may not be a priority for them. This may not be as much a case of fear of U.S. military attacks within their borders as it is a case of moving toward their own agenda. That agenda could include attack on convenient Western symbols like personnel or local assets, but achieving specific objectives and goals may not center on those Western symbol attacks. Boko Haram is a good example of this. They have learned they can achieve national attention by manipulating the West when emotional response issues are tapped and public opinion pressures for Western leadership to act in order to achieve a desired result. If they can trigger Western deployment of troops onto their land, this would be a coup, and Boko Haram recruitment, marketing, and hate mongering would benefit.

Al Qaeda never veers far from the tactic of employing a distractor. At times that tactic has been used to incite infighting between known opponents like India-Pakistan or perceived opponents like the United States and Islam.[18] Pulling those levers exacts a known response, permitting al Qaeda to implement whatever next step in its strategy it desires.[19]

We also recognize that the nation-states within which al Qaeda functions are being manipulated by al Qaeda, the same way targeted countries in the West are. This al Qaeda manipulation is juxtaposed to the manipulation some target countries have played on Western nations. Syria, Yemen, and Nigeria may leverage their relationships with the West on terrorism to acquire increased funding and military equipment to counter that terrorism. The resource allocations acquired this way may or may not be used for the intended purpose of fighting the "terror menace." Al Qaeda knows it is a win-win for such governments, so it has busily established itself within the boundaries of these failed or failing governments, functioning as if they are one continuous territory up for grab. There is no one country that is the source of al Qaeda recruitment, funding, or control. Nor is any one leader a pivot point. Individuals such as Zawahiri, bin Laden, and Abdelmalek Droukdal, the leader of al Qaeda in the Islamic Maghreb, are replaceable. They are opportunistic and will continue activities such as land transport of illegal goods for trusted clients through routes carved out in their continuous territory, particularly in Northern Africa.

But the international community can learn from the past and the lack of effectiveness of its most recent approaches. Killing individual participants in this movement will not end the opposition. As far back as 1948, this approach had been tried and the results were the same as today. When the murder of Hassan al-Banna by an unknown assailant occurred under the Nasser administration, and Sadat carried out a campaign against the Muslim Brotherhood, these acts did nothing to instill fear in the Brotherhood.[20] Rather, it acted as fuel to a fire that heated interest in and greater membership for Muslim Brotherhood.[21]

Nassar continued to harass the Brotherhood, putting Sayyid Qutb on trial where he was sentenced to death. But that act created a martyr and generations of angry young supporters who cite his history, "chapter and verse," to justify turning from government to individual war against authority.[22,23] We must ensure we do not fall prey to the same tactic. Ayman Zawahiri is a result of such behavior. Born in Egypt, Zawahiri came of age in the jihad movement during the chaos of Nasser trying to control the Brotherhood. Zawahiri was jailed, tortured, and forced to reveal the whereabouts of friends and colleagues. His reputation as a jihadi suffered with many never forgiving him for the betrayal.[24] While it did create some known animosities between the fighters, it did not quell the desire for change. United States' imprisonments at Abu Ghraib could have a similar impact in the future.

Instead we must find a way to have young people who reflect the demographic of al Qaeda review the online world of the jihadi; give us ideas on how they, as individuals, respond to these beckonings and suggest a road forward; and give us ideas on what they would do. The crowdsourcing approach is currently in use with the intelligence community as they compare the world events prediction success rate of members of the general public to that of so-called experts.[25] They can assess and use tools like those developed at the International Center for Political Violence and Terrorism Research (ICPVTR). Both crowdsourcers and experts can work together, particularly through the Terrorism Venture Index to harness available information and expand the reach of our analysis programs for their response and assessment capabilities. The new members of the team can even identify cultural aspects of approaches being proposed and critique them for potential exploit by both al Qaeda and the Western governments considering them. This method uses the home team members as offensively as possible. One of the first tasks could be identifying how the transition of a key ideologue from advocate of violence to an opponent of it can be incorporated into our counter-attacks strategy. Dr. Fadl wrote two of the most respected, if not seminal, works on jihad, "Al-Umda fi l-dad Al-Udda" in 1988 and "Al-Jami' fi Talab Al-Ilm Al-Sharif" in 1993 (The Essentials of Preparation for Jihad and A Compendium for the Pursuit of Divine Knowledge, respectively).[26] They were written during the heyday of al Qaeda and its drive for support. Nation-states had not started their concerted effort against al Qaeda, and their works were easily disseminated via magazines or the Internet. However, after capture and imprisonment in an Egyptian jail cell, he began to contemplate the violent approach and decided it was not correct from a theological perspective. He wrote as much in his 2007 work "Wathiqat Tarshid Al-'Amal Al-Jihadi fi Misr wal-'Alam" (Guidance Document for Jihad Activity in Egypt and the World).[27] The recant charged that al Qaeda's troubles were a direct accusation from Allah that the group was not following the Qur'an in its attacks. It charged that Zawahiri carried the weight of the deaths of the innocents in Iraq and Afghanistan on his head. It also called the attack of September 11, 2001, unwise. This, of course, did not sit well with Zawahiri and the two began a "back and forth" that included Sharif calling Zawahiri a liar and accusing him of colluding with the Sudanese and taking $100,000 in exchange for executing 10 Egyptian attacks; Zawahiri inferred that the recant is not worth the paper on which it is written.[28]

The ideological argument presented by Sharif can act as an input to any future total plan developed to redirect our future response against the criminal and violent acts that attack, kill, and do harm. Its guidance may put the Western response on a more successful track..

It also combats the current practice the West uses of forcing young people to choose between their religion and some perceived "better." Instead there is a need to incorporate a stronger understanding of the significance Islam has in the everyday life of its followers and the role it plays in the decisions made by every level of action, from individual to international. Individuals in the United States must come to realize that to acknowledge the religion of Islam as a force that governs the actions of almost three-quarters of the world's population is not an acknowledgment of defeat for Western democracy. The West must also recognize that the resulting "democracy" that works for a country filled with followers of Islam may include incorporating "Church and state." It is not a defeat for Western democracy if it ends the disputes and initiates a governance that works for the people under its purview.

We also have to acknowledge that al Qaeda will continue to expand its reach to "sell its product" in new markets or to prime previously underperforming ones. So as we focus on Nigeria and Boko Haram, we should monitor al Qaeda as it trains its sights on Japan.[29] A December 2011 *Taipei Times* article presented Vanguards of Khorasan's (an AQ magazine) objections to the treatment it articulated China and Japan used toward the elderly. It took the two countries to task for following the West's "materialistic" approach to life.[30] According to Hossam Abdul Raoul, the *Vanguard* magazine's editor, "If those poor people had been blessed with Islam, their state would have been different, whereas the elderly would receive appreciation, respect and good treatment." According to Raoul even non-Muslim elderly would fare well under the Islamic state.[31] While many have watched targeted Christians die in al Qaeda-initiated attacks in other already cultivated al Qaeda markets, we can seek to mitigate some of the anticipated future growth al Qaeda hopes to secure if we direct attention and resources toward blunting the potential for new markets like Japan. Should they expect targeted improvised explosive device attacks or suicide bomber attacks in retribution for its participation in Iraq, or should China worry because of the potential for revenge for the deaths of Muslim Uighurs?[32] That may be answered if a crowdsourcing approach is employed in this new growth area.

But we have to also look at South America and the opportunities al Qaeda ties with organized crime represent. These opportunities hold little transaction costs to increase local influence and fan the fires of dissent and displeasure with Western powers. Look at Suriname. While it is only a small country, it has already been the center stage for controversy, with Dino Bouterse, son of Suriname's President Desi Bouterse, charged with trying to establish a training base for Lebanon's Hezbollah.

History has proven that use of "military might" has no long-term effect on eliminating the simmering anger and discontent that nurtures and is nurtured by terrorist groups.[33]

We also have to acknowledge that young idealist Western citizens will support a cause in which they believe. Our citizens will go where they believe an oppressed people need support. That support will range from nongovernmental organization humanitarian support to fighting in the grand fight for which they are willing to lay down their lives. One of the most striking examples of that was Alabama-born and -raised Omar Shafik Hammami.[34] Known as Abu Mansour, Hammami professed his support for the fight for right and traveled to Somalia to join al Shabaab in order to be a part of that fight.[35] Michael Adebolajo professed the same sentiment. At his trial, Adebolajo, he too said, fought for right when he fought for the cause of the women of Afghanistan. He made himself a fighter who turned to the external vague "West" to find an enemy. He saw his action as fighting for right in his own backyard. He did not travel to Iraq, Syria, or Somalia. Instead he identified a near representation of the fight against the West, an enemy he came to believe represented an evil that must be eliminated.

Killing Fusilier Lee Rigby personified the vague West permitting him to take action and eliminate the enemy in one fell swoop.

In "The Rise of Muslim Foreign Fighters," Hegghamer correctly states that the foreign fighters supporting the struggle between Afghanistan and Russia were not directly United States or Saudi Arabian state supported. But the tacit approval of the actions, the "making room" so they could fight alongside the state-sponsored players, must be acknowledged as an approval of sorts. It appears disingenuous and a continuation of colonial betrayal.[36] As we move forward, the direction we take must reflect a collaborative international intent to protect our young men and women who fall prey to the beguiling message presented just one website away. But to do that we must represent the entire field that supports that "beguiling message." If we do not, then al Qaeda will continue to ply its wares, convincing our young they are doing the right thing when they execute the missions. Whether from the Internet or any other instrument, like the old "revolutionary's" manifesto, the end result is an inspiring declaration that motivates the violence they believe will coerce the target government into the social objective they want. It is not viewed as unlawful violence, and they are assured it is not political. But to achieve what is desired, they are actually both. One tactic often employed to force the desired behavior is to exploit any sense of guilt. This stratagem was used with early recruits to the fight for Afghanistan, and it is employed today. One of the most well known of the early recruits against whom this tactic was used was Ahmed Said Khadr.[37] In the early 1980s Khadr is said to have felt for his family wealth.[38] He subsequently joined the fight in Afghanistan, reportedly helped found al Qaeda, and funded the attack on the Egyptian Embassy in Islamabad. In 2013 Sabirhan Hasanoff too acted partially out of guilt when he bought "an advanced remote control for explosives attacks and reported information about the New York Stock Exchange."[39,40] He sought to salve that guilt with aid to al Qaeda. As with other times, al Qaeda exploited a target's feeling of guilt to ensure participation; the guilt-ridden follower of Islam commits the act al Qaeda needs performed and, if captured by law enforcement, the guilt-ridden follower can only plead that he or she succumbed to the pressure applied by al Qaeda (or ISIS, take your pick). The follower is also the only one who suffers with jail time.

WHAT ARE THEY THINKING? HOW WILL THEY GROW?

Foreign fighters are the growth area for al Qaeda. As it recruits foreign fighters, al Qaeda will seek to shore up areas it currently considers lacking and try to make inroads into new areas for growth. In theory, central Asia and Israel will remain high on the list of "must haves" for Zawahiri and anyone who takes his place.[41,42] Zawahiri and Osama bin Laden allocated resources as needed and leveraged opportunities as they appeared. One resource that was allocated sparingly was trained seasoned fighters. Both bin Laden and Zawahiri handled this limited resource with care and introduced it into an attack or strategy equation only when appropriate. They both welcomed and fanned the fires of a Wild West atmosphere the "cyberhadists" promulgated. One of the best examples was that of the CIA attacker Humam Khalil Abu-Mulal al-Balawi. The media response to his suicide attack immortalized his act and probably fed the fire for a similar end of other Web-based participants.

Each perpetrator acted on a commitment to a higher cause, even if it was participation in or the preplanning of violence. These actions furthered al Qaeda's objectives, and they were technically in support of the asymmetrical war against the United States. The U.S. government has a right to protect itself and should execute that right. When it does, the individuals who are duped into supporting the virtually sovereign al Qaeda are in violation of U.S. law. A war against a nonstate limits the U.S. response. The idea of war is to extinguish the desire to fight your opponent and to impose your will as a victor on a subjugated people. If it is a just war, the vanquished are not annihilated. The victor must make the vanquished whole again. But the Sykes-Picot Agreement did not. The Ottoman Empire division did not. But there are models that did work. The Marshall Plan worked. If we go to the young people who the terror industry recruitment drives target and seek their help, we may be able to develop plans and achieve success rates that far exceed current rates.

DON'T FORGET OUR LEGAL WEAPONS

Of course, we have to recognize the roles of intelligence and law enforcement in any strategy designed to move forward against these fear mongers. But with that recognition comes the reality that these two critical tools have limits. Intelligence gathering is rightfully limited by the constitution, and law enforcement has the obligation of fairness and reason.[43] Deferring to these criteria permits us to enforce the laws and statutes that are challenged when al Qaeda, and any other terrorist organization, commit their calculated acts of violence. It is that very capability to function with fairness and reason when we are treated so viciously and with such violence that will resonate with the young recruitment targets of al Qaeda and its affiliates.[44]

We must redirect attention so that prosecuting the perpetrators of those acts is an active tool in our kit to strategically whittle away at the mystique and heroism the Internet videos attach to the role each individual considering joining will play.

We also have to recognize that al Qaeda and its media specialists will frame that prosecution in an anti-Islam propaganda campaign, one that taunts us for being the un-Islamic "other" just as they did when troops were introduced onto Afghanistan soil in response to the attacks of September 11,

2001. At that time the United States' stated desire was to have the government of Afghanistan turn over a specific individual (Osama bin Laden) for prosecution and cease harboring terrorists. Understanding that the primary purpose for using military resources to engage an adversary outside our borders is to force that adversary to capitulate and accept our terms, the war in Afghanistan was against a sovereign (Taliban) government for not turning over a "known" terrorist.

Relying only on intelligence and diplomacy channels immediately after the attacks could not provide a response as quickly as the anger in the country appeared to demand. Normally, when intelligence assets and diplomacy are employed, the United States' diplomats have sufficient time to negotiate an equitable solution; this is particularly true when data may not support the immediate use of force.[45] In the case of Afghanistan in 2001, that road was not fast enough for the palpable anger the U.S. people felt. When the United States communicated with the then Afghanistan leadership, it requested the Taliban's Supreme Leader Mullah Muhammad Omar to turn over Osama bin Laden. Both sides had stipulations; neither side had all its requirements met. When no agreement was reached, the United States used kinetic force against another sovereign state.[46] This use of force led to the retreat of the Taliban, creation of a government void, and the establishment of an interim government, under Hamid Karzai, after the signing of the Agreement on Provisional Arrangements in Afghanistan Pending the Re-Establishment of Permanent Government Institutions. New rules for security and "governance" were established. As the rules evolved, so did a civilian law enforcement model[47] and a need for development, building everything from roads to companies to houses of worship. This critical piece demands both sides of the governance equation (government and people) bargain from a confidence of trust in the other side, creating an agreement on identity and social norms for the nation. Promoting that equation was supposed to be a step toward trust in the West as well. It did not. U.S. missteps and al Qaeda framing the United States as the un-Islamic other—the opponent permitted the Islamic aspect of the resistance to frame the discussion so that it became an international liberation from imperialist domination.

Crafting a delicate balance of law enforcement, intelligence, and military response is needed to fight the asymmetrical threat of al Qaeda.[48] The law enforcement response is secular and the rules of engagement come from this definition. The violation of law can center on any al Qaeda and affiliated organization's activities from the perspective of a criminal matter where the rules of engagement come from responsibilities of law enforcement.[49] The focus will remain within the terms of community-based policing, intelligence-based policing, and law enforcement evidence/problem-based policing. Intelligence will focus on predicting, where that prediction fits intelligence policing as an enforcement of law.[50] Today's military response is a sparingly applied viable option that has so much more available than boots on the ground or drone attacks. Exploiting those capabilities, particularly the invaluable ideas, insight, and background information that can be crowdsourced from returned Iraqi, Afghanistan, and Northern Africa veterans, increases the chance for a more accurately calculated response. The task is to correlate the intelligence, law enforcement, and military response to prevent, predict, and prepare a response for the crime.[51]

OVERCOMING PREVIOUS APPROACHES

The same Afghanistan we supported as it began to build its own self-defined democratic future was the same Afghanistan targeted for pursuit of al Qaeda using drone attacks. Drone attacks on Afghanistan, Pakistan, and Yemen eliminated many targeted key command and control elements, but the result was not what Western allies envisioned. While this approach removed individual members of al Qaeda from the target list, it did not remove al Qaeda, the organization, or al Qaeda influence. Instead al Qaeda responded by remodeling itself into a distributed organization, one that exploited the asymmetrical relationships of the ongoing confrontation between the United States, its allies, and the elements of the al Qaeda operating entity. But instead of going away altogether, there was a redirection toward the "message" that increased the importance of individuals such as Anwar al Awlaki. Al Qaeda started using more social media sites to project a sense of "leaderless resistance," promoting more of individual violence, smaller cells, and attacks. This emulated the work of groups like the Weather Underground, which once was a hierarchical group. The Underground started as a nonviolent organization, the Students for a Democratic Society (SDS). But it morphed into the more violent version after the Days of Rage in Chicago. After the Weather Underground formed, it, like al Qaeda, used more adaptive methods to respond to the policing techniques employed against it. There was a connection to a new set of rules. Ultimately the result is difference in response because of different missions and definitions.

From a behavioral perspective, the people that the military engages offer opportunities for preventive policing and community policing to instill trust even when the needs and cultural values of the engaged people are different. But there is still the underlying requirement to facilitate for a set of norms that empower the people and the individuals from the community to see the forces as facilitator. This offers opportunity to fill gaps of knowledge and intelligence in order to mitigate a potential growing threat. Anger value goes down, which can act as prevention. But prevention is different from eliminating. It requires mitigation. If we can develop preventive measures that identify community-oriented focus, then most policing (whether national or international) supports law-abiding citizens.[52] There are no concerted efforts to reach out to those who pose a particular threat. If a group or an individual is isolated, understanding the interpersonal relationships to determine trust, control, empathy, fear, or intimidation reduces group think that a young person exposed to violence could perceive as an accepted definition of behavior.

These efforts need support from other areas. We must remain investigative. We must look into data that are available and assess them for the patterns and trends they reveal.

As Western nations' government officials respond to the attacks executed against their citizens, they must segregate the crime from the religion. If an attack is executed against citizens, then "the perpetrators killed xx." We remove the religion from the discussion and focus attention on the criminal act. The hardest part will be to curtail reference to Muslim citizens of the West as if they are not. A citizen must be treated as such. We must learn to use this to our advantage. Just as perpetrators of these acts know how to leverage the Western judicial system to their advantage, the West must learn to do the same. If a crime of murder was perpetrated, charge accordingly.

OPPORTUNITIES TO EXPLOIT

The West did not exploit the defection of Omar Hammami, when he left al Shabaab, after a dispute with Ahmed Abdi Godane, head of al Shabaab. Hammami did not want to leave the struggle but rather wanted to expose what he called "The cause of the problem." Hammami stated "that [Godane] left the principles of our religion and he is trying to change al-Shabaab into an organization that oppresses every single Muslim in an effort to make him the next Siad Barre."[53] When al Shabaab gunmen killed Hammami, he was counted as just another jihadist.[54] Instead we could have exploited the transition of Hammami. This same defiant had made a recruitment video touting the life and mission of al Shabaab. He had left the group but he had not left the fight. That transition step alone should have been used to work to the West's anti-perpetrator/anti-recruitment advantage.

Al Shabaab has had periods of difficulty convincing local Somali to support its fight. It relies on reinforcements from distant lands, new bodies with arms to carry weapons and legs to run into a firefight, and bodies connected to heads that have romanticized the fight. To accept the life of an al Shabaab, new blood must come with the al Shabaab framed concept of "true knowledge of the actual life."[55]

We must also recognize al Qaeda will exploit the West's vulnerabilities. For instance, the UN Security Council has not been able to articulate and implement an effective antiterrorism program, one that actually reduces the negative impact of terrorist activities. The United States has entered two of the 57 Muslim countries, perpetrated war activity, and had to exit without a clear victory. The public image of the United States in the 57 Muslim countries is significantly depressed because of the impact drone strikes have had on women and children who have suffered or died. Al Qaeda continues to use this in videos, fatwas, and social media recruitment.

Attack data analysis indicates al Qaeda may assess potential associations by group efficiency, among other characteristics. This efficiency can be detected and response to group activity developed and executed.

We must recognize that as technology has become more complex, al Qaeda and affiliate attack perpetrators moved in the other direction and adhered to the Kiss method (Keep it simple, Shirley). *Homemade* became the word of the day, keeping everything below the radar of suspicion. Both the Boston Marathon bombers and the Westgate Mall attackers breeched secure areas using low-tech, low-cost, highly mobile strategies in a highly visible, high-payoff target. They had no way to go but up on the chart of win-win.[56]

As we look at the many faces of al Qaeda, the West in particular has to come to terms with the fact that it may not hold the key to success in eliminating the threat al Qaeda represents. There is no way to totally eliminate al Qaeda, the entity that houses individuals who are dissatisfied with the current situation, and they are certain the only way to remove the reason for their dissatisfaction is extreme violence. That national security problem will remain. But the al Qaeda exploits a situation, leverages vulnerabilities, and focuses on keeping "the fight" going rather than the transition to a solution.

The West can do the same by exploiting a vulnerability to make it a part of the solution. For instance, the rampant drought can offer opportunity for technology that can be used to turn the river conditions to those of pre-2003. Water is a critical resource for the entire Middle East. Yemen is short of this precious resource; Iraq's rivers no longer support the fishing industries that were so plentiful in previous years. Nor can they support the water demands of pre-2003.[57] Nigeria's polluted waterways do not support the same abundant species from previous years. Technology could support solutions in several affected areas.

Are Lebanon and Turkey next? What are the signs? We are aware of the African continent and South America as areas of concern, but what about places like Suriname?

Al Qaeda has long had coalition links and distributed cells. As early as 1989 it had affiliations with the Abu Sayyaf Group in the Philippines, al-Ansar in Chechnya, and the Islamic Group of Egypt.[58] Cells were known to span Italy, Germany, Britain, Canada, the United States, South Africa, Tanzania, Yemen, Kenya, Albania, Singapore, Malaysia, Algeria, Libya, Indonesia, Somalia, and the Sudan. This does not ignore the originating places like Pakistan and Saudi Arabia.[59] By 2007 the struggle in North Africa and the elections of Morocco epitomized the difficulty of managing the ever more powerful neo-Salafists. It was becoming very evident that the leaders of governments being pressed for change would have to accommodate the Islamic leadership-focused groups into official discussion of the countries' governing procedures. Saudi Arabia and Qatar watched Morocco with interest. But change does not come overnight, and as the same struggle with the Al Qaeda neo-Salafists, continued violence and radicalism rose sharply.[60]

Al Qaeda continued to pursue the connection to history for its members whenever they were to execute a mission. The letter of instruction and encouragement to the September 11, 2001, hijackers compared their actions to those of the Prophet in the seventh century.[61]

The struggle for Yemen is similar in that it is a fight for leadership to implement Islamic Sharia al Qaeda style.[62]

PHANTOM OF THE FOREVER

In the beginning, bin Laden and Zawahiri were central to al Qaeda direction and focus. But as operations and executed attacks expanded, command and control moved beyond Al Qaeda central. "The company" had morphed into a visible hydra with talons everywhere. Attention followed that redirection away from "individuals" in charge to the organization as a whole to the development of "signature" tactics, messages, goals, and threats. Several times al Qaeda had to modify procedures in order to take advantage of its ability to exploit opportunities that did not involve weaponry. When the American people did not understand the difference between North Waziristan and South Waziristan, al Qaeda delivered a knock-out punch by having Maulana Abdul Ghazi, of Lal Masjid, issue a fatwa declaring all Pakistani soldiers killed in the battle against Muslim militants in South Waziristan ineligible to receive a proper Islamic burial. It is reported that some families refused to accept the body of their loved ones because of the decree.[63] This ultimately reduced the number of Pakistani soldiers willing to battle the militants.

Abu-Jandal went to Bosnia filled with zeal and little theological training. He viewed his "jihad" as a voluntary duty. But by the time he left he had searched within and found that he believed his "jihad" was a "religious duty, like prayers, fasting, alms-giving, and pilgrimages."[64]

When bin Laden died, it was said al Qaeda suffered a serious blow. But that has not proven correct. Al Qaeda had evolved to the point that it was ready to transition to a non-Middle East-centric organization. Yes, it still wants the Middle East rulers to rule within the confines of the Quran, as defined by al Qaeda. But it also wants to create a Sharia law by its own definition. The people of Radda in Yemen's Abyan province have had that distinction. The result was people maimed or stoned for infractions that did not warrant such punishment.

We recognize Zawahiri is quite comfortable at the helm, as he has had the reins for quite some time. But his control of all factions touting the al Qaeda brand is suspect. The management of ISIS is a perfect example. That is a plus for us. His thinking is along the lines of AQIM and AQAP. Violent action is key to his approach. But viciousness is not. But we still have to ask, Even if Zawahiri was granted everything he wanted, could he transition to a world with no "jihad?" That answer is critical to our response plan.

Osama bin Laden's goal was to "unite all Muslims and establish a government which follows the rule of the Caliphs."[65] Bin Laden had little respect for the American military. To him, they frightened easily, running away at the first difficulty.[66] Adding Somalia to the other defeats, he saw "Vietnam, Beirut, Aden and Somalia" as precursors to Iraq and Afghanistan. Now that the United States is leaving the Holy Lands, elements of al Qaeda will continue its pursuit of the United States attempting to niggle it to annoyance with cyber attacks, cripple it with infrastructure demolishment, and frighten it to immobility with threats, attempts, and recruitment of our young. The last is the most devastating. Our young are the real targets for al Qaeda; and their success with that target would dissolve hope of later success in ending the plague of terrorist attacks. We can rebuild a dam, or return funds stolen in an account. But to steal our young has no replacement for us as a nation.

We have learned that "droning" the leaders of al Qaeda will not eliminate the threat. If anything it complicates the threat, throwing the advantage to the militant for "framing the problem." The problem has evolved beyond al Qaeda, or at least the al Qaeda of 1989, or even the al Qaeda of 2001. The al Qaeda of today has become a myelin sheath on the backbone of frustrated discontent—a discontent that extends across the developing and emerging nations of the Middle East, Asia, and Africa. All have had a "history" with Western nations. A history that al Qaeda has demonstrated can be exploited using today's youth as its instrument of power. Al Qaeda has taught us not to underestimate the discontent or the forces that can be marshaled to act on that discontent.[67]

While the drone strikes actually started in 2002, they were the response of choice from 2009 on. It was hoped this would eliminate the opposition force without Western "boots on the ground" political difficulty. When the strikes intensified in 2009, the United States insisted 300 targets were in the Yemen area, but by 2012 the estimate was 700. The goal of reducing the number did not seem achievable as the United States relied on this tool in lieu of "boots on the ground." Fallout from the growing number was a reinforcement of antagonists' message of discontent with the West.

The history of colonialism is not so far in the past that purveyors of anti-West sentiment (it need not be an al Qaeda member!) cannot find someone who remembers, someone who can regale the young with tales of personal abuse, discrimination, or disregard at the hands of the colonialists. Taken together these tales and their message demonstrate the "disrespect" our current actions display. The message becomes "US Drones over Yemen airspace kill Yemen women and children, all without Yemen permission, a modern day colonial action. The US is doing this because it can."

Does that mean not to "strike" back or to remove a sworn enemy with the stated objective of killing us? No, on the contrary, removing that enemy is paramount. But creating additional ones along the way must be avoided. Afghanistan and the Soviet occupation is within the current memory of many. Those memories may not acknowledge the truth of U.S. support for the freedom fight, or they may couch the help in terms of U.S. interests being our motivation. However the U.S. tie to the Afghanistan-Soviet fight is framed, it will be a call to action to the next generation (whether or not they participated).

We have been down this road before. We permitted bin Laden to frame the message to our young when we did not respond to his first World Islamic Front statement urging jihad against Jews and crusaders. We permitted him to frame the ground rules, and our dismissal of him reinforced his "US has no regard or respect" mantra. It gave bin Laden a grand opportunity to go "door-to-door" with his grassroots campaign. Each individual listener, whether a follower of Islam or not, assessed the situation based on the information in front of them at the time. Bin laden made more information available than we did. By the time we awoke to the need to address bin Laden's claims, our catch-up position was perceived as slights to the religion. In the war of words, we are equal if we remain focused. We must move the discussion from the specific of the middle east of North Africa to the specific of the individual. In an attrition on shores in the mid-east or Africa, we become vulnerable to the same crusader-invader campaign. Neither our economy nor out diplomatic relations can absorb that alternative.

Affiliations during 1998 were conducted through face-to-face meetings like the 1998 discussion between Abu Doha speaking for the London cell of GSPC and Osama bin Laden speaking for al Qaeda.[68] Just killing the members may not always eliminate the organization. It will not eliminate the threat. When Sabri al-Banna, leader of the group named for his "nom de guerre" Abu Nidal (ANO), reportedly died in Iraq in 2002, the organization had no further reported major events associated with them. But that assumption was questioned in 2008 when an ANO member was caught planning attacks aimed at Jordan.[69] Another is Abdel Ghani Meskini. Apprehended in 1999, Meskini cooperated with the state and testified for the prosecution. After serving a very short time, he was released in 2005; by 2007 he was back in business ordering an AK-47 for attacks on Western targets.[70] The individuals remain—they are key.

But we also have to consider where the growth area for attacks may occur. The Sahel and Northern Africa are ripe with opportunity for illicit activity, no government oversight, and successful stories of acts executed with no real ramifications. In addition, we also need to take heed of a study that indicated young Nigerian computer science college graduates' desire to join the ranks of those who execute cyber crime. A proactive counter now may be a wise approach. Al Qaeda's presence in Africa is old, ingrained, and accepted. The Nairobi cell was already established before 1994. That plus the 1993 move of Khader Abu Hosher to Yemen, where he connected with the Palestinian Islamic Jihad, makes the al Qaeda presence in Yemen and the Maghreb long before the existence of AQIM and AQAP. The creation of a formal link between the Saudi AQ and the Yemen AQ was more than convenience. It offered an avenue to continue the distancing away from the bin Laden approach to attacks. This plus the fact that bin Laden established London link to GSPC created the groundwork very early for what was later deemed by the press (and some experts) as "new organizations." Assessing crowdsourced data for these patterns can increase our ability to successfully respond.

The use of al Awlaki as the frequently named influence to execute missions also indicated that the guidance for mission accomplishment was moving from the need for psychological approval of AQ central to the individual attacker. While the Internet facilitated that move, it was not the only prompter. Use of English, change in tone, and language as well created a welcoming atmosphere for an audience not previously pursued. Al Awlaki is a different threat from earlier years when the dangerous common link was a planner or trainer. With al Awlaki the threat was the ethereal inspiration. There was no specific "mode of operation." That is left to the individual. Al Qaeda began to look at the individual as a unit of attack.

This new threat definition offered al Qaeda several pluses. Al Awlaki was an American working against America. He achieved key successes without imposing on al Qaeda logistic assets. Major Nidal Hasan struck on U.S. soil killing 13 fellow military members. Resource acquisition and attack execution were left to the individual. Al Qaeda could decide to associate itself or not. This cherry-picking posture keeps the victim nation-state off kilter because no official claim of responsibility leaves judicial prosecution in a limbo predicament.

We must cease to acknowledge astonishment at the use of technology or an advancement or change in al Qaeda's management style. These offer opportunities for al Qaeda flacks to exploit our incredulity as an insult to Islam.

We must identify the strategy used over several countries and find elements of vulnerability that transcend them. That includes looking at perceived strengths and determining all the factors that contribute to those strengths and then analyzing them for vulnerabilities. The self-initiated attacks all have elements to them that can be examined. For instance, the Boston Marathon bombing was executed without al Qaeda or Chechnya rebel sanction. Both received media exposure after the event. We know that when these events occur, a video message in support usually follows. The direct target of these videos is the young individual listener. We have no counter to those messages. We do not release videos days later shaping the message of the attack or incident to our goal or objective. Al Qaeda does.

Items that have not worked include state-sponsored decrees. Nor did the state-sponsored debates, as both opened windows on the frailty of the states in adherence to Islam.[71]

One especially successful tactic that has worked for al Qaeda is targeting young followers of Islam with little or no structured religious training. They practice and inculcate Islam into their hearts based on exposure to al Qaeda's web of communication tools. As they watch events or incidents unfold, the prime objects of the strategy may question a specific act because it may not make them uncomfortable, but if al Qaeda reference can be identified within the Qur'an or Hadith, then nonresistance may result. This nonresistance is separate from acceptance. It offers opportunity for al Qaeda to continue its objectives. It could also be a vulnerability for examination.

Al Qaeda emphasis on individuals resulted in horizontal expansion, and while it may seem paradoxical, expansion in this direction has actually given "al Qaeda the concept" of depth that will be hard to eliminate, like that of a spider web that silently grows while no one is watching.[72]

We must also look at the al Qaeda relationships from the perspective of longevity and power. All relationships including Haqqani and the Tablighi must be analyzed. As we have seen in the past, quiet background Haqqani influence, is where to find the one who wields the most power.

Al Qaeda's regional associations, like those with al Shabaab are significant. But how long will they exist, and what trends in the organization may determine the organization has outgrown the al Qaeda concept? What is the African geographic and affiliate contribution to the al Qaeda brand? That most definitely must not be shortchanged. Nor should the volatile relationship between the failing or fragile governments of the regional desperately trying to continue. These areas in particular present a challenge because they offer significant opportunity for future improvement of relations and reduced terrorist activity.

Last, al Qaeda uses Islam as a tool to achieve its goals. We in the West are realistically hampered from having any semblance of trying to manipulate Islam to solve the terrorism problem. Even if support is extended such that it focuses only[73] on statehood management and humanitarian aid through Islamic sources, the al Qaeda media machine will reframe those same efforts to appear they are for our own benefit and not that of international good. However, the 57 nations that follow Islam have that right and are the ones we must support as they wrestle with the problem of reclaiming Islam. U.S. policy toward the sovereign governments targeted by al Qaeda must include overtures that indicate the relationship is equal not paternalistic.[74]

Appendix A

Maps

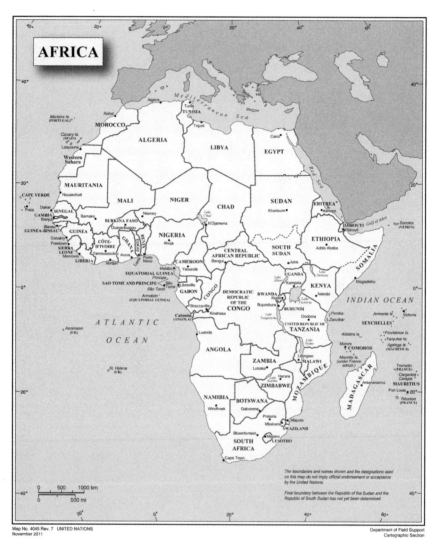

Africa, Map No. 4045 Rev.7, November 2011. Used by permission of the United Nations Publications Board.

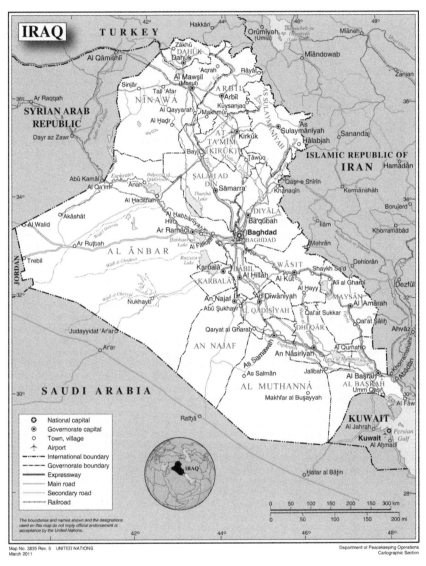

Iraq, Map No. 3835 Rev.5, March 2011. Used by permission of the United Nations Publications Board.

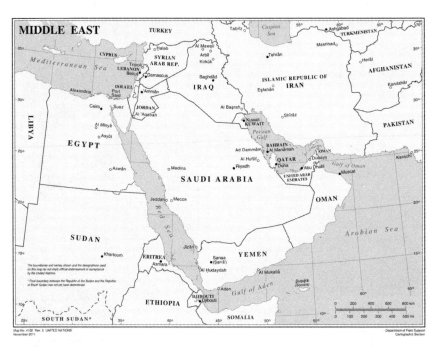

Middle East, Map No. 4102 Rev.5, November 2011. Used by permission of the United Nations Publications Board.

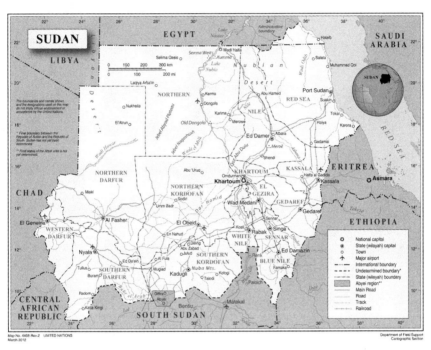

Sudan, Map No. 4458 Rev.2, March 2012. Used by permission of the United Nations Publications Board.

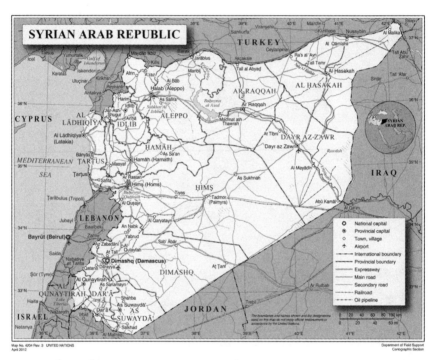

Syrian Arab Republic, Map No. 4204 Rev.3, April 2012. Used by permission of the United Nations Publications Board.

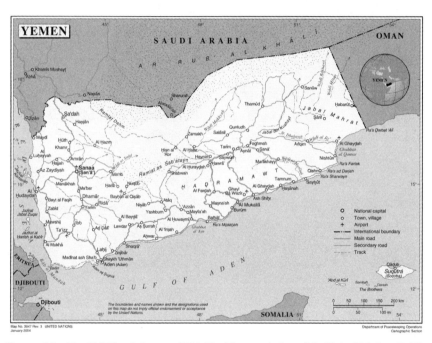

Yemen, Map No. 3847 Rev.3, January 2004. Used by permission of the United Nations Publications Board.

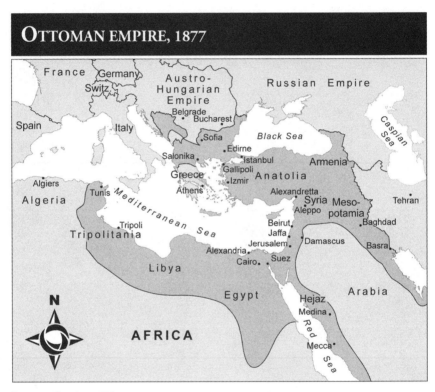

OTTOMAN EMPIRE, 1877

Ottoman Empire, 1877.

THE OTTOMAN EMPIRE TO 1914

GREAT BRITAIN NETHERLANDS
BELGIUM GERMAN EMPIRE
LUXEMBOURG
FRANCE
SWITZERLAND
AUSTRO-HUNGARIAN EMPIRE
TRANSYLVANIA
Belgrade
ITALY BOSNIA SERBIA ROMANIA
HERZEGOVINA BULGARIA
MONTENEGRO San Stefano
ALBANIA Istanbul
GREECE (Constantinople)
Smyrna
SARDINIA
SPAIN
SICILY
Cyprus
ALGERIA Mediterranean Crete
Sea
TUNISIA
Tripoli
TRIPOLI
EGYPT
AFRICA

Vistula R.
Dnieper R.
RUSSIA Volga R. Aral Sea
BESSARABIA
Odessa
CRIMEA Caspian Sea
Sevastopol Balaklava
Black Sea GEORGIA
Varna ARMENIA
Sinope
Trebizond
Ankara OTTOMAN EMPIRE PERSIA
Euphrates R.
Baghdad
Damascus
KUWAIT Persian Sea
PALESTINE
Jerusalem
Alexandria
Cairo ARABIA
Red Sea

Ottoman Empire
⬚ Territory lost, 1829-1877
⬚ Territory lost, 1878-1913
⬚ Ottoman Empire in 1914
Russian Empire
▓ Russia in 1802
▓ Territory gained, by 1914

0 ——— 800 mi
0 ——— 800 km

N

Ottoman Empire, before 1914.

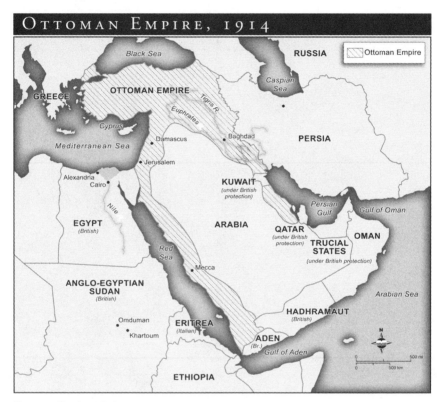

OTTOMAN EMPIRE, 1914

Black Sea

RUSSIA

Ottoman Empire

OTTOMAN EMPIRE

Caspian
Sea

GREECE

Tigris R.

Cyprus

Euphrates

PERSIA

Mediterranean Sea

Damascus

Baghdad

Jerusalem

Alexandria
Cairo

KUWAIT
(under British
protection)

Nile

Persian
Gulf

Gulf of Oman

EGYPT
(British)

ARABIA

QATAR
(under British
protection)

OMAN

Red
Sea

TRUCIAL
STATES
(under British protection)

Mecca

Arabian Sea

ANGLO-EGYPTIAN
SUDAN
(British)

HADHRAMAUT
(British)

Omduman

ERITREA
(Italian)

Khartoum

ADEN
(Br.)

N

Gulf of Aden

ETHIOPIA

0   500 mi

0   500 km

Ottoman Empire, 1914.

Appendix B

―∞∞∞―

Timelines

Timelines courtesy of Jasmin Ullah.

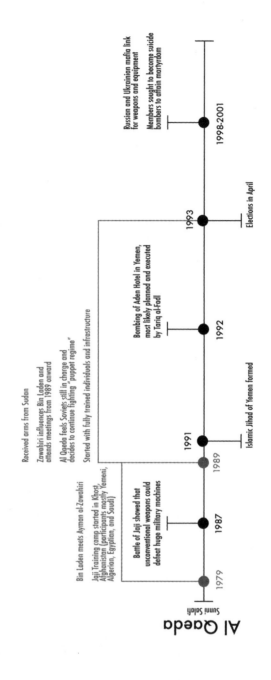

184

Al Qaeda in the Arabian Peninsula

centered in Yemen, homeland of Bin Laden's father

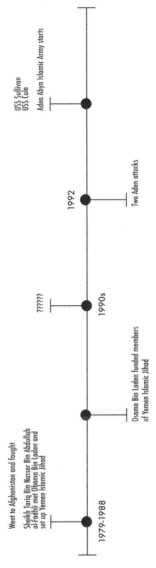

1979-1988

Went to Afghanistan and fought

Sheikh Tariq Bin Nasser Bin Abdullah al-Fadhli met Obama Bin Laden and set up Yemen Islamic Jihad

Osama Bin Laden funded members of Yemen Islamic Jihad

1990s

??????

1992

Two Aden attacks

USS Sullivan
USS Cole

Aden Abyn Islamic Army starts

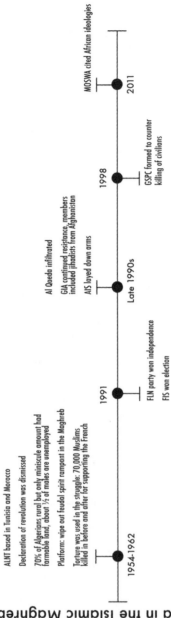

Al Qaeda in the Islamic Maghreb

1954-1962

ALNT based in Tunisia and Morocco

Declaration of revolution was dismissed

70% of Algerians rural but only miniscule amount had farmable land, about 1/2 of males are unemployed

Platform: wipe out feudal spirit rampant in the Maghreb

Torture was used in the struggle: 70,000 Muslims killed in before and after for supporting the French

1991

FLN party won independence

FIS won election

Late 1990s

Al Qaeda infiltrated

GIA continued resistance, members included jihadists from Afghanistan

AIS layed down arms

1998

GSPC formed to counter killing of civilians

2011

MOSWA cited African ideologies

Al Shabaab

Wahdat Al Shabaab/Al Jama'a Al Islamiyya/Al Ittihab Al Islamiya (AIAI)

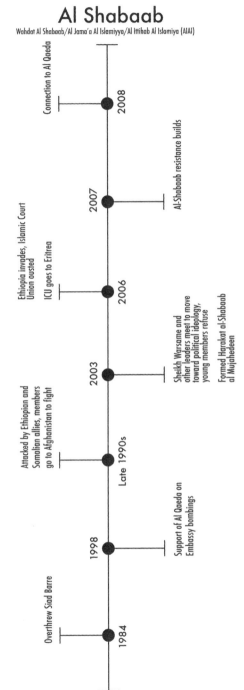

Connection to Al Qaeda

2008

Al-Shabaab resistance builds

2007

Ethiopia invades, Islamic Court Union ousted

ICU goes to Eritrea

2006

Sheikh Warsame and other leaders meet to move toward political ideology, young members refuse

Formed Harakat al-Shabaab al Mujahedeen

2003

Attacked by Ethiopian and Somalian allies, members go to Afghanistan to fight

Late 1990s

Support of Al Qaeda on Embassy bombings

1998

Overthrew Siad Barre

1984

Notes

INTRODUCTION

1. Stephen Chan, "Fanon. The Octogenarian of International Revenge and the Suicide Bomber of Today," *Cooperation and Conflict: Journal of the Nordic International Studies Association* 42, no. 2 (June 1, 2007): 151–68.

2. "Lee Rigby Named as Woolwich Victim," *BBC*, May 23, 2013, sec. UK, http://www.bbc.co.uk/news/uk-22644857.

3. Susan Sevareid, "Israel Tries to Learn Motives of Suicide Bombers," *The Free Lance–Star*, June 20, 2002.

4. "Watch Now: Al Qaeda in Yemen | FRONTLINE | PBS Video," http://video.pbs.org/video/2240325626. Interviews with Ali Soufan, FBI agent and chief investigator in the *USS Cole* investigation, highlight information he was able to secure from Fahd Mohammed Ahmed al-Quso during interrogations. During those interrogation sessions, Soufan was able to determine al Qaeda presence in locations not previously known by the U.S. intelligence community.

5. "Charlie Hebdo Attack: Three Days of Terror," BBC News, http://www.bbc.com/news/world-europe-30708237.

6. "French Police Raid Two Sites, Kill Charlie Hebdo Suspects | Al Jazeera America," http://america.aljazeera.com/articles/2015/1/9/duel-hostage-situationsinparisendwithassailantshostageskilled.html.

7. Aminu Abubaker, "Strategic City Falls in Nigeria's Battle against Boko Haram—CNN.com," CNN, http://www.cnn.com/2015/01/25/africa/nigeria-boko-haram-battle-maiduguri/index.html.

8. Paul Cruickshank, Tim Lister, and Nic Robertson, "Al-Qaida Document Reveals U.S. Attack Plans," KRCRTV, March 20, 2013, http://www.krcrtv.com/news/Al-Qaida-document-reveals-U-S-attack-plans/-/14286064/19390212/-/up8vae/-/index.html.

9. Ibid.

10. Robin Simcox, "Boko Haram and Defining the 'Al-Qaeda Network,'" *Al Jazeera*, June 6, 2014, http://www.aljazeera.com/indepth/opinion/2014/06/boko-haram-al-qaeda-201463115816142554.html.

11. Priyanka Boghani, "What Makes Boko Haram's Atrocities So Hard to Track? – Hunting Boko Haram," *FRONTLINE*, http://www.pbs.org/wgbh/pages/frontline/foreign-affairs-defense/hunting-boko-haram/what-makes-boko-harams-atrocities-so-hard-to-track/.

12. Mona El-naggar, "Houthi Leader Blames Separatists in South Yemen for Political Stalemate," *New York Times*, January 27, 2015, http://www.nytimes.com/2015/01/28/world/middleeast/houthi-leader-blames-separatists-in-south-yemen-for-political-stalemate.html.

13. Matthew Mpoke Bigg and Kwasi Kpodo, "West African Leaders Mull New Force to Fight Boko Haram Insurgents," *Reuters*, January 16, 2015, U.S. edition, http://www.reuters.com/article/2015/01/16/us-nigeria-violence-africa-idUSKBN0KP1FN20150116.

CHAPTER 1

1. Ben Brumfield, "Officials: 3 Denver Girls Played Hooky from School and Tried to Join ISIS," *CNN*, October 23, 2014, http://www.cnn.com/2014/10/22/us/colorado-teens-syria-odyssey/index.html.

2. Brian Fishman and Joseph Felter, "Al-Qa'ida's Foreign Fighters in Iraq: A First Look at the Sinjar Records," Report of the Harmony Project Combatting Terrorism Center, January 2, 2007, https://www.ctc.usma.edu/posts/al-qaidas-foreign-fighters-in-iraq-a-first-look-at-the-sinjar-records.

3. Ibid.

4. Daniel L. Byman, *Breaking the Bonds between Al-Qa'ida and Its Affiliate Organizations*, Analysis Paper 27 (Brookings Institution, 2012), http://www.brookings.edu/~/media/Research/Files/Papers/2012/7/alqaida%20terrorism%20byman/alqaida%20terrorism%20byman.pdf.

5. Anders Strindberg and Mats Warn, "Realities of Resistance: Hizballah, the Palestinian Rejectionists, and Al-Qa`ida Compared," *Journal of Palestine Studies* 34, no. 3 (May 2004), http://www.palestine-studies.org/jps/fulltext/41571.

6. Jane Corbin, *Al-Qaeda: In Search of the Terror Network That Threatens the World* (New York: Nation Books, 2003).

7. Bruce Lawrence, *Messages to the World: The Statements of Osama bin Laden*, annotated ed. (London/New York: Verso, 2005).

8. Ibid.

9. Gilles Kepel, *Jihad: The Trail of Political Islam* (Cambridge: Belknap Press of Harvard University Press, 2002).

10. Gilles Kepel, *Muslim Extremism in Egypt: The Prophet and Pharaoh* (Berkeley: University of California Press, 1985).

11. Corbin, *Al-Qaeda*.

12. John Turner, "From Cottage Industry to International Organisation: The Evolution of Salafi-Jihadism and the Emergence of the Al Qaeda Ideology," *Terrorism and Political Violence* 22, no. 4 (September 14, 2010): 541–58, doi:10.1080/09546553.2010.485534.

13. Mark Sedgwick, "Al-Qaeda and the Nature of Religious Terrorism," *Terrorism and Political Violence* 16, no. 4 (January 1, 2004): 795–814, doi:10.1080/0954655090906098.

14. David Fromkin, *A Peace to End All Peace: The Fall of the Ottoman Empire and the Creation of the Modern Middle East* (New York: Henry Holt and Company, 2009).

15. Tinka Veldhuis and Jørgen Staun, *Islamist Radicalisation: A Root Cause Model* (Netherlands: Institute of International Relations Clingendael, 2009).

16. Edward Newman, "Failed States and International Order: Constructing a Post-Westphalian World," *Contemporary Security Policy* 30, no. 3 (December 1, 2009): 421–43, doi:10.1080/13523260903326479.

17. Ibid.

18. Alan B. Krueger and Jitka Maleckova, *Education, Poverty, Political Violence and Terrorism: Is There a Causal Connection?*, Working Paper (National Bureau of Economic Research, July 2002), http://www.nber.org/papers/w9074.

19. Jessica Stern, *Terror in the Name of God: Why Religious Militants Kill*, 1st ed. (New York: Ecco, 2003).

20. Richard Barrett, *Foreign Fighters in Syria* (New York: The Soufan Group, June 2014), http://soufangroup.com/wp-content/uploads/2014/06/TSG-Foreign-Fighters-in-Syria.pdf.

21. Jeffrey Haynes, "Al Qaeda: Ideology and Action," *Critical Review of International Social and Political Philosophy* 8, no. 2 (June 1, 2005): 177–91, doi:10.1080/13698230500108868.

22. Quintan Wiktorowicz, "Anatomy of the Salafi Movement," *Studies in Conflict & Terrorism* 29, no. 3 (May 4, 2006): 207–39, doi:10.1080/10576100500497004.

23. Ibid.

24. Kepel, *Jihad.*

25. Lise Storm, "The Persistence of Authoritarianism as a Source of Radicalization in North Africa," *International Affairs* 85, no. 5 (September 2009): 997–1013, doi:10.1111/j.1468-2346.2009.00843.x.

26. Gilles Kepel, *Jihad.*

27. Ibid.

28. Gilles Kepel, *The Roots of Radical Islam* (London: Saqi Books, 2005).

29. Kepel, *Muslim Extremism in Egypt.*

30. Ibid.

31. Kepel, *The Roots of Radical Islam.*

32. Diego Gambetta and Steffen Hertog, "Engineers of Jihad," Paper presented at a workshop at the Peace Research Institute in Oslo, August 10, 2006.

33. Kepel, *The Roots of Radical Islam.*

34. Thomas Hegghammer, *The Faiure of Jihad in Saudi Arabia*, Occasional Paper Series (West Point, NY: Combat Terrorism Center at West Point, February 25, 2010), http://www.ctc.usma.edu/wp-content/uploads/2010/10/CTC_OP_Hegghammer_Final.pdf.

35. Henri Lauziere, "The Construction of Salafiyya: Reconsidering Salafism from the Perspective of Conceptual History," *International Journal of Middle East Studies* 42, no. 3 (August 2010):369–89, doi:10.1017/S0020743810000401.

36. Ibid.

37. Ibid.

38. Hegghammer, *The Faiure of Jihad in Saudi Arabia.*

39. Kepel, *Jihad.*

40. Mohamed Sheishaa, "A Study of the Fatwa by Rashid Rida on the Translation of the Qur'an | Islamic Writings," *Journal of the Society for Qur'anic Studies* 1, http://www.islamicwritings.org/quran/language/a-study-of-the-fatwa-by-rashid-rida-on-the-translation-of-the-quran/.

41. Ibid.

42. Turner, "From Cottage Industry to International Organisation."

43. Kepel, *Jihad*, 66.

44. Kepel, *The Roots of Radical Islam*.

45. Kepel, *Jihad*.

46. Camille Tawil and Robin Bray, trans., *Brothers in Arms: The Story of Al Qa'ida and the Arab Jihadists* (London: Saqi Books, 2007).

47. Ibid.

48. Reza Ekhtiari Amiri, Ku Hasnita Binti Ku Samsu, and Hassan Gholipour Fereidouni, "Iran's Economic Considerations after the War and Its Role in Renewing of Iran-Saudi Diplomatic Relations" [Considérations Économiques de l'Iran Après la Guerre et Son Rôle Dans le Renouvellement des Relations Diplomatiques Entre l'Iran et l'Arabie Saoudite], *Cross-Cultural Communication* 6, no. 3 (2010): 45–54.

49. Wiktorowicz, "Anatomy of the Salafi Movement."

50. Ibid.

51. Lauziere, "The Construction of Salafiyya."

52. Ibid.

53. Ashaf Moghadam, *The Globalization of Martyrdom: Al Qaeda, Salafi Jihad, and the Diffusion of Suicide Attacks* (Baltimore: Johns Hopkins University Press, 2008).

54. Ibid.

55. Umbreen Javaid and Nighat Noureen, "An Insight into the Philosophical Dynamics of Al-Qaeda," *Journal of Political Studies* 20, no. 2 (Winter 2013): 201–18.

56. Lawrence, *Messages to the World*.

57. Abdel Bari Atwan, *The Secret History of Al Qaeda* (London: Saqi Books, 2012).

58. Muhammad Saed Abdul-Rahman, *Islam Questions and Answers. Volume 8, Schools of Thought, Religions and Sects* (London: MSA Publication Ltd, 2003).

59. Wiktorowicz, "Anatomy of the Salafi Movement."

60. Ibid.

61. Wiktorowicz, "Anatomy of the Salafi Movement."

62. Turner, "From Cottage Industry to International Organisation."

63. Ibid.

64. Bruce Livesey, *The Salafist Movement*, http://www.pbs.org/wgbh/pages/front line/shows/front/special/sala.html, and Christopher Henzel, "The Origins of the Al Qaeda Ideology: Implications for U.S. Strategy," *Parameters* (Spring, 2005): 72.

65. Lawrence, *Messages to the World*.

66. Youssef H. Aboul-Enein and USAF Counterproliferation Center, "Ayman Al-Zawahiri: The Ideologue of Modern Islamic Militancy" (USAF Counterproliferation Center, Air University, 2004).

67. Olivier Roy, "Al-Qaeda Brand Name Ready for Franchise: The Business of Terror," *Le Monde Diplomatique* (September 1, 2004).

68. Ibid.

69. Moghadam, *The Globalization of Martyrdom*.

70. Fawaz A Gerges, *The Far Enemy: Why Jihad Went Global*, 2nd ed. (Cambridge: Cambridge University Press, 2009).

71. Wiktorowicz, "Anatomy of the Salafi Movement."

72. Ibid.

73. S. Khatab, "Hakimiyyah and Jahiliyyah in the Thought of Sayyid Qutb," *Middle Eastern Studies* 38, no. 3 (2002): 145–70.

74. Muhammad Zubayr Siddiqi, *Hadith Literature: Its Origins, Development, and Special Features* (Cambridge: The Islamic Text Society, 1993), 31–6.

75. Danny Orbach, "Tyrannicide in Radical Islam: The Case of Sayyid Qutb and Abd Al-Salam Faraj," *Middle Eastern Studies* 48, no. 6 (November 1, 2012): 961–72, doi:10.1080/00263206.2012.723629.

76. Sayed Khatab, "'Hakimiyyah' and 'Jahiliyyah' in the Thought of Sayyid Qutb," *Middle Eastern Studies* 38, no. 3 (July 1, 2002): 145–70.

77. Orbach, "Tyrannicide in Radical Islam."

78. Khatab, "'Hakimiyyah' and 'Jahiliyyah' in the Thought of Sayyid Qutb."

79. Peter Sluglett and Andrew Currie, *Atlas of Islamic History* (London: Routledge, 2014), http://mutex.gmu.edu/login?url=http://search.ebscohost.com/login.aspx?direct=true&db=nlebk&AN=945788&site=ehost-live&scope=site.

80. Ibid.

81. Ibid.

82. Sujata Ashwarya Cheema, "Sayyid Qutb's Concept of Jahiliyya as Metaphor for Modern Society," in *Beyond Textual Islam*, 2008, https://www.academia.edu/3222569/Sayyid_Qutbs_Concept_of_Jahiliyya_as_Metaphor_for_Modern_Society.

83. Sayed Khatab, "'Hakimiyyah' and 'Jahiliyyah' in the Thought of Sayyid Qutb," *Middle Eastern Studies* 38, no. 3 (July 1, 2002): 145–70.

84. Hossam Taman, "The Muslim Brotherhood and Saudi Wahhabism" (al-akhbar, January 22, 2009), http:www.al-akhbar.com/ar/node/114449.

85. Syed Asas Gilani, *Maududi: Thought and Movement*, 1st ed. (Lahore, Pakistan: Islamic Publications LTD, 1984).

86. Khatab, "'Hakimiyyah' and 'Jahiliyyah' in the Thought of Sayyid Qutb."

87. Robert Rozehnal, "Gabriele Marranci: Jihad beyond Islam," *Contemporary Islam* 2, no. 2 (July 1, 2008): 159–62, doi:10.1007/s11562-008-0041-3.

88. John L. Esposito, *Unholy War: Terror in the Name of Islam* (Oxford: Oxford University Press, 2003).

89. Khatab, "'Hakimiyyah' and 'Jahiliyyah' in the Thought of Sayyid Qutb."

90. Ibid.

91. Ibid.

92. Olivier Roy, *Globalized Islam: The Search for a New Ummah* (New York: Columbia University Press, 2006).

93. Esposito, *Unholy War: Terror in the Name of Islam*.

94. Ibid.

95. Quintan Wiktorowicz, "Anatomy of the Salafi Movement," *Studies in Conflict & Terrorism* 29, no. 3 (May 4, 2006): 207–39, doi:10.1080/10576100500497004.

96. Ibid.

97. Ibid.

98. Trevor Stanley, "Taqi Al-Deen Ahmad Ibn Taymiyya," in *Perspectives on World History and Current Events*, 2004, http://www.pwhce.org/taymiyyah.html.

99. Ibid.

100. Ibid.

101. Albert Hourani, *Arabic Thought in the Liberal Age, 1798-1939*, 1983.

102. Ibid.

103. Daniel Benjamin, *The Age of Sacred Terror*, 1st ed. (New York: Random House, 2002).

104. Jason Burke, *Al-Qaeda: Casting a Shadow of Terror* (London; New York: IB Tauris, 2003).

105. Ibid.

106. Kepel, *Muslim Extremism in Egypt.*

107. Khatab, "'Hakimiyyah' and 'Jahiliyyah' in the Thought of Sayyid Qutb."

108. Ali Rahnama, *Pioneers of Islamic Revival* (London; Atlantic Highlands, NJ: Zed Books, 1994).

109. Majid Khadduri, *The Islamic Conception of Justice* (Baltimore: JHU Press, 2001).

110. Charles Tripp, "Sayyid Qutb," in *Pioneers of Islamic Revival*, Ali Rahhnema, ed. (London: Zed Books, 1994).

111. Kepel, *Muslim Extremism in Egypt.*

112. Fawaz A Gerges, *The Far Enemy: Why Jihad Went Global*, 2nd ed (Cambridge; New York: Cambridge University Press, 2009).

113. Benjamin, *The Age of Sacred Terror.*

114. Ibid.

115. Gerges, *The Far Enemy.*

116. Ibid.

117. Ibid.

118. Ibid.

119. Roy, *Globalized Islam.*

120. Nimrod Raphaeli, "Ayman Muhammad Rabi' Al-Zawahiri: The Making of an Arch-Terrorist," *Terrorism and Political Violence* 14, no. 4 (December 1, 2002): 1–22, doi:10.1080/714005636.

121. Dominc Casciani, "Profile: Abu Qatada," *BBC News*, June 26, 2014, http://www.bbc.com/news/uk-16584923.

122. Abu Bakr Naji and William McCants, trans., "The Management of Savagery: The Most Critical Stage Through Which the Umma Will Pass" (Harvard: John M. Olin Institute for Strategic Studies, Harvard University, May 23, 2006), http://azelin.files.wordpress.com/2010/08/abu-bakr-naji-the-management-of-savagery-the-most-critical-stage-through-which-the-umma-will-pass.pdf.

123. Raphaeli, "Ayman Muhammad Rabi' Al-Zawahiri."

124. Ibid.

125. Gerges, *The Far Enemy.*

126. Gilles Kepel, *The Roots of Radical Islam* (London: Saqi Books, 2005).

127. Thomas Hegghammer, "Global Jihadism After the Iraq War," *Middle East Journal* 60, no. 1 (2006), http://hegghammer.com/_files/Global_Jihadism_after_the_Iraq_War.pdf.

128. Moghadam, *The Globalization of Martyrdom.*

129. Ibid.

130. "Exclusive: Al-Shumoukh Forum Member Calls for Lone Wolf Attacks on Churces, Hotels, Shopping Centers-Jihad and Terrorism Threat Monitor (JTTM) Weekend Summary," *MEMRI—The Middle East Media Research Institute*, January 3, 2015, http://www.memri.org/report/en/0/0/0/0/0/0/8359.htm.

131. Terrence McCoy, "The Calculated Madness of the Islamic State's Horrifying Brutality," *Washington Post*, August 12, 2014, http://www.washingtonpost.com/news/morning-mix/wp/2014/08/12/the-calculated-madness-of-the-islamic-states-horrifying-brutality/.

132. Assaf Moghadam, *The Globalization of Martyrdom.*

133. Hegghammer, "Global Jihadism After the Iraq War."

CHAPTER 2

1. Jason Burke, *Al-Qaeda: Casting a Shadow of Terror* (New York: IB Tauris, 2003).

2. Fawaz Gerges, "The Rise and Fall of Al-Qaeda: Debunking the Terrorism Narrative," news, *The World Post*, January 3, 2012, http://www.ispu.org/GetArticles/48/2401/Publications.aspx.

3. Rohan Gunaratna, *Inside Al Qaeda: Global Network of Terror* (New York, NY: Columbia University Press, 2002).

4. Vahid Brown and Don Rassler, *Fountainhead of Jihad: The Haqqani Nexus, 1973–2012* (New York, NY: Oxford University Press, 2013).

5. Ted Carpenter, "U.S. Aid to Anti-Communist Rebels: The 'Reagan Doctrine' and Its Pitfalls," *Cato Institute*, June 24, 1986, http://www.cato.org/publications/policy-analysis/us-aid-anticommunist-rebels-reagan-doctrine-its-pitfalls.

6. Gunaratna, *Inside Al Qaeda*.

7. Syed Saleem Shahzad, *Inside Al-Qaeda and the Taliban: Beyond Bin Laden and 9/11* (New York: Pluto Press, 2011).

8. Brown and Rassler, *Fountainhead of Jihad*.

9. Ibid.

10. Ibid.

11. Ibid.

12. Abdul Waheed Wafa and Carlotta Gall, "State Funeral for Afghan Leader Slain in '78 Coup," *New York Times*, March 18, 2009, sec. International/Asia Pacific, http://www.nytimes.com/2009/03/18/world/asia/18afghan.html.

13. Brown and Rassler, *Fountainhead of Jihad*.

14. Ibid.

15. Ibid.

16. Don Rassler and Vahid Brown, "The Haqqani Nexus and the Evolution of Al-Qa'ida," Harmony Project (New York: Combating Terrorism Center at West Point, July 14, 2011), https://www.ctc.usma.edu/posts/the-haqqani-nexus-and-the-evolution-of-al-qaida.

17. Ibid.

18. Ibid.

19. Ibid.

20. Ibid.; and "Cracks in the Foundation: Leadership Schisms in al-Qa'ida from 1989–2006," Harmony Project, 2007.

21. Fawaz Gerges, *The Rise and Fall of al-Qaeda*, 67–73.

22. Bruce O. Riedel, *The Search for Al Qaeda: Its Leadership, Ideology, and Future* (Washington, D.C.: Brookings Institution Press, 2008).

23. Ibid.

24. Peter L. Bergen, "Espionage & Intelligence Gathering" (Booknotes), *Holy War, Inc.: Inside the Secret World of Osama Bin Laden* (New York: Free Press, 2001).

25. Rohan Gunaratna and Aviv Oreg, "Al Qaeda's Organizational Structure and Its Evolution," *Studies in Conflict & Terrorism* 33, no. 12 (December 2010): 1043–78, doi:10.1080/1057610X.2010.523860.

26. Ibid.

27. "Beware of Imitators Al-Qa'ida through the Lens of Its Confidential Secretary," Harmony Project, June 2012, and "Founding Documents of Al Qaeda Recovered from Bosnia," *ICPVTR Database* (Singapore, January 2008).

28. Ibid.; and "Cracks in the Foundation: Leadership Schisms in al-Qa'ida from 1989–2006," Harmony Project, 2007.

29. Vahid Brown, *Cracks in the Foundation: Leadership Schisms in al-Qaida from 1989-2006*, CTC Report (West Point, NY: US Military Academy, Combating Terrorism Center, 2007).

30. Rohan Gunaratna and Aviv Oreg, "Al Qaeda's Organizational Structure and Its Evolution," *Studies in Conflict & Terrorism* 33, no. 12 (December 2010): 1043–78, doi:10.1080/1057610X.2010.523860.

31. Fawaz Gerges, "The Rise and Fall of Al-Qaeda: Debunking the Terrorism Narrative," news, *The World Post*, January 3, 2012, http://www.ispu.org/GetArticles/48/2401/Publications.aspx.

32. Peter Bergen and Paul Cruickshank, "Revisiting the Early Al Qaeda: An Updated Account of Its Formative Years," *Studies in Conflict & Terrorism* 35, no. 1 (2012): 1–36.

33. Iibid.

34. Bergen and Cruickshank, "Revisiting the Early Al Qaeda"; Gunaratna and Oreg, "Al Qaeda's Organizational Structure and Its Evolution."

35. Jason Burke, *Al Qaeda: Casting a Shadow of Terror* (New York: IB Taurus, 2003): 12–20.

36. Bergen, *The Osama bin Laden I Know*, 49–73.

37. Ibid.

38. Thomas Hegghamer, "The Origins of Global Jihad: Explaining the Arab Mobilization to 1980s Afghanistan" (Policy Memo, *International Security Program, Belfer Center for Science and International Affairs, Harvard Kennedy School*, January 22, 2009).

39. Ibid.

40. Peter Bergen, *Holy War, Inc.: Inside the Secret World of Osama Bin Laden* (New York: Touchstone, 2002): 88–101.

41. Gerges, "The Rise and Fall of Al-Qaeda: Debunking the Terrorism Narrative," 65–80; Peter and Cruickshank, "Revisiting the Early Al Qaeda."

42. Riedel, *The Search for al-Qaeda,*73–88.

43. Bergen and Cruickshank, "Revisiting the Early Al Qaeda."

44. Gerges, *Rise and Fall of al-Qaeda*, 65–72.

45. Ibid.

46. Ibid.

47. *Cracks in the Foundation: Leadership Schisms in al-Qaida from 1989–2006* and http://www.ctc.usma.edu/wpcontent/uploads/2011/06/Abul-Walid.pfd.

48. Rassler and Brown, "The Haqqani Nexus and the Evolution of Al-Qa'ida."

49. Ibid.

50. Ibid.

51. Denis McAuley, "The Ideology of Osama Bin Laden: Nation, Tribe and World Economy," *Journal of Political Ideologies* 10, no. 3 (October 2005): 269–287.

52. Bergen, *Holy War, Inc.*, 88–101.

53. Thomas Hegghamer, "Islamist Violence and Regime Stability in Saudi Arabia," *International Affairs* 84, no. 4 (2008): 701–715.

54. Bergen, *The Osama bin Laden I Know*.

55. Gerges, *The Rise and Fall of al-Qaeda*, 52–65.

56. Lee Smith, *Sudan's Osama, The Islamist Roots of Darfur Genocide*, Slate, August 5, 2004.

57. Max Taylor and Mohamed E. Elbushra, "Research Note: Hassan al-Turabi, Osama bin Laden, and Al Qaeda in Sudan," *Terrorism and Political Violence* 18, no. 3 (2006): 449–464.

58. "The Five Letters of the African Corps," Letter 3, CTC's Harmony Document Database, West Point Combating Terrorism Center, released February 14, 2006.

59. Taylor and Elbushra, "Research Note: Hassan al-Turabi, Osama bin Laden, and Al Qaeda in Sudan."

60. Millard Burr and Robert O. Collins, *Revolutionary Sudan: Hasan al-Turabi and the Islamist State, 1989–2000* (Leiden: Koninklijke Brill, 2003), 68–73.

61. Ibid.

62. Ibid.

63. Mare Sageman, *Understanding Terror Networks* (Philadelphia: University of Pennsylvania Press, 2004), 39.

64. Ann Lesch, "Osama bin Laden's business' in Sudan," *Current History* (May 2002): 101, 655; A. Fever, "Bin Laden Group Had Extensive Network of Companies, Witness Says," *New York Times*, February 13, 2001.

65. Ibid.

66. Ibid.

67. Ibid.

68. Rassler and Brown, "The Haqqani Nexus and the Evolution of Al-Qa'ida."

69. "Al Qaida's (Mis)Adventures in the Horn of Africa," Harmony Project, Combating Terrorism Center at West Point, 5–8.

70. Gerges, *The Rise and Fall of al-Qaeda*.

71. Bergen, *Holy War, Inc.*, 63–65, 88–89.

72. Lesch, "Osama bin Laden's business' in Sudan."

73. John Hunwick, "Sub-Saharan Africa and the Wider World of Islam: Historical and Contemporary Perspectives," *Journal of Religion in Africa* 26, Fasc. 3 (August, 1996): 230–257.

74. Ken Menkhaus, "Political Islam in Somalia," *Middle East Policy* (March 2002): 111–115; David H. Shinn, "Somalia: US Government Policy and Challenges," Hearing Before the Subcommittee on African Affairs of the Committee on Foreign Relations, U.S. Senate, July 11, 2006.

75. "Al Qaida's (Mis)Adventures in the Horn of Africa."

76. Menkhaus, "Political Islam in Somalia"; J. Stephen Morrison, "Testimony before the Subcommittee on Africa, Committee on International Relations, U.S. House of Representatives," 107th Cong., 1st Sess., November 15, 2001, http://commdocs.house.gov/committees/intlrel/hfa76191.000/hfa76191_0.HTM.

77. "Al Qaida's (Mis)Adventures in the Horn of Africa."

78. Ibid., 29–38.

79. Ibid.; and "Cracks in the Foundation-Leadership Schisms in Al Qaeda from 1989–2006," 5–11.

80. Peter Bergen, *Holy Terror, Inc.: Inside the Secret World of Osama bin Laden* (New York: Free Press, 2001), 47–49.

81. Bergen, *Holy War, Inc.*, 47–59, 89, 141; "Al Qaida's (Mis)Adventures in the Horn of Africa," 2, 29–47.

82. Burr and Collins, *Revolutionary Sudan*, 60–72.

83. Lesch, "Osama bin Laden's business' in Sudan"; Burr and Collins, *Revolutionary Sudan*, 111, 123, 223.

84. For a detailed account, see Richard Miniter, *Losing Bin Laden: How Bill Clinton's Failures Unleashed Global Terror* (Washington, D.C.: Regnery Publishing, 2004).

85. Ibid.

86. Abu Walid al Misri, "History of Arab Afghans," serialized in *Asharq al Awsat*, December 8–14, 2004; Mohammed Hafez, "*Jihad* after Iraq: Lessons from the Arab Afghans," *Studies in Conflict and Terrorism* 32, (2009): 75.

87. Bergen, *The Osama bin Ladin I Know*, 49–63, 74–88.

88. Riedel, *The Search for Al Qaeda*.

89. Ibid.

90. "Beware of the Imitators: Al-Qaida through the Lens of Its Confidential Secretary," Harmony Project, New York Combating Terrorism Center at West Point, 2012, 5–11.

91. Riedel, *The Search for Al Qaeda*.

92. Jason Burke, *Al Qaeda: Casting a Shadow of Terror* (New York: IB Taurus, 2003), 160–171.

93. Ahmed Rashid, "Pakistan, the Taliban and the U.S.," *Nation*, October 8, 2001.

94. "The Haqqani Nexus."

95. Riedel, *The Search for Al Qaeda*.

96. Bergen and Cruickshank, "Revisiting the Early Al Qaeda."

97. Ibid.

98. "Cracks in the Foundation"; Riedel, Cruickshank, *The Search for Al Qaeda*.

99. Gerges, *The Rise and Fall of al-Qaeda*, 68–75.

100. Riedel, *The Search for Al Qaeda*, 113–20; Ahmed Rashid, "Afghanistan Heart of Darkness," *Far Eastern Economic Review*, August 5, 2001.

101. "Cracks in the Foundation."

102. Fawaz Gerges, *The Far Enemy: Why Jihad Went Global* (Cambridge: Cambridge University Press, 2005), chapter 4; Gerges, *The Rise and Fall of Jihad*, 42–49.

103. Gerges, *The Rise and Fall of al-Qaeda*, 55–72.

104. Ibid.

105. Ibid.

106. Ibid.

107. BBC Monitoring Service, "Profile of Al-Qa`idah Leader for Horn of Africa Fazul `Abdullah,'" November 29, 2009.

108. Jeremy Prestholdt, "Phatom of the Forever War: Fazul Abdullah Muhammad and the Terrorist Imaginary," *Public Culture* 21, no. 3 (2009): 451–464.

109. Brian Whitaker, "Who Dunnit," *Middle East International*, October 27, 2000.

110. Brian Whitaker, "Who Sank the Cole?," *Middle East International*, November 10, 2000.

111. Ibid.

112. Brian Whitaker, "Abu Hamza Collared," *Middle East International*, March 26, 1999.

113. Gerges, *The Rise and Fall of al-Qaeda*, chapter 4; *The Far Enemy*, chapters 3 and 4.

114. Ibid.

115. "Cracks in the Foundation," 11–15; Alan Cullison, "Inside Al-Qaeda's Hard Drive: A Fortuitous Discovery Reveals Budget Squabbles, Baby Pictures, Office Rivalries—and the Path to 9/11," *The Atlantic Monthly* 294(2), no. 2 (September 2004): 63–64.

116. Bruce Hoffmann, "The Changing Face of Al Qaeda and the Global War on Terrorism," *Studies in Conflict & Terrorism* 27, no. 6 (2004): 549–560.

117. Paul Cruickshank and Mohannad Hage Ali, "Abu Musab Al Suri: Architect of the New Al Qaeda," *Studies in Conflict & Terrorism* 30, no. 1 (2007): 1–14.

118. International Crisis Group, Terrorism in Indonesia, Noordin's Network Crisis Group Asia, May 5, 2006, 5–8.

119. Robert Wesley, "The Madrid Attacks, Results of Investigations Two Years Later," *Terrorism Monitor* 4, no. 5 (March 9, 2006); Lawrence Wright, "The Terror Web: Were the Madrid Bombings Part of a New Far Reaching Jihad Being Plotted in the Internet?" *New Yorker*, August 2004.

120. Gerges, *The Rise and Fall of al-Qaeda*, 75–93.

121. Ibid.

122. http://www.chathamhouse.org/sites/default/files/public/International% 20Affairs/2010/86_6dodge.pdf.

123. Ibid.

124. Gerges, *The Rise and Fall of al*-Qaeda, 110–23.

125. Mark Danner, "US Torture: Voices from Black Sites," *New York Review of Books*, April 9, 2009.

126. Gerges, *The Rise and Fall of al-Qaeda*.

127. Hoffman, "The Changing Face of Al Qaeda and the Global War on Terrorism."

128. Jason Burke, *The 9/11 Wars* (Allen Lane, 2010), 88–100.

129. Ibid.

130. For more on al-Suri, see Cruickshank and Ali, "Abu Musab Al Suri."

131. Burke, *The 9/11 Wars*.

132. Walter Pincus, "CIA Studies Provide Glimpse of Insurgents in Iraq; Analysis Describes Groups of Fighters, Gives Clearer Picture of Their Operations," *Washington Post*, February 6, 2005, 19; Gerges provides an account of how AQI and AQAP were not connected in *The Rise and Fall of al-Qaeda*; see chapter 3.

133. Ibid.

134. Ibid.

135. Burke, *The 9/11 Wars*; Riedel, *The Search for Al* Qaeda; Ibid.

136. "Cracks in the Foundation."

137. The differences between al-Zarqawi's religious worldview and that of al-Qaeda and bin Laden are also reported by Sayf al-`Adl, "Abu Mus`ab al-Zarqawi: al-Sira al-Dhatiyya," in Fuad Hussein, ed., *Al-Zarqawi: aljil al-thani li-al-Qa`ida* (Beirut: Dar al-khayal, 2005), 115–42.

138. Gerges, *The Rise and Fall of al-Qaeda*, 88–101.

139. Ibid.

140. Gerges, *The Far Enemy*.

141. http://www.understandingwar.org/files/reports/IraqReport03.pdf_.

142. Cruickshank and Ali,) "Abu Musab Al Suri."

143. Burke, *The 9/11 Wars*.

144. Ahmed Hashim, "Foreign Involvement in the Iraqi Insurgency," *Terrorism Monitor*, August 2004.

145. Ibid.

146. Joas Wagemakers, "A Purist Jihadi-Salafi: The Ideology of Abu Muhammad al-Maqdisi," *British Journal of Middle Eastern Studies* 36, no. 2 (2009): 281–297.

147. Hoffman, "The Changing Face of Al Qaeda and the Global War on Terrorism."

148. Ibid.

149. Burke, *The 9/11 Wars*.

150. Gerges, *The Rise and Fall of al-Qaeda*, 182–191.

151. Brynjar Lia and Thomas Hegghammer, "Jihadi Strategic Studies," *Studies in Conflict and Terrorism* 27, no. 5 (2004).

CHAPTER 3

1. Vikram Dodd, "Man Killed in Deadly Terror Attack in London Street," *Guardian*, May 22, 2013, sec. UK news, http://www.guardian.co.uk/uk/2013/may/22/police-respond-serious-incident-woolwich.

2. *Woolwich Attack: Nigerian Community in London Mourns Lee Rigby*, 2013, http://www.youtube.com/watch?v=DChKbLxvHq4&feature=youtube_gdata_player.

3. *Muslims Butcher British Soldier in Woolwich, England. Western Media and Politicians Clueless*, 2013, http://www.youtube.com/watch?v=Jx5qWtK3KK4&feature=youtube_gdata_player.

4. Andrew Wander, "A History of Terror: Al-Qaeda 1988-2008," *Guardian*, July 12, 2008, sec. World news, http://www.theguardian.com/world/2008/jul/13/history.alqaida.

5. Ibid.

6. "1998: US Embassies in Africa Bombed," *BBC*, August 7, 1998, sec. 7, http://news.bbc.co.uk/onthisday/hi/dates/stories/august/7/newsid_3131000/3131709.stm.

7. Bruce Lawrence, *Messages to the World: The Statements of Osama Bin Laden*, annotated edition (London/New York: Verso, 2005).

8. Poynter Institute for Media Studies, *September 11, 2001* (Kansas City, MO: Andrews McMeel Publishing, 2001).

9. Sheila Musaji, "The American Muslim (TAM)," Reference materials, *The American Muslim*, 2005, http://theamericanmuslim.org/tam.php/features/articles/muslim_voices_against_extremism_and_terrorism_part_i_fatwas/.

10. Thanassis Cambanis, "Grand Ayatollah Fadlallah, Shiite Cleric, Dies at 75," *New York Times*, July 4, 2010, sec. World/Middle East, http://www.nytimes.com/2010/07/05/world/middleeast/05fadlallah.html.

11. Jean-Charles Brisard, *Zarqawi, The New Face of Al Qaeda* (New York: Other Press, 2005).

12. Robert Lindsay, "Robert Lindsay Returns: Nick Berg Beheading Video," *Robert Lindsay Returns*, November 19, 2009, http://robert-lindsay.blogspot.com/2009/10/nick-berg-beheading-video.html.

13. Brisard, *Zarqawi, The New Face of Al Qaeda*.

14. Islamic State of Iraq and al-Sham, *Al-Naba—Islamic State of Iraq and Al-Sham Annual Report, November 2011–2012*, Iraq, 2013, http://azelin.files.wordpress.com/2013/08/islamic-state-of-iraq-and-al-shc481m-22harvest-of-operations-for-the-year-1433-h-in-iraq22.pdf.

15. Alex Bilger, "ISIS Annual Reports Reveal a Metrics-Driven Military Command," *Institute for the Study of War*, May 22, 2014, http://understandingwar.org/backgrounder/ISIS-Annual-Reports-Reveal-Military-Organization.

16. Shashank Bengali, "Long-Dead Militant's Battle Plan Resurrected in Iraq," *Los Angeles Times*, June 22, 2014, http://www.latimes.com/world/middleeast/la-fg-iraq-militants-caliphate-20140623-story.html#page=1.

17. CBS and AP, "Militants Post Grisley Images of Mass Killing in Iraq," *CBS News*, June 14, 2014, /viz/5f4cbfdc-f244-11e3-b1e6-0e10bcd91c2b/embed_map?title=false&description=false&search=false&shareable=true&cartodb_logo=false&layer_selector=true&legends=true&scrollwheel=false&fullscreen=true&sublayer_options=1%7C1%7C1%7C1&sql=&sw_lat=32.93492866908233&sw_lon=39.056396484375&ne_lat=37.413800350662875&ne_lon=48.31787109375.

18. Ibid.

19. Ibid.

20. Ibid.

21. Alexander Smith, "ISIS Militants' Offensive Spreads Fear in Baghdad, Iraq," *NBC News*, June 13, 2014, http://www.nbcnews.com/storyline/iraq-turmoil/isis-militants-offensive-spreads-fear-baghdad-iraq-n130306.

22. AP, "Nigeria Soldiers Left Checkpoint Hours before Boko Haram Attacked School, Official Says," *CBS News*, February 26, 2014, http://www.cbsnews.com/news/nigeria-soldiers-left-checkpoint-hours-before-boko-haram-attacked-school-official-says/.

23. NBC News, "Boko Haram Terror Increases in Nigeria," *WNCN*, June 14, 2014, http://www.wncn.com/story/25778375/boko-haram-terror-increases-in-nigeria.

24. Ibid.

25. Ibid.

26. David Blair, "Al-Qaeda's Hand in Boko Haram's Deadly Nigerian Attacks," *Telegraph.co.uk*, February 5, 2012, http://www.telegraph.co.uk/news/worldnews/al-qaeda/9062825/Al-Qaedas-hand-in-Boko-Harams-deadly-Nigerian-attacks.html.

27. Robin Simcox, "Boko Haram and Defining the 'Al-Qaeda Network,'" *Al Jazeera*, June 6, 2014, http://www.aljazeera.com/indepth/opinion/2014/06/boko-haram-al-qaeda-201463115816142554.html.

28. Associated Press, "Al-Qaeda Exploiting Syria Rebellion to Wage War on Shiites across Mideast," *South China Morning Post*, January 9, 2014, http://www.scmp.com/news/world/article/1401617/al-qaeda-exploiting-syria-rebellion-wage-war-shiites-across-mideast.

29. Raul Caruso and Friedrich Schneider, "Brutality of Jihadist Terrorism: A Contest Theory Perspective and Empirical Evidence in the Period 2002-2010," *Journal of Policy Modeling* 35, no. 5 (2013): 685–96, doi:http://dx.doi.org/10.1016/j.jpolmod.2012.12.005.

30. David Rohde, "Our Fear of Al-Qaeda Hurts Us More Than Al-Qaeda Does," *The Atlantic*, October 27, 2013, http://www.theatlantic.com/international/archive/2013/10/our-fear-of-al-qaeda-hurts-us-more-than-al-qaeda-does/280897/.

31. Greg Myre, "In One Map, The Dramatic Rise of ISIS in Iraq and Syria," *NPR.org*, June 13, 2014, http://www.npr.org/blogs/parallels/2014/06/13/321678737/in-one-map-the-dramatic-rise-of-isis-in-iraq-and-syria.

32. Al Jazeera and Other Agencies, "Iraq City of Tikrit Falls to ISIL Fighters," *Al Jazeera*, June 12, 2014, http://www.aljazeera.com/news/middleeast/2014/06/iraqi-city-tikrit-falls-isil-fighters-2014611135333576799.html.

33. Michael Jansen, "Isis Dogma Shows Zero Tolerance of Dissent," *Irish Times*, June 13, 2014, http://www.irishtimes.com/news/world/middle-east/isis-dogma-shows-zero-tolerance-of-dissent-1.1830368.

34. Ibid.

35. Ibid.

36. Ibid.

37. "Qur'an," Reference Materials, *Qur'an* (n.d.), http://quran.com/2.

38. Ben Mathis-Lilley, "By the Way, 'Al-Qaida-Inspired Militants' Now Control Two Major Iraqi Cities," *Slate*, June 10, 2014, http://www.slate.com/blogs/the_slatest/2014/06/10/al_qaida_iraq_mosul_fallujah_controlled_by_militants.html.

39. Al Jazeera and Other Agencies, "Iraq City of Tikrit Falls to ISIL Fighters."

40. Sarah Almukhtar et al., "Where ISIS Is Gaining Control in Iraq and Syria," *New York Times*, June 11, 2014, http://www.nytimes.com/interactive/2014/06/11/world/middleeast/isis-control-map.html.

41. Rod Nordland and Alissa J. Rubin, "Massacre Claim Shakes Iraq," *New York Times*, June 15, 2014, http://www.nytimes.com/2014/06/16/world/middleeast/iraq.html.

42. Chris Hughes, Melissa Thompson, and Christopher Bucktin, "Police Chief Beheaded by Jihadist Rebels Who Tweeted: 'This Is Our Ball. It Is Made of Skin. #WorldCup,'" *Mirror*, 2014, http://www.mirror.co.uk/news/world-news/police-chief -beheaded-jihadist-rebels-3690513.

43. Scott Neuman and Bill Chappell, "Militants Reportedly Overrun Tikrit, As 500,000 Flee Mosul," *NPR.org*, June 13, 2014, http://www.npr.org/blogs/thetwo-way/ 2014/06/11/320932929/500-000-people-reportedly-flee-mosul-after-iraqi-city-falls.

44. Conflict Casualties Monitor, "Iraq Body Count," Reference Materials, *Iraq Body Count*, June 12, 2014, https://www.iraqbodycount.org/database/.

45. Ibid.

46. Jeffrey Hendricks, "US-Iraq War, Timeline, 1990-2011," Reference Materials, *ProCon.org*, December 19, 2011, http://usiraq.procon.org/view.resource.php?resour ceID=000670.

47. Conflict Casualties Monitor, "Iraq Body Count."

48. Ibid.

49. Ibid.

50. Ibid.

51. Neuman and Chappell, "Militants Reportedly Overrun Tikrit, As 500,000 Flee Mosul."

52. A. D. Kendall, "Al Qaeda Makes Millions from Mosul Shakedowns," *Money Jihad*, July 8, 2013, http://moneyjihad.wordpress.com/2013/07/08/al-qaeda-makes -millions-from-mosul-shakedowns/.

53. Al Jazeera and Other Agencies, "Iraq City of Tikrit Falls to ISIL Fighters."

54. Rohan Gunaratna, *Inside Al Qaeda: Global Network of Terror* (New York, NY: Columbia University Press, 2002).

55. Gilles Kepel, Jean-Pierre Milelli, and Pascale Ghazaleh, *Al Qaeda in Its Own Words* (Cambridge, MA: Harvard University Press, 2008).

56. Ibid.

57. "UN General Assembly Resolution 181 (II), Palestine," *Council on Foreign Rela-tions*, June 5, 2013, http://www.cfr.org/un/un-general-assembly-resolution-181-ii -palestine/p11191.

58. Youssef Ibrahim, "P.L.O. Proclaims Palestine to be an Independent State; Hints at Recognizing Israel," *New York Times*, November 15, 1988, http://www.nytimes.com/ 1988/11/15/world/plo-proclaims-palestine-to-be-an-independent-state-hints-at-recognizing -israel.html?pagewanted=all&src=pm.

59. Kepel, Milelli, and Ghazaleh, *Al Qaeda in Its Own Words*.

60. Ibid.

61. Abdullah Azzam, "Defense of the Muslim Lands - The First Obligation After Imam," Brothers in Ribatt, trans., n.d., http://www.kalamullah.com/Books/defence.pdf.

62. Gunaratna, *Inside Al Qaeda*.

63. "Al-Qaeda Criticizes Treatment of Elderly in Japan and China," *Taepei Times*, December 18, 2011, http://www.taipeitimes.com/News/world/archives/2011/12/18/ 2003521049.

64. Caruso and Schneider, "Brutality of Jihadist Terrorism."

65. Ibid.

66. Fawaz A. Gerges, *Journey of the Jihadist: Inside Muslim Militancy*, 1st ed (Orlando, FL: Harcourt, 2006).

67. Ibid.

68. Ibid.

69. Ibid.

70. Ibid.

71. Ibid.

72. Abdullah Azzam denies this support in his "Defense of the Muslim Lands—The First Obligation After Imam." Bin Laden continued to carry that same denial message to his fighters, recognizing that if he said it enough he would be believed and not the United States.

73. Gunaratna, *Inside Al Qaeda*.

74. Chris Greenwood, Rebecca Evans, and Martin Robinson, "Fiancée and Estranged Wife of Soldier Lee Rigby Flee Murder Trial in Tears as Jury Is Shown CCTV Footage of Moment 'Muslim Converts Ran Him down before Almost Decapitating Him with Meat Cleaver and Knives,'" *Mail Online*, November 29, 2013, http://www.dailymail.co.uk/news/article-2515493/Soldier-Lee-Rigby-murdered-mutilated-decapitated-Woolwich-attack-court-hears.html.

75. Paul Cockerton, "Woolwich Trial Live: Lee Rigby Murder Accused Michael Adebolajo and Michael Adebowale Appear in Court," *Mirror*, November 29, 2013, http://www.mirror.co.uk/news/uk-news/woolwich-trial-live-lee-rigby-2863956.

76. Lawrence Wright, *The Looming Tower: Al-Qaeda and the Road to 9/11*, 1st ed. (New York: Knopf, 2006).

77. Ibid.

78. "What Are Al Qaeda's Capabilities," *Frontline*, April 24, 2003.

79. Ibid.

80. Ibid.

81. Angeligue Chrisafis, "Former Cern Scientist Faces Terror Trial in France," *Guardian*, March 29, 2012, sec. World news, http://www.guardian.co.uk/world/2012/mar/29/cern-scientist-terror-trial-france.

82. "Al Qaeda Chemist Killed in U.S. Strike: Pakistani Agents," *Reuters*, July 29, 2008, http://www.reuters.com/article/2008/07/29/us-pakistan-security-idUSISL9039020080729.

83. Rita Katz and Michael Kern, "Terrorist 007, Exposed," *Washington Post*, March 26, 2006, sec. Technology, 007, http://www.washingtonpost.com/wp-dyn/content/article/2006/03/25/AR2006032500020.html.

84. Eileen Sullivan and Kimberley Dozier, "Abu Anas Al-Libi, Al Qaeda Suspect Captured in U.S. Raid, Arrives in New York," *Huffington Post*, October 14, 2013, http://www.huffingtonpost.com/2013/10/14/abu-anas-al-libi-us_n_4098458.html.

85. Gilad Zahavi, "Al-Qaeda Electronic Army Online Jihadists Express Interest in Cyber Warfare and Cyber Security," Blog, *SenseCy*, February 24, 2014, http://blog.sensecy.com/tag/al-qaeda-electronic-army/.

86. Gianluca Mezzofiore, "Boko Haram Leaks Data of Nigeria's Top Spies," *International Business Times*, August 30, 2012, http://www.ibtimes.co.uk/articles/379074/20120830/boko-haram-leaks-data-nigeria-s-top.htm.

87. AP, "Nigeria Soldiers Left Checkpoint Hours before Boko Haram Attacked School, Official Says."

88. Jack Cloherty, "Virtual Terrorism: Al Qaeda Vid Calls for 'Electronic Jihad,'" *ABC News*, May 22, 2012, http://abcnews.go.com/Politics/cyber-terrorism-al-qaeda-video-calls-electronic-jihad/story?id=16407875.

89. John Rollins, *Al Qaeda and Affiliates: Historical Perspective, Global Presence, and Implications for U.S. Policy* (Washington, D.C., January 25, 2011), http://www.fas.org/sgp/crs/terror/R41070.pdf.

90. Ayman Al-Zawahiri, "Letter from Ayman Al-Zawahiri to Abu Musab Al-Zarqawi," *Council on Foreign Relations*, July 9, 2005, http://www.cfr.org/iraq/letter-ayman-al-zawahiri-abu-musab-al-zarqawi/p9862.

91. Ibid.

92. Agencies, "Iraq Crisis: 500,000 Flee Mosul as Sunni Jihadists Pose 'Mortal Threat' to Nation," *Telegraph.co.uk*, June 11, 2014, http://www.telegraph.co.uk/news/world news/middleeast/iraq/10891354/Iraq-crisis-500000-flee-Mosul-as-Sunni-jihadists -pose-mortal-threat-to-nation.html.

93. Adam Taylor, "The Rules in ISIS' New State: Amputations for Stealing and Women to Stay Indoors," *Washington Post*, June 12, 2014, http://www.washington post.com/blogs/worldviews/wp/2014/06/12/the-rules-in-isis-new-state-amputations -for-stealing-and-women-to-stay-indoors/.

94. Yemen Post Staff, "Top Salafi Leader in Yemen Calls on Al Qaeda to Give Allegiance to ISIL Caliphate," *YemenPost.net*, July 19, 2014, http://www.yemenpost.net/ Detail123456789.aspx?ID=3&SubID=8009.

95. Taylor, "The Rules in ISIS' New State."

96. Ibid.

97. Michael Page, Lara Challita, and Alistair Harris, "Al Qaeda in the Arabian Peninsula: Framing Narratives and Prescriptions," *Terrorism and Political Violence* 23, no. 2 (2011): 150–72, doi:10.1080/09546553.2010.526039.

98. Ibid.

99. Ibid.

100. Yemen Post Staff, "Iran Wants Its Diplomat Released Now," *YemenPost.net*, July 28, 2014, http://www.yemenpost.net/Detail123456789.aspx?ID=3&SubID=8014 &MainCat=3.

101. Richard Esposito and Brian Ross, "Investigators: Northwest Bomb Plot Planned by Al Qaeda in Yemen," *ABC News*, December 29, 2009, http://abcnews.go.com/Blotter/ al-qaeda-yemen-planned-northwest-flight-253-bomb-plot/story?id=9426085.

102. Jonathan Masters and Zachary Laub, "Al-Qaeda in the Arabian Peninsula (AQAP)," *Council on Foreign Relations*, August 22, 2013, http://www.cfr.org/yemen/ al-qaeda-arabian-peninsula-aqap/p9369.

103. Camille Tawil, *The Al Qaeda Organization in the Islamic Maghreb: Expansion in the Sahel and Challenges from Within Jihadist Circles* (New York: The Jamestown Foundation, April 2010), file:///Users/shieldanalysis/Downloads/Jamestown %20Foundation-Tawil_Al%20Qaeda%20in%20the%20Islamic%20Maghreb-Expansion %20in%20the%20Sahel%20and%20Challenges%20from%20Within%20Jihadist% 20Circles-2010%20(1).pdf.

104. David Blair, "Timbuktu: Al-Qaeda's Terrorist Training Academy in the Mali Desert," *Telegraph.co.uk*, February 11, 2013, http://www.telegraph.co.uk/news/world-news/africaandindianocean/mali/9860822/Timbuktu-al-Qaedas-terrorist-training-academy-in-the-Mali-desert.html.

105. The word *mission* is an overarching term for an event, large or small, violent or nonviolent. It applies to any activity that is specifically executed to further the organization-defined "jihad."

106. D. Baken, "An Analysis of the Potential Direct or Indirect Influence Exerted by an Al Qaeda Social Network Actor on Future Biological Weapon Mission Planning," 2007, http://digilib.gmu.edu:8080/xmlui/handle/1920/2881.

107. Bilger, "ISIS Annual Reports Reveal a Metrics-Driven Military Command."

108. "ISIS 'Annual Report Boasts over a 1000 Murders,' " *ITV News*, June 19, 2014, http://www.itv.com/news/update/2014-06-18/isis-annual-report-boasts-over-a-1000 -murders/.

109. Baken, "An Analysis of the Potential Direct or Indirect Influence Exerted by an Al Qaeda Social Network Actor on Future Biological Weapon Mission Planning."

110. David Kimble, "Operational Aftermath: Measuring the Threat of Terrorism Through Attack Efficiency," *Searching for Balance in the Middle East and Africa* (presented at the Association for the Study of the Middle East and Africa, Washington, D.C, 2014).

111. Ibid.

112. Katherine Zimmerman, *The Al Qaeda Network: A New Framework for Defining the Enemy* (American Enterprise Institute, September 2013), http://www.critical threats.org/sites/default/files/pdf_upload/analysis/Zimmerman_the_al_Qaeda_Network _September_2013.pdf.

113. Kimble, "Operational Aftermath: Measuring the Threat of Terrorism Through Attack Efficiency."

114. Ibid.

115. Paul Gill, *Tracing the Moivations and Antecedent Behaviors of Lone-Actor Terrorism* (International Center for the Study of Terrorism, August 2012).

116. Ibid.

117. Alastair Crooke, "The ISIS' 'Management of Savagery' in Iraq," *Huffington Post*, June 30, 2014, http://www.huffingtonpost.com/alastair-crooke/iraq-isis-alqaeda _b_5542575.html.

118. Abu Bakr Naji and William McCants, trans., "The Management of Savagery: The Most Critical Stage Through Which the Umma Will Pass" (John M. Olin Institute for Strategic Studies, Harvard University, May 23, 2006), http://azelin.files.word press.com/2010/08/abu-bakr-naji-the-management-of-savagery-the-most-critical -stage-through-which-the-umma-will-pass.pdf.

119. Leela Jacinto, "Middle East—Analysis: Fallujah, Mosul, Tikrit Down—Iraq's Perfect Storm of Crises," *France 24*, June 12, 2014, http://www.france24.com/en/ 20140611-iraq-mosul-jihadist-syria-perfect-storm/.

120. Naji and McCants, "The Management of Savagery: The Most Critical Stage Through Which the Umma Will Pass."

121. Dexter Filkins, "ISIS vs. the Kurds," *New Yorker*, September 22, 2014, http:// www.newyorker.com/magazine/2014/09/29/fight-lives.

122. Lizzie Dearden, "This Is How the Kurds Are Celebrating Turfing ISIS out of Kobani," *Independent*, February 3, 2015, http://www.independent.co.uk/news/world/ middle-east/kurdish-fighters-celebrate-victory-over-isis-in-kobani-with-traditional -dance-through-streets-10018377.html.

123. Alice Fordham, "For Extremists in Syria, Extortion Brings Piles of Cash from Iraq," *NPR.org*, April 21, 2014, http://www.npr.org/blogs/parallels/2014/04/21/ 304542370/for-extremists-in-syria-extortion-brings-piles-of-cash-from-iraq.

124. Terrence McCoy, "ISIS, Beheadings and the Success of Horrifying Violence," *Washington Post*, June 13, 2014.

125. Farouk Chothia, "Boko Haram Crisis: How Have Nigeria's Militants Become so Strong?," *BBC News*, February 1, 2015, http://www.bbc.com/news/world-africa -30933860.

126. Monica Mark in Mark, "Thousands Flee as Boko Haram Seizes Military Base on Nigeria Border," *Guardian*, January 5, 2015, http://www.theguardian.com/world/2015/jan/05/boko-haram-key-military-base-nigeria-chad-border.

127. J. Peter Pham, "Boko Haram Has Become Africa's ISIS," *TheHill*, January 7, 2015, http://thehill.com/blogs/pundits-blog/international/228721-boko-haram-has-become-africas-isis.

128. Mezzofiore, "Boko Haram Leaks Data of Nigeria's Top Spies."

129. Ibid.

130. Doina Chiacu, "U.S. NSA Chief Says Monitoring Tech-Savvy Islamic State," *Reuters*, September 16, 2014, http://www.reuters.com/article/2014/09/16/us-cybersecurity-usa-islamic-state-idUSKBN0HB22A20140916.

131. "Exclusive: Top ISIS Leaders Revealed," February 13, 2014, http://english.alarabiya.net/en/News/2014/02/13/Exclusive-Top-ISIS-leaders-revealed.html.

CHAPTER 4

1. Gunaratna, *Inside Al Qaeda*, 2002.

2. Ibid.

3. Giraldo and Trinkunas, *Terrorism Financing and State Responses*, 2007.

4. Ibid.

5. Ibid.

6. Chulov, "How an Arrest in Iraq Revealed ISIS's $2bn Jihadist Network."

7. Masters, "Al-Qaeda in the Islamic Maghreb (AQIM)."

8. *The 9/11 Commission Report.*

9. John Roth, Douglas Greenburg, and Serena Wille, "National Commission on Terrorist Attacks Upon the United States: Monograph on Terrorist Financing," 26–35, 134–148.

10. Bergen, *Holy War, Inc.*

11. Ibid.

12. *The 9/11 Commission Report.*

13. Ibid.

14. "Terrorism Financing, Roots and Trends of Saudi Terrorism Financing," Report Prepared for the President of the United Nations Security Council, December 19, 2002, New York, United States, 6–12.

15. Jane Corbin. *Al Qaeda: The Terror Network That Threatens the World* (New York: Thunder's Mouth Press, 2002), 15–25.

16. Gunaratna, *Inside Al Qaeda*, 61; Rohan Gunaratna and Aviv Oreg, "Al Qaeda's Organizational Structure and Its Evolution," *Studies in Conflict & Terrorism* 33, no. 12 (2010): 1043–78.

17. Roth, Greenburg, and Wille, "National Commission on Terrorist Attacks Upon the United States," 26, 134.

18. Mark Basile, "Going to the Source: Why Al Qaeda's Financial Network Is Likely to Withstand the Current War on Terrorist Financing," *Studies in Conflict & Terrorism* 27, no. 3, 169–85.

19. Zachary Abuza, "Funding Terrorism in Southeast Asia: The Financial Network of Al Qaeda and Jemaah Islamiyah," *The National Bureau of Asian Research* 14, no. 5 (December 2003): 20–1.

20. Max Taylor and Mohamed E. Elbushra, "Research Note: Hassan al-Turabi, Osama bin Laden, and Al Qaeda in Sudan," *Terrorism and Political Violence* 18, no. 3 (2006): 449–64; Bergen, *Holy Terror, Inc.*, 47–49.

21. Ann Lesch, "Osama bin Laden's business' in Sudan," *Current History* 101, no. 655 (May 2002): 203.

22. Lesch, "Osama bin Laden's business' in Sudan."

23. "Terrorism Financing, Roots and Trends of Saudi Terrorism Financing."

24. Ibid.

25. Ibid.

26. Roth, Greenburg, and Wille, "National Commission on Terrorist Attacks Upon the United States," 26, 134.

27. Michael Freeman and Moyara Ruehsen, "Terrorism Financing Methods: An Overview," *Perspectives on Terrorism* 7, no. 4, 1–24, 2013.

28. Ibid.

29. Ibid.

30. Roth, Greenburg, and Wille, "National Commission on Terrorist Attacks Upon the United States," 26–35, 134–148.

31. Jean-Charles Brisard, "Terrorism Financing (Roots and Trends of Saudi Terrorism Financing)," Report prepared for the President of the Security Council, United Nations, JCB Consulting, New York, December 19, 2002, 20.

32. Financial Action Task Force on Money Laundering, "Guidance for Financial Institutions in Detecting Terrorist Financing," April 2002, http://www.fatf-gafi.org/TerFinance_en.htm.

33. Gunaratna and Oreg, "Al Qaeda's Organizational Structure and Its Evolution."

34. Matthew Epstein, and Ben Schmidt, "Operation Support System Shutdown," *National Review Online*, September 4, 2003, http://www.nationalreview.com/comment/comment-epsteinschmidt090403.

35. Juan Miguel del Cid Gómez, "Perspectives on Terrorism, a Financial Profile of the Terrorism of Al-Qaeda and Its Affiliates, 4, no. 4 (2010).

36. Philip Shenon, "U.S.-Based Muslim Charity Raided by NATO in Kosovo," *New York Times*, December 18, 2001.

37. Robin Wright and Joseph Meyer, "America Attacked: Mapping a Response," *Los Angeles Times*, September 12, 2001.

38. United Nations, Tenth Report of the Analytical Support and Sanctions Implementation Monitoring Team submitted pursuant to Resolution 1822 (2008) Concerning Al-Qaida and the Taliban and Associated Individuals and Entities, 2009, New York: United Nations, note 47, 22.

39. "Terrorism Financing, Roots and Trends of Saudi Terrorism Financing."

40. Garry Mason, "Profits of Doom: How Al Qaeda Makes Millions to Fund Terror," Jane's Terrorism Intelligence Center, October 24, 2003.

41. Ibid.

42. U.S. Congress. House. Committee on Financial Services, Subcommittee on Oversight and Investigations, *Progress since 9/11: The Effectiveness of U.S. Anti-Terrorist Financing Efforts*, 108th Cong. 1st sess., March 11, 2003.

43. Nimrod Raphaeli, "Financing Terrorism: Sources, Methods and Channels," *Terrorism and Political Violence* 15, no. 4 (2003): 59–82.

44. Gunaratna, *Inside Al Qaeda*; Gunaratna and Oreg, "Al Qaeda's Organizational Structure and Its Evolution."

45. Ibid.

46. Al-Sharq Al-Awsat, December 16, 2002.

47. Al-Sharq Al-Awsat, March 14, 2003.

48. U.S. General Accounting Office, *Terrorist Financing: U.S. Agencies Should Systematically Assess Terrorists' Use of Alternative Financing Mechanisms*, United States General Accounting Office, November 2003, GAO-04-163, 19.

49. Ibrahim Warde, *Islamic Finance in the Global Economy* (Edinburgh: Edinburgh University Press, 2000), 144–153.

50. Ibid., 227–232.

51. "Terrorism Financing, Roots and Trends of Saudi Terrorism Financing."

52. United Nations, Tenth Report of the Analytical Support and Sanctions Implementation Monitoring Team.

53. Ibid.

54. Raphaeli, "Financing Terrorism: Sources, Methods and Channels."

55. Dennis M. Lormel, "Combating Terrorist Financing at the Agency and Interagency Levels," *CTC Sentinel* 1, no. 4 (2008).

56. "Drug Cartels Begin Cracking West Africa," Jane's Foreign Report (London: Jane's Information Group, August 23, 2007).

57. Lormel, "Combating Terrorist Financing at the Agency and Interagency Levels."

58. Ibid.

59. Alex Schmid, "The Links Between Transnational Organized Crime and Terrorist Crimes," *Transnational Organized Crime* 2 (1996): 40–82.

60. Wolfram Lacher, *Organized Crime and Conflict in the Sahel-Sahara Region* (New York: Carnegie Endowment for International Peace, 2012).

61. United Nations Development Programme, World Human Development Report 2012 (New York, 2012).

62. Lacher, *Organized Crime and Conflict in the Sahel-Sahara Region.*

63. UNODC Regional Office for West Africa, "Cocaine Trafficking in Western Africa," unpublished report, July 2007, cited in Antonio Mazziteli, "Transnational Organized Crime in West Africa: The Additional Cchallenge," *International Affairs* 83, no. 6 (2007).

64. Lacher, *Organized Crime and Conflict in the Sahel-Sahara Region.*

65. Lacher, "Challenging the Myth of the Drug-Terror Nexus in the Sahel; WACD Background Paper No. 4."

66. Ibid.

67. Ibid.

68. Ibid.

69. Ibid.

70. David Lewis and Adama Diarra, "Special Report: In the land of 'gangster-jihadists,'" Reuters, October 25, 2012, http://www.reuters.com/article/2012/10/25/us-mali-crisis-crime-idUSBRE89O07Y20121025.

71. "Drug Seizures in West Africa Prompt Fears of Terrorist Links," *Observer*, November 29, 2009.

72. National Commission on Terrorist Attacks Upon the United States.

73. William Billingslea, "Illicit Cigarette Trafficking and the Funding of Terrorism," *The Police Chief* 71, no. 2 (2004); Financial Action Task Force (FATF), "Illicit Tobacco Trade," June 2012, and Doward Jamie, "How Cigarette Smuggling Fuels Africa´s Islamist Violence," *Guardian*, January 27, 2013, http://www.guardian.co.uk/world/2013/jan/27/cigarette-smuggling-mokhtar-belmokhtar-terrorism.

74. Ibid.

75. UNODC, *Trafficking in Persons: Global Patterns* (New York, 2009); Office to Monitor and Combat Traffi cking in Persons, Victims of Traffi cking and Violence Protection Act of 2000: Trafficking in Persons Report 2009 (Washington, D.C.: Department of State, June 12, 2009).

76. Ibid.

77. Lacher, *Organized Crime and Conflict in the Sahel-Sahara Region.*

78. Luis de la Corte Ibáñez, To what extent do global terrorism and organised criminality converge, *Revista del Instituto Español de Estudios Estratégicos Núm.* 1 (2013): 353–380.

79. Ibid.

80. Ibid.

81. Mantzikos Ioannis, "Somalia and Yemen: The Links between Terrorism and State Failure," *Digest of Middle East Studies* 20, no. 2, 242–260.

82. Ibid.

83. Ibid.

84. Saul and Reed, "Shabaab-Somali Pirate Links: UN Advisor."

85. D.H., "Somalia and Piracy: The Cost on Land as Well as at Sea."

86. Ibid.

87. U.S. Committee on Foreign Relations, *Al Qaeda in Yemen and Somalia: A Ticking Time Bomb* (Washington, D.C.: U.S. Government Printing Office, 2010).

88. CNN Wire Staff, "Al-Shabaab Joining Al Qaeda, Monitor Group Says."

89. Thompson, "Al-Shabaab Attacks Kenyan College."

90. Ibid.

91. Ibid.

92. Gail Wannenburg, "Links between Organised Crime and Al-Qaeda," *South African Journal of International Affairs* 10, no. 2 (2003): 77–90.

93. Ibid.

94. Ibid.

95. Financial Action Task Force on Money Laundering, "Guidance for Financial Institutions in Detecting Terrorist Financing," April 2002, http://www.fatf-gafi.org/Ter-Finance_en.htm; National Commission on Terrorist Attacks Upon the United States, http://govinfo.library.unt.edu/911/staff_statements/911_TerrFin_Monograph.pdf.

96. National Commission on Terrorist Attacks Upon the United States, http://govinfo.library.unt.edu/ 911/staff_statements/911_TerrFin_Monograph.pdf.

97. Richard A. Oppel Jr., "Iraq's Insurgency Runs on Stolen Oil Profits," *New York Times*, March 16, 2008.

98. D.H., "Somalia and Piracy: The Cost on Land as Well as at Sea."

99. Labi, "Jihad 2.0."

100. Aransiola and Asindemade, "Understanding Cybercrime Perpetrators and the Strategies They Employ in Nigeria."

101. CBS News, "Money Lost in Internet Scams Hits New High."

102. Stephen Jeffrey Weaver, "Modern Day Money Laundering: Does the Solution Exist in An Expansive System of Monitoring and Record Keeping Regulations?," *Annual Review of Banking and Finance Limited* 24 (2005): 443, 444.

103. CNN, "IPL Spot-Fixing: Dawood, Chhota Shakeel Are Suspects, Say Sources," June 10, 2013.

104. National Commission on Terrorist Attacks Upon the United States, http://govinfo.library.unt.edu/ 911/staff_statements/911_TerrFin_Monograph.pdf.

105. Financial Action Task Force, "Trade Based Money Laundering," June 23, 2006, http://www."ncen.gov/news_room/rp/"les/ fatf_typologies.pdf.

106. Ibid.

107. Chad Bray, "Plea in Bomb-Link Case," *Wall Street Journal*, August 19, 2011.

108. Robert Feldman, "Fund Transfers – African Terrorists Blend Old and New: Hawala and Satellite Telecommunications," *Small Wars and Insurgencies* 17, no. 3 (September 2006): 356–66.

109. National Commission on Terrorist Attacks Upon the United States, http:// govinfo.library.unt.edu/ 911/staff_statements/911_TerrFin_Monograph.pdf.

110. Maurice R. Greenberg (chairman), "Terrorist Financing: Report of an Independent Task Force Sponsored by the Council for Foreign Relations," Council for Foreign Relations. November 14, 2002.

111. Ibid.

112. "Principles of Islamic Banking," *Nida'ul Islam*, November–December 1995, http://www.usc.edu/dept/MSA/economics/nbank1.html.

113. House of Commons, "Report of the Official Account of the Bombings in London on 7th July 2005."

114. "Islamic Banking."

115. Gary C. Gambill and Ziad K. Abdelnour, "The Al-Madina Bank Scandal," *Middle East Intelligence Bulletin*, January 2004.

116. [106] U.S. Senate Report, "U.S. Vulnerabilities to Money Laundering, Drugs, and Terrorist Financing: HSBC Case History," July 17, 2012, Permanent Subcommittee on Investigations, 189–95.

117. Ibrahim Warde, *Islamic Finance in the Global Economy* (Edinburgh: Edinburgh University Press, 2000), 144–53.

118. "Big Interest, No Interest."

119. Ibid.

120. Ibid.

121. Great Britain., *British Somaliland and Sokotra.*

122. Gunaratna, *Inside Al Qaeda*, 2013.

123. Ibid.

124. Chulov, "How an Arrest in Iraq Revealed ISIS's $2bn Jihadist Network."

125. Kendall, "ISIS Steals $429 Million in Mosul; IB Times Cites Money Jihad in Comparison of Richest Terror Groups."

126. Aronson, Samuel. 2014. "AQIM's Threat to Western Interests in the Sahel." *CTC Sentinel* 7 (4), https://www.ctc.usma.edu/v2/wp-content/uploads/2014/04/CTCSentinel-Vol7Iss4.pdf.

127. Chulov, "How an Arrest in Iraq Revealed ISIS's $2bn Jihadist Network."

CHAPTER 5

1. J. Bowyer Bell, "Terrorist Scripts and Live-Action Spectaculars," *Columbia Journalism Review* 17, no. 1 (June 1978): 47–50.

2. John L. Scott, "Media Congestion Limits Media Terrorism," *Defence & Peace Economics* 12, no. 3 (May 2001): 215.

3. Dominic Rohner and Bruno S. Frey, "Blood and Ink! The Common-Interest-Game between Terrorists and the Media," *Public Choice* 133, no. 1 (October 2007): 129–45, doi:10.1007/s11127-007-9182-9.

4. Bruno S. Frey and Dominic Rohner, "Blood and Ink! The Common-Interest-Game Between Terrorists and the Media," *SSRN eLibrary*, April 2006, http://papers.ssrn.com/sol3/papers.cfm?abstract_id=900353.

5. Chris Greenwood, Rebecca Evans, and Martin Robinson, "Fiancée and Estranged Wife of Soldier Lee Rigby Flee Murder Trial in Tears as Jury Is Shown CCTV Footage of Moment 'Muslim Converts Ran Him Down before Almost Decapitating Him with Meat Cleaver and Knives,'" *Mail Online*, November 29, 2013, http://www.daily mail.co.uk/news/article-2515493/Soldier-Lee-Rigby-murdered-mutilated-decapitated -Woolwich-attack-court-hears.html.

6. Paul Cockerton, "Woolwich Trial Live: Lee Rigby Murder Accused Michael Adebolajo and Michael Adebowale Appear in Court," *Mirror*, November 29, 2013, http://www.mirror.co.uk/news/uk-news/woolwich-trial-live-lee-rigby-2863956.

7. Lawrence Wright, *The Looming Tower: Al-Qaeda and the Road to 9/11*, 1st ed. (New York: Knopf, 2006).

8. Fawaz A. Gerges, *Journey of the Jihadist: Inside Muslim Militancy*, 1st ed. (Orlando, FL: Harcourt, 2006).

9. Ibid.

10. Ibid.

11. Ibid.

12. Ibid.

13. Ibid.

14. Ibid.

15. Donald Holbrook, "Alienating the Grassroots: Looking Back at Al Qaeda & Its Communicative Approach Toward Muslim Audiences," *Studies in Conflict & Terrorism* 36, no. 11 (2013): 883–98, doi:10.1080/1057610X.2013.832116.

16. Brynjar Lia, "Al-Qaida's Appeal: Understanding Its Unique Selling Points," *Perspectives on Terrorism* 2, no. 8 (2008).

17. Gerges, *Journey of the Jihadist*.

18. Ibid.

19. Ibid.

20. Ibid.

21. Bruce Lawrence, *Messages to the World: The Statements of Osama Bin Laden*, annotated edition (London/New York: Verso, 2005).

22. Ibid.

23. Abdel Bari Atwan, *The Secret History of Al Qaeda* (London: Saqi Books, 2012).

24. The correspondents invited were: Abdel Bari Atwan, editor-in-chief of *al-Quds al-Arabi*; Robert Fisk, of the *Independent*; Peter Bergen, CNN; and British Channel Four. The United States' CBS was invited but it declined the offer, as did the United Kingdom's BBC.

25. Atwan, *The Secret History of Al Qaeda*.

26. Phillip Seib, "The Al Qaeda Media Machine," *Military Review*, June 2008.

27. Gerges, *Journey of the Jihadist*.

28. Ibid.

29. Karen Nikos, "Will Bin Laden's Tapes Reshape His Legacy?," *Futurity*, May 3, 2012, http://www.futurity.org/society-culture/will-bin-ladens-tapes-reshape-his-legacy/.

30. Syed Saleem Shahzad, *Inside Al-Qaeda and the Taliban: Beyond Bin Laden and 9/11* (New York: Pluto Press, 2011).

31. Ibid.

32. Ibid.

33. Ibid.

34. Ibid.

35. Ibid.

36. Gerges, *Journey of the Jihadist.*

37. Ibid.

38. Shahzad, *Inside Al-Qaeda and the Taliban.*

39. David Blair, "Charlie Hebdo Attack: Anwar Al-Awlaki—the Al-Qaeda Ideologue Who May Have Inspired the Massacre," January 9, 2015, sec. World, http://www.telegraph.co.uk/news/worldnews/europe/france/11335327/Charlie-Hebdo-attack-Anwar-al-Awlaki-the-al-Qaeda-ideologue-who-may-have-inspired-the-massacre.html.

40. Evan Kohlmann, *Testimony of Evan F. Kohlmann with Josh Lefkowitz and Laith Alkhouri before the House Committee on Homeland Security "Jihadist Use of Social Media—How to Prevent Terrorism and Preserve Innovation"* (Washington, D.C.: Government Printing Office, 2011), http://homeland.house.gov/sites/homeland.house.gov/files/Testimony%20Kohlmann%5B1%5D.pdf.

41. Siobhan Gorman, Anand Gopal, and Yochi J. Dreazen, "CIA Blast Blamed on Double Agent," *Wall Street Journal*, January 6, 2010, sec. Politics, http://online.wsj.com/article/SB126264256099215443.html.

42. Florian Flade, "Death of a Online-Jihadi – From Cyberspace to Battlefield," *Jih@d*, December 21, 2010, http://ojihad.wordpress.com/2010/12/21/death-of-a-online-jihadi-from-cyberspace-to-battlefield/.

43. Atwan, *The Secret History of Al Qaeda.*

44. Ibid.

45. Ibid.

46. Ibid.

47. Ibid.

48. Allan Hall, " 'Kosovan Muslim Who Shouted Islamic Slogans' before Shooting Dead Two U.S. Airmen at Frankfurt Airport Was an Employee," *Mail Online*, March 4, 2011, http://www.dailymail.co.uk/news/article-1362247/Arid-Uka-Frankfurt-airport-Kosovan-Muslim-employee-shot-dead-2-US-airmen.html.

49. Matthias Bartsch and Matthias Gebauer, "The Radical Islamist Roots of the Frankfurt Attack," *Spiegel Online*, March 3, 2011, http://www.spiegel.de/international/germany/facebook-jihad-the-radical-islamist-roots-of-the-frankfurt-attack-a-748910.html.

50. Guido Steinberg, *Jihadismus und Internet: Eine deutsche Perspektive* (Berlin: Stiftung Wissenschaft und Politik Deutsches Institut für Internationale Politik und Sicherheit, October 2012).

51. Janet Reitman, "Jahar's World," *Rolling Stone*, July 17, 2013, http://www.rollingstone.com/culture/news/jahars-world-20130717.

52. Yoree Koh, "African Militants Turn More to Social Media," *Wall Street Journal*, September 22, 2013, sec. World, http://online.wsj.com/news/articles/SB10001424052702304713704579091720477473610?mg=reno64-wsj&url=http%3A%2F%2Fonline.wsj.com%2Farticle%2FSB10001424052702304713704579091720477473610.html.

53. Ibid.

54. Y Feldner and G Lustig, "Al-Rai TV – A Syrian Platform for Iraqi Terror Broadcasts," *MEMRI – The Middle East Media Research Institute*, March 10, 2014, http://www.memri.org/report/en/0/0/0/0/0/0/2907.htm.

55. Jon Jensen, "Syria's Al-Rai TV Goes off the Air," GlobalPost, *The Casbah*, December 13, 2011, http://www.globalpost.com/dispatches/globalpost-blogs/the-casbah/syria-s-al-rai-tv-goes-the-air.

56. Philip Ross, "ISIS Recruitment Reaches 'Unprecedented Scale' with 15,000 Foreign Jihadists Joining Militant Fighters," *International Business Times*, October 30, 2014, http://www.ibtimes.com/isis-recruitment-reaches-unprecedented-scale-15000-foreign-jihadists-joining-militant-1716684.

57. Reza Ekhtiari Amiri, Ku Hasnita Binti Ku Samsu, and Hassan Gholipour Fereidouni, "Iran's Economic Considerations after the War and Its Role in Renewing of Iran-Saudi Diplomatic Relations/considérations économiques de l'iran après la guerre et son rôle dans le renouvellement des relations diplomatiques entre l'iran et l'arabie saoudite," *Cross-Cultural Communication* 6, no. 3 (2010): 45–54.

58. Jane Corbin, *Al-Qaeda: In Search of the Terror Network That Threatens the World* (New York: Nation Books, 2003).

59. *Michael Adebolajo Woolwich Terrorist*, 2013, https://www.youtube.com/watch?v=B9DbRMIlQ5A&feature=youtube_gdata_player.

60. Farouk Chothia, "Why Is Boko Haram so Strong?," *BBC News*, February 1, 2015, http://www.bbc.com/news/world-africa-30933860.

61. Thomas Fessy, "Niger Hit by Nigeria's Boko Haram Fallout," *BBC News*, April 22, 2014, http://www.bbc.com/news/world-africa-27111884.

62. Ibid.

63. "Fears in Cameroon of Boko Haram Recruitment," *IRINnews*, April 16, 2014, http://www.irinnews.org/Report/99949/Fears-in-Cameroon-of-Boko-Haram-recruitment.

CHAPTER 6

1. Jean-Charles Brisard, *Zarqawi, the New Face of Al Qaeda* (New York: Other Press, 2005).

2. Ibid.

3. Rita Katz and Michael Kern, "Terrorist 007, Exposed," *Washington Post*, March 26, 2006, sec. Technology, http://www.washingtonpost.com/wp-dyn/content/article/2006/03/25/AR2006032500020.html.

4. Ibid.

5. "Chicago Cousins Sentences in Terrorism Case," ADL, July 13, 2010, http://archive.adl.org/main_Terrorism/ahmed_cousins_guilty.htm.

6. Jane Corbin, *Al-Qaeda: In Search of the Terror Network That Threatens the World* (New York: Nation Books, 2003).

7. "Ramzi Yousef," The Investigative Project on Terrorism, July 9, 2008, http://www.investigativeproject.org/profile/105.

8. Craig Whitlock, "Briton Used Internet As His Bully Pulpit," *Washington Post*, August 8, 2005, sec. World, http://www.washingtonpost.com/wp-dyn/content/article/2005/08/07/AR2005080700890.html.

9. Rachel Nuwer, "Mapping the Dark Web of Terrorist Sites," *Tech Page One*, March 19, 2013, http://www.techpageone.com/technology/mapping-the-dark-web-of-terrorist-sites/.

10. Steven Hipple and Karen Kosanovich, "Computer and Internet Use at Work in 2001," *Monthly Labor Review* (February 2003): 26–35.

11. Steve Coll and Susan B. Glasser, "Terrorists Turn to the Web as Base of Operations," *Washington Post*, August 7, 2005, sec. World, http://www.washingtonpost.com/wp-dyn/content/article/2005/08/05/AR2005080501138.html.

12. John Pike, "Al-Qaida / Al-Qaeda Terrorist Training Camps," *GlobalSecurity.org*, June 14, 2012, http://www.globalsecurity.org/military/world/para/al-qaida-camps.htm.

13. Gabriel Weimann, *Terror on the Internet* (Washington, D.C.: United States Institute of Peace Press, 2006).

14. Ibid.

15. In January 2004, Judge Audrey B. Collins struck a portion of the USA Patriot Act saying "that a provision in the law banning certain types of support for terrorist groups was so vague that it risked running afoul of the First Amendment." It was a case prosecuting individuals from New York, Oregon and Michigan.

16. John Schwarz, "Threats and Responses: The Internet; Revamped Proposal Suggests Strategies to Tighten Online Security," *New York Times*, September 18, 2002, http://www.nytimes.com/2002/09/18/us/threats-responses-internet-revamped-proposal-suggests-strategies-tighten-online.html. Reported in 2002 by John Schwarz of the New York Times, this report outlined an effort that sought better sharing of information on cyber attacks and perpetrators of those attacks.

17. *The National Strategy to Secure Cyberspace* (Washington, D.C., February 2003), http://www.us-cert.gov/sites/default/files/publications/cyberspace_strategy.pdf.

18. al Shahab Media, 2012, د كـــــاروان غازيـــــ) ١ (http://vimeo.com/51606425. This sophisticated video transmits a message of professionalism that is not lost on the young who watch it.

19. Aaron Zelin and Richard Fellow, "The State of Global Jihad Online – A Qualitative, Quantitative, and Cross-Lingual Analysis," New America Foundation, January 2013.

20. Curt Hopkins, "Terrorist Group behind Westgate Shooting Livetweeted the Attack," *The Daily Dot*, September 22, 2013, http://www.dailydot.com/news/westgate-al-shabaab-hsm-press-twitter/.

21. AAP, "Sabirhan Hasanoff, the Aussie Accountant Who Turned to Terror," *Sydney Morning Herald*, October 1, 2013, http://www.smh.com.au/world/sabirhan-hasanoff-the-aussie-accountant-who-turned-to-terror-20131001-2upqd.html.

22. Susan B. Glasser and Steve Coll, "The Web as Weapon," *Washington Post*, August 9, 2005, sec. World, http://www.washingtonpost.com/wp-dyn/content/article/2005/08/08/AR2005080801018.html.

23. Ibid.

24. Ibid.

25. Evan Kohlmann, "Al-Qa'ida's 'MySpace' – Terrorist Recruitment on the Internet," *CTC Sentinel* 1, no. 2 (January 2008), https://www.ctc.usma.edu/wp-content/uploads/2010/06/Vol1Iss2-Art4.pdf.

26. Glasser and Coll, "The Web as Weapon."

27. Jarret Brachman and Alix Levine, "The World of Holy Warcraft," *Foreign Policy*, April 13, 2011, http://www.foreignpolicy.com/articles/2011/04/13/the_world_of_holy_warcraft?wp_login_redirect=0.

28. Coll and Glasser, "Terrorists Turn to the Web as Base of Operations."

29. Corbin, *Al-Qaeda*

30. Compiled from Wire Reports, "Al Qaeda's Second Fatwa," PBS News, February 23, 1998, http://www.pbs.org/newshour/updates/military/jan-june98/fatwa_1998.html.

31. "Bin Laden's Fatwa," *PBS Newshour*, August 23, 1996, http://www.pbs.org/news hour/updates/military/july-dec96/fatwa_1996.html. Ibid.

32. Hanna Rogan, *Jihadism Online – A Study of How Al-Qaida and Radical Islamist Groups Use the Internet for Terrorist Purposes* (Kjeller, Norway: Forsvarets Forskning-sinstitutt Norwegian Defense Research Establishment, March 20, 2006), http://rapporter.ffi.no/rapporter/2006/00915.pdf.

33. Ibid.

34. Ibid.

35. "Majority and Minority Staff Senate Committee on Homeland Security and Governmental Affairs," *Zachary Chesser: A Case Study in Online Islamist Radicalization and Its Meaning for the Threat of Homegrown Terrorism*, U.S. Senate, February 2012, http://www.hsgac.senate.gov/imo/media/doc/CHESSER%20FINAL%20REPORT (1).pdf.

36. IPT News, "The Awlaki Effect," *The Investigative Project on Terrorism*, November 15, 2010, http://www.investigativeproject.org/2323/the-awlaki-effect.

37. "Majority and Minority Staff Senate Committee on Homeland Security and Governmental Affairs."

38. Rogan, *Jihadism Online*.

39. John Warrick and Peter Finn, "Bomber of CIA Post Was Trusted Informant," *Washington Post*, January 5, 2010, http://articles.washingtonpost.com/2010-01-05/world/36901444_1_balawi-actionable-intelligence-jordanian-informant.

40. Siobhan Gorman, Anand Gopal, and Yochi J. Dreazen, "CIA Blast Blamed on Double Agent," *Wall Street Journal*, January 6, 2010, sec. Politics, http://online.wsj.com/article/SB126264256099215443.html.

41. Evan Kohlmann, "Exclusive: Interview with a Foreign Fighter from Al-Qaida's 'Islamic State of Iraq,'" *Counterterrorism Blog*, May 12, 2007, http://counterterrorism blog.org/2007/05/interview_with_a_foreign_fight.php. The two hour session was supposed to "offer an accurate picture of the jihad in Mesopotamia."

42. D. Baken, "An Analysis of the Potential Direct or Indirect Influence Exerted by an Al Qaeda Social Network Actor on Future Biological Weapon Mission Planning," 2007, http://digilib.gmu.edu:8080/xmlui/handle/1920/2881. Ibid.

43. Ibid.

44. Rogan, *Jihadism Online*.

45. Ibid.

46. Mustafa Hamid, "The Airport 1990 (English Translation)," reference materials, *Combatting Terrorism Center*, http://www.ctc.usma.edu/posts/the-airport-1990-english-translation. Ibid.

47. Coll and Glasser, "Terrorists Turn to the Web as Base of Operations."

48. Whitlock, "Briton Used Internet as His Bully Pulpit." Ahmad's 2004 arrest did not stop his electronic anti-Western campaign. He found a way to use the Web to protest his extradition from the United Kingdom to the United States. He cited fear of being sent to Guantanamo Bay or receiving the death penalty, if convicted

49. Ibid.

50. "Azzam Publications – for Jihad and Mujahideen," November 18, 2000.

51. Whitlock, "Briton Used Internet as His Bully Pulpit."Ibid.

52. Pike, "Al-Qaida/Al-Qaeda Terrorist Training Camps."

53. Evan Kohlmann, *Expert Report on the ~AQCORPO WebsiteK*, August 2006. .

54. Ibid.

55. Ibid.

56. Coll and Glasser, "Terrorists Turn to the Web as Base of Operations."

57. "Al Battar Issue 6 – Northeast Intelligence Network," *Northeast Intelligence Network*, http://www.homelandsecurityus.com/archives/3294.

58. Coll and Glasser, "Terrorists Turn to the Web as Base of Operations."

59. Ibid.

60. Paul Cruickshank and Mohannad Hage Ali, "Abu Musab Al Suri: Architect of the New Al Qaeda," *Studies in Conflict & Terrorism* 30, no. 1 (2007): 1–14, doi:10.1080/10576100601049928.

61. Coll and Glasser, "Terrorists Turn to the Web as Base of Operations."

62. Jarret M. Brachman, *High-Tech Terror: Al-Qaeda's Use of New Technology*, 2006, http://stinet.dtic.mil/oai/oai?&verb=getRecord&metadataPrefix=html&identifier=ADA458499. Ibid.

63. Ibid.

64. Gabriel Weimann, "Lone Wolves in Cyberspace," *Journal of Terrorism Research* 3, no. 2 (September 22, 2012), http://ojs.st-andrews.ac.uk/index.php/jtr/article/view/405.

65. Evan Kohlmann, "Al-Qaida's Online Couriers: The Al-Fajr Media Center and the Global Islamic Media Front (GIMF)," *Flashpoint Partners*, May 2009, http://www.globalterroralert.com/fajrchart9_final.php.

66. David Clarke, *Technology and Terrorism* (New Brunswick, NJ: Transaction Publishers, 2004).

67. Corbin, *Al-Qaeda*. Ibid.

68. Glasser and Coll, "The Web as Weapon."

69. Ibid.

70. Ibid.

71. Ibid.

72. Ibid.

73. Ibid.

74. Ibid.

75. Ibid.

76. Ibid.

77. Ibid.

78. Ibid.

79. Paul Cruickshank and Tim Lister, "Al Qaeda Calling?," *Security Clearance*, August 8, 2013, http://security.blogs.cnn.com/2013/08/08/al-qaeda-calling/.

80. Katz and Kern, "Terrorist 007, Exposed."

81. Ibid.

82. 304th MI Bn OSINT Team, *Supplemental to the 304th MI Bn Periodic Newsletter – Sample Overview: Al Qaida-Like Mobile Discussions & Potential Creative Uses*, October 16, 2008.

83. Ibid.

84. Ibid.

85. Ibid.

86. Ibid.

87. IPT News, "New English-Language Jihad Forum: The Investigative Project on Terrorism," January 12, 2011, http://www.investigativeproject.org/2490/new-english-language-jihad-forum.

88. Daniel Williams, "The Search for White Jihadists," *New York Times*, April 20, 2010, sec. World/Middle East, http://www.nytimes.com/2010/04/21/world/middleeast/21iht-letter.html. Ibid.

89. IPT News, "New English-Language Jihad Forum."

90. IPT News, "New Jihadi Publications Group: Al-Qadisiyyah Media," *The Investigative Project on Terrorism*, January 10, 2011, http://www.investigativeproject.org/2484/new-jihadi-publications-group-al-qadisiyyah-media.

91. Cii, "Who Is Muhammad Bin Qasim Al-Thaqafi?," *Cii Broadcasting*, October 2009, http://www.ciibroadcasting.com/2012/02/15/who-is-muhammad-bin-qasim-al-thaqafi/. Ibid.

92. Ibid.

93. Sheikh Abu Sa'd al Amili, "The Reality and the Role of the Jihadist Media," Ansar al Mujahideen English Forum, September 10, 2010, http://ia700404.us.archive.org/19/items/theRealityAndTheRoleOfTheJihadistMedia/Heart_of_the_Matter.pdf. Ibid.

94. Ibid.

95. Ibid.

96. Nur Aziemah Binte Azman, "Al Qaeda's Internet Strategy a Failure? Online Jihadists Disprove," International Center for Political Violence and Terrorism Research, S. Rajaratnam School of International Studies, February 2012, http://www.pvtr.org/pdf/CTTA/2012/CTTA-February12.pdf. Ibid.

97. Brian Jenkins, "Is Al Qaeda's Internet Strategy Working?," Product Page, *Rand*, 2011, http://www.rand.org/pubs/testimonies/CT371.html. Ibid.

98. Ibid.

99. Binte Azman, "Al Qaeda's Internet Strategy A Failure? Online Jihadists Disprove."

100. Ibid.

101. Ibid.

102. Harun Maruf, *Interview with Omar Hammami by Harun Maruf*, audio tape, 2013, http://www.voasomali.com/audio/audio/324662.html.

103. MEMRI, *Jihadis Collaborate to Create "Center For Electronic Terrorism" Aimed At Virtually Attacking Infrastructure in U.S., U.K., France* (Washington, D.C: The Middle East Media Research Institute, June 11, 2011).

104. "Al-Qaeda in Iraq Looks for Fundraising Ideas," *Telegraph.co.uk*, July 26, 2011, sec. World news, http://www.telegraph.co.uk/news/worldnews/al-qaeda/8664536/Al-Qaeda-in-Iraq-looks-for-fundraising-ideas.html.

105. Brian Krebs, "Three Worked the Web to Help Terrorists," *Washington Post*, July 6, 2007, sec. Technology, http://www.washingtonpost.com/wp-dyn/content/article/2007/07/05/AR2007070501945.html.

106. Ibid.

107. Ibid.

108. Rogan, *Jihadism Online*

109. "Prominent Writer on Jihadi Forum Outlines Program for Spreading Al-Qaeda Ideology in US by Infiltrating Forums and Facebook Pages, Hacking Websites," *The MEMRI Blog*, http://www.thememriblog.org/blog_personal/en/41625.htm.

110. Gabriel Weimann, "Cyber-Fatwas and Terrorism," *Studies in Conflict & Terrorism* 34, no. 10 (2011): 765–81, doi:10.1080/1057610X.2011.604831.

CHAPTER 7

1. Mouna Succarieh and Rani Geha, trans., "Rise of Radical Islam in Yemen Altering Its Tribalism, Book Finds – Al-Monitor: The Pulse of the Middle East," *Al-Monitor*, September 23, 2012, http://www.al-monitor.com/pulseen/politics/2012/09/weekenda-detailed-look-at-islamism-in-yemen.html.

2. The Global Realm, "Yemen and the Militarization of Strategic Waterways," *The Global Realm*, February 7, 2010, http://theglobalrealm.com/2010/02/07/yemen-and-the-militarization-of-strategic-waterways/.

3. Ibid.

4. Robert F. Worth and Laura Kasinof, "Chaos in Yemen Drives Economy to Edge of Ruin," *New York Times*, June 2, 2011, sec. World/Middle East, http://www.nytimes.com/2011/06/03/world/middleeast/03yemen.html.

5. Charles Schmitz, "Building a Better Yemen," *Carnegie Endowment for International Peace*, April 3, 2012, http://carnegieendowment.org/2012/04/03/building-better-yemen/a67j.

6. Jomana Farhat, "The Untouchables of Yemen," *Al Akhbar English*, December 5, 2012, http://english.al-akhbar.com/content/untouchables-yemen.

7. Craig R. Prentiss, *Religion and the Creation of Race and Ethnicity: An Introduction* (New York: NYU Press, 2003).

8. "Profile: Yemen's Houthi Fighters," *Al Jazeera.com*, August 12, 2009, http://www.aljazeera.com/news/middleeast/2009/08/200981294214604934.html.

9. Succarieh and Geha, "Rise of Radical Islam in Yemen Altering Its Tribalism, Book Finds – Al-Monitor."

10. Farea al-Muslimi and Kamal Fayad, trans., "Yemen's Brotherhood: Early Losses and an Unknown Future – Al-Monitor: The Pulse of the Middle East," *Al-Monitor*, September 25, 2013, http://www.al-monitor.com/pulseen/originals/2013/09/yemen-brotherhood-losses-unknown-future.html.

11. Ibid.

12. Succarieh and Geha, "Rise of Radical Islam in Yemen Altering Its Tribalism, Book Finds – Al-Monitor."

13. Barak Salmoni, Bryce Loidolt, and Madeleine Wells, "Regime and Periphery in Northern Yemen," Product Page, *Rand*, 2010, http://www.rand.org/pubs/monographs/MG962.html.

14. al-Muslimi and Fayad, "Yemen's Brotherhood."

15. Arafat Madabish, "The Kingdom of the Houthis," *ASHARQ AL-AWSAT*, September 9, 2013, http://www.aawsat.net/2013/08/article55310983.

16. Ibid.

17. Ibid.

18. Juliane von Mittelstaedt, "'Operation Scorched Earth': A US Hand in Yemen's Civil War," *Spiegel Online*, March 12, 2010, http://www.spiegel.de/international/world/operation-scorched-earth-a-us-hand-in-yemen-s-civil-war-a-732734.html.

19. "History of Yemen," *History of Nations*, 2004, http://www.historyofnations.net/asia/yemen.html.

20. "Zaydi Shias," *World Directory of Minorities and Indigenous People*, 2005, http://www.minorityrights.org/4730/yemen/zaydi-shias.html.

21. Madabish, "The Kingdom of the Houthis."

22. Human Rigths Watch, "World Report 2013: Yemen," *Human Rights Watch*, 2013, http://www.hrw.org/world-report/2013/country-chapters/yemen.

23. Mark Durie, "Salafis and the Muslim Brotherhod: What Is the Difference?," *Middle East Forum*, June 6, 2013, http://www.meforum.org/3541/salafis-muslim-brotherhood.

24. Ibid.

25. Ibid. According to Abdul Malik Issa in his book *Islamist Movements in Yemen*, there are three Salafist branches: one as defined by the Salafist founder Sheikh Moqbel al-Wadii; one called the Wisdom society movement guided by Sheikh Abdul Rahman Khaliq in Kuwait; and the Ihsan Society, sometimes known as the Syrian Current, from Sheikh Mohammad Srour.

26. Mawassi Lahcen, "As Al-Qaeda Falls, Ansar Al-Sharia Rises," *Magharebia*, October 5, 2012, http://magharebia.com/en_GB/articles/awi/reportage/2012/10/05/reportage-01.

27. J. A. C. Brown, *Salafis and Sufis in Egypt*, The Carnegie Papers (Washington, D.C.: Carnegie Endowment for International Peace, 2011), http://edoc.bibliothek .uni-halle.de:8080/servlets/MCRFileNodeServlet/HALCoRe_derivate_00005803/ CEIP_salafis_sufis.pdf.

28. Ibid.

29. "International Reactions to Morsi's Removal," *Al Jazeera*, July 4, 2013, http:// www.aljazeera.com/news/middleeast/2013/07/201373223029610370.html.

30. Jamal Jubran, "Yemen's Salafis: In the Service of the Regime?," *Al Akhbar English*, December 9, 2011, http://english.al-akhbar.com/content/yemen%E2%80%99s-salafists -service-regime.

31. Yemen Post Staff, "Yemen Salafis Fight Back," *Yemen Post*, January 19, 2014, http://www.yemenpost.net/Detail123456789.aspx?ID=3&SubID=7511.

32. Ibid.

33. Yemen Post Staff, "Salafis Are Driven out of Dammaj," *YemenPost.net*, January 13, 2014, http://yemenpost.net/Detail123456789.aspx?ID=3&SubID=7493.

34. Ibid.

35. "CIA 'Killed Al-Qaeda Suspects' in Yemen," *BBC*, November 5, 2002, sec. Middle East, http://news.bbc.co.uk/2/hi/2402479.stm.

36. David S. Cloud, "U.S. Drone Strike in Yemen Kills U.S.-Born Al Qaeda Figure Awlaki," *Los Angeles Times*, October 1, 2011, http://articles.latimes.com/2011/oct/01/ world/la-fg-awlaki-killed-20111001.

37. International Fund for Agricultural Development (IFAD), "Rural Poverty Portal," *Rural Poverty Portal*, http://www.ruralpovertyportal.org/country/home/tags/yemen.

38. Bernard Haykel, "Opinion: Yemen's Unsteady Transition," *ASHARQ AL-AWSAT*, April 16, 2013, http://www.aawsat.net/2013/04/article55298896.

39. Rory Barrett, *Yemen: A Different Political Paradigm in Context* (MacDill Airforce Base: Joint Special Operations University, May 2011), https://jsou.socom.mil/JSOU% 20Publications/JSOU11-3barrettYemen_final.pdf.

40. CIA, "The World Factbook 2001" (Central Intelligence Agency, n.d.), https:// www.cia.gov/library/publications/download/download-2001/index.html.

41. Ibid.

42. Ibid.

43. Ibid.

44. Abdulkareem Al-Arhabi, *Yemen in Figures 2009* (San'a, Yemen: Ministry of Planning & Int. Cooperation Central Statistical Organization, October 2010).

45. Anna Fedec and Antonio Sousa, "Trading Economics," 2013, http:// www.tradingeconomics.com/yemen/unemployment-rate.

46. "The WorldFactBook."

47. Laura Kasinof, "Yemenis Say They Have Bigger Problems Than Al Qaeda," *New York Times*, September 30, 2011, sec. World/Middle East, http://www.nytimes.com/ 2011/10/01/world/middleeast/yemenis-say-they-have-bigger-problems-than-al-qaeda.html.

48. Mittelstaedt, "'Operation Scorched Earth.'"

49. Ibid.

50. Worth and Kasinof, "Chaos in Yemen Drives Economy to Edge of Ruin."

51. Yemen Fox, "Sheikh Al-Ahmar: Civil State Required by Tribe," *Yemen Fox.net*, February 14, 2012, http://www.yemenfox.net/news_details.php?lng=english &sid=2052.

52. *Al Qaeda Insurgents Blows Yemen's Pipeline*, 2011, http://www.youtube.com/watch?v=dnTg402w5N4&feature=youtube_gdata_player.

53. "Yemeni Tribes Clash with Al-Qaeda in Marib," *Al-Shorfa*, http://al-shorfa.com/en_GB/articles/meii/newsbriefs/2013/09/23/newsbrief-04.

54. Glevum Associates, "2011 Yemen Stability Survey," March 2011, http://www.fpri.org/pubs/2011/glevum.yemen2011stabilitysurveyvi.pdf.

55. Haykel, "Opinion."

56. Barrett, *Yemen: A Different Political Paradigm in Context*.

57. Ibid.

58. Ibid.

59. Sherman Kent, "CIA Office of National Estimates Special Memorandum No. 9–65" (Central Intelligence Agency, February 18, 1965), https://history.state.gov/historical documents/frus1964-68v21/d360.

60. Policy Analysis Unit, "Yemen and Al-Qaeda," *Arab Center for Research & Policy Studies*, June 11, 2012.

61. Mittelstaedt, "'Operation Scorched Earth.'"

62. Ghaith Abdul-Ahad, "Al Qaeda in Yemen | FRONTLINE | PBS Video," *PBS.org*, May 12, 2012, http://video.pbs.org/video/2240325626.

63. Ibid.

64. Edward Burke, *Yemen: Make Haste Slowly*, Policy Brief, FRIDE, January 2010, http://edoc.bibliothek.uni-halle.de:8080/servlets/MCRFileNodeServlet/HALCoRe_derivate _00004396/FRIDE_PB33_Yemen_AlQaeda_EN_Ene10.pdf.

65. Daily Mail Reporter, "Amputations, Beheadings and a Crucifixion: Horrific Stories from Yemen Where Al Qaeda Has Imposed Sharia Law," *Mail Online*, December 4, 2012, http://www.dailymail.co.uk/news/article-2242719/Al-Qaeda -committed-truly-shocking-human-rights-abuses-power-Yemens-Abyan-region-says -Amnesty-report.html.

66. "Yemen: Al-Qaeda Suspect Found Dead in Ja'ar, Abyan," *Aden Tribune*, April 9, 2013, http://www.adentribune.com/yemen-al-qaeda-suspect-found-dead-in-jaar-abyan/.

67. Abdul-Ahad, "Al Qaeda in Yemen | FRONTLINE | PBS Video."

68. "Lahij Governor Says Hundreds of Citizens Support Army against Al-Qaeda," *Al-Shorfa*, April 24, 2012, http://al-shorfa.com/en_GB/articles/meii/newsbriefs/2012/04/24/newsbrief-02.

69. "Watch Now: Al Qaeda in Yemen | FRONTLINE | PBS Video," *PBS.org*, http://video.pbs.org/video/2240325626.

70. Mohammed Mukhashaf, "Yemen's Army Retakes Base Seized by Qaeda Militants," *Reuters*, September 30, 2013, http://www.reuters.com/article/2013/09/30/us-yemen-violence-idUSBRE98T0BS20130930.

71. Tik Root and Casey Coomes, "A Sheikh's Life," *Free Speech TV*, April 30, 2012, https://www.freespeech.org/text/sheikhs-life.

72. "States of the Aden Protectorates" (Ben Cahoon), http://www.worldstatesmen.org /Yemen_protectorate.html. There were 16 plus Aden. The entire list: Aden, Alawi

Aqrabi, Audhali, Beihan, Dathina, Dhala, Fadhli Haushabi, Lahej, Lower Aulaqi, Lower Yafa, Maflahi, Shaib, Upper Aulaqi Sheikhdom, Upper Aulaqi Sultanate, and Wahidi

73. Ibid.

74. King-yuh Chang, "The United Nations and Decolonization: The Case of Southern Yemen," *International Organization* 26, no. 1 (May 22, 2009): 37–61, doi:10.1017/S0020818300002873.

75. Ibid.

76. Ibid.

77. Ibid.

78. Robert F. Worth, "In Yemen's South, Protests Could Cause More Instability," *New York Times*, February 28, 2010, sec. A.

79. Ibid.

80. Ibid.

81. Sheila Carapico, "Yemen and the Aden-Abyan Islamic Army," Research, *Middle East Research an Information Project*, October 18, 2000, http://www.merip.org/mero/mero101800.

82. "Tariq Al-Fadhli: An Influential Man's Story," *National Yemen*, February 21, 2011, http://nationalyemen.com/2011/02/21/tariq-al-fadhli-an-influential-man%E2%80%99s-story/.

83. Camille Tawil and Robin Bray, trans., *Brothers in Arms: The Story of al-Qa'ida and the Arab Jihadists* (London: Saqi Books, 2007).

84. Ibid.

85. Jane Corbin, *Al-Qaeda: In Search of the Terror Network That Threatens the World* (New York: Nation Books, 2003).

86. Tawil and Bray, *Brothers in Arms*.

87. Fernando Carvajal, "Deepening Crises Breed Local Support for Ansar Al-Sharia: Part 1," *Fair Observer*, July 3, 2012, http://www.fairobserver.com/article/deepening-crises-breed-local-support-ansar-al-sharia-part-1.

88. Ibid.

89. Charles Schmitz, "Understanding the Role of Tribes in Yemen," *CTC Sentinel* 4, no. 10 (October 2011), http://www.ctc.usma.edu/wp-content/uploads/2011/11/CTCSentinel-Vol4Iss106.pdf.

90. Prentiss, *Religion and the Creation of Race and Ethnicity*.

91. Succarieh and Geha, "Rise of Radical Islam in Yemen Altering Its Tribalism, Book Finds – Al-Monitor."

92. Barrett, *Yemen: A Different Political Paradigm in Context*.

93. Succarieh and Geha, "Rise of Radical Islam in Yemen Altering Its Tribalism, Book Finds – Al-Monitor."

94. Prentiss, *Religion and the Creation of Race and Ethnicity*.

95. Schmitz, "Understanding the Role of Tribes in Yemen."

96. Sigurd Neubauer, "Tensions at the Saudi-Yemeni Border," *Carnegie Endowment for International Peace*, October 8, 2013, http://carnegieendowment.org/sada/2013/10/08/tensions-at-saudi-yemeni-border/gpez.

97. Ibid.

98. Ibid.

99. Fernando Carvajal, "Deepening Crises Breed Local Support for Ansar Al-Sharia: Part 2," *Fair Observer*, July 4, 2012, http://www.fairobserver.com/article/deepening-crises-breed-local-support-ansar-al-sharia-part-2.

100. Abdul-Ahad, "Al Qaeda in Yemen | FRONTLINE | PBS Video."

101. Alistair Harris, *Yemen on the Brink – Exploiting Grievances Al-Qaeda in the Arabian Peninsula*, Middle East Program, Carnegie Papers Series (Washington, D.C.: Carnegie Endowment for International Peace, May 2010), http://carnegieendowment.org/2010/06/08/exploiting-grievances-al-qaeda-in-arabian-peninsula/692.

102. Ibid.

103. John Moore, "The Evolution of Islamic Terrorism: An Overview," *FRONTLINE*, October 2001, http://www.pbs.org/wgbh/pages/frontline/shows/target/etc/modern.html.

104. Barrett, *Yemen: A Different Political Paradigm in Context.*

105. Root and Coomes, "A Sheikh's Life."

106. Ibid.

107. Ibid.

108. "Tariq Al-Fadhli: An Influential Man's Story."

109. Ibid.

110. Ibid.

111. Ibid.

112. "Sheikh Tariq Al-Fadli: I'm Not an Al-Qaeda Member," *ASHARQ AL-AWSAT*, February 7, 2010, http://www.aawsat.net/2010/02/article55251895.

113. Christopher Swift, "Arc of Convergence: AQAP, Ansar Al-Sharia and the Struggle for Yemen," *CTC Sentinel* 5, no. 6 (June 2012).

114. Ibid.

115. "The WorldFactBook."

116. Abdul-Ahad, "Al Qaeda in Yemen | FRONTLINE | PBS Video."

117. "15 AQAP Suspects Escape Yemen Prison," December 17, 2011, http://yemenpost.net/printpage.aspx.

118. Ibid.

119. Ibid.

120. Fawaz Gerges, "The Rise and Fall of Al-Qaeda: Debunking the Terrorism Narrative," news, *The World Post*, (January 3, 2012), http://www.ispu.org/GetArticles/48/2401/Publications.aspx.

121. Jonathan Masters and Zachary Laub, "Al-Qaeda in the Arabian Peninsula (AQAP)," *Council on Foreign Relations*, August 22, 2013, http://www.cfr.org/yemen/al-qaeda-arabian-peninsula-aqap/p9369.

122. Ken Dilanian, "Al Qaeda Group Is Operating on Ransom Money from the West," *Los Angeles Times*, October 21, 2013, http://www.latimes.com/world/la-fg-yemen-ransom-20131021,0,5305947.story#axzz2iVFBEXry.

123. Joe Hemba, "Boko Haram Boarding School Attack: Nigerian Islamists Kill 29 Students," *Huffington Post*, February 25, 2014, http://www.huffingtonpost.com/2014/02/25/boko-haram-boarding-school-attack_n_4852306.html?utm_hp_ref=mostpopular.

124. Yemen Times Staff, "BREAKING NEWS: Abducted Foreigners Handed over to Omani Authorities," *Yemen Times*, May 9, 2013, http://www.yementimes.com/en/1675/news/2329/BREAKING-NEWS-Abducted-foreigners-handed-over-to-Omani-authorities.htm.

125. Jonathan Masters, "Al-Qaeda in the Islamic Maghreb (AQIM)," *Council on Foreign Relations*, January 24, 2013, http://www.cfr.org/world/al-qaeda-islamic-maghreb-aqim/p12717.

126. Thomas Hegghamer, *The Failure of Jihad in Saudi Arabia*, Occasional Paper Series (West Point, NY: Combat Terrorism Center at West Point, February 25, 2010), http://www.ctc.usma.edu/wp-content/uploads/2010/10/CTC_OP_Hegghammer_Final.pdf.

127. "The WorldFactBook."

128. "Yemen – Introduction," Communication with Crisis-Affected Communities, *Infoasaid*, February 2012, http://www.google.com/imgres?imgurl=http://infoasaid.org/sites/infoasaid.org/files/internal_displacement_of_people_in_yemen.jpg&imgrefurl=http://infoasaid.org/guide/yemen/introduction&h=494&w=1029&sz=47&tbnid=3LOaw6DE74QIMM:&tbnh=90&tbnw=187&zoom=1&usg=__H4SgdoTsv07PC H9xo3ywXKnbk9Y=&docid=IymX3tClIBlFSM&sa=X&ei=CtekUppPuKu_lsAT-h YHACg&sqi=2&ved=0CFEQ9QEwBQ.

129. "The WorldFactBook."

CHAPTER 8

1. Library of Congress, *Iraq: A Country Study*, Helen Chapin Metz, ed., 4th ed, Area Handbook Series 550-31 (Washington, D.C: The Division: For sale by the Supt. of Docs., U.S. G.P.O, 1990).

2. Ibid.

3. John R. Ballard, *Fighting for Fallujah a New Dawn for Iraq* (Westport, CT: Praeger Security International, 2006), http://mutex.gmu.edu/login?url=http://search.ebscohost.com/login.aspx?direct=true&scope=site&db=nlebk&db=nlabk&AN=226330.

4. Ibid.

5. Jessica Lewis, "Black Flags over Fallujah," *Weekly Standard*, January 20, 2014.

6. Ibid.

7. Jean-Charles Brisard, *Zarqawi, the New Face of Al Qaeda* (New York: Other Press, 2005).

8. Ibid.

9. Ibid.

10. Ibid.

11. Ibid.

12. AFP, "Daash Impose Pay 'Tribute' to the Christians of Tenderness," *Al Arabiya*, February 27, 2014, http://www.alarabiya.net/ar/arab-and-world/syria/2014/02/27/%D8%AF%D8%A7%D8%B9%D8%B4-%D8%AA%D9%81%D8%B1%D8%B6-%D8%AF%D9%81%D8%B9-%D8%A7%D9%84%D8%AC%D8%B2%D9%8A%D8%A9-%D8%B9%D9%84%D9%89-%D9%85%D8%B3%D9%8A%D8%AD%D9%8A%D9%8A-%D8%A7%D9%84%D8%B1%D9%82%D8%A9-%D9%81%D9%8A-%D8%B3%D9%88%D8%B1%D9%8A%D8%A7.html.

13. Ibid.

14. Anne Applebaum, "Syria's Slow Death," *Slate*, February 5, 2014, http://www.slate.com/articles/news_and_politics/foreigners/2014/02/bashar_al_assad_killing_syrians_through_starvation_the_syrian_dictator_is.html.

15. Dan Rivers, ITV News Correspondent Damascus, "The Struggle to Survive in the Suburb Starved by Bashar Al-Assad," *Telegraph.co.uk*, 20:26, sec. World news, http://www.telegraph.co.uk/news/worldnews/middleeast/syria/10598212/The-struggle-to-survive-in-the-suburb-starved-by-Bashar-al-Assad.html.

16. Ibid.

17. Ruth Sherlock and Richard Spencer, "Syria's Assad Accused of Boosting Al-Qaeda with Secret Oil Deals," *Telegraph.co.uk*, January 20, 2014, sec. World news, http://www.telegraph.co.uk/news/worldnews/middleeast/syria/10585391/Syrias-Assad -accused-of-boosting-al-Qaeda-with-secret-oil-deals.html.

18. Ibid.

19. Ruth Sherlock, Gaziantep, and Tom Whitehead, "Al-Qaeda Training British and European 'Jihadists' in Syria to Set Up Terror Cells at Home," *Telegraph.co.uk*, January 19, 2014, sec. World news, http://www.telegraph.co.uk/news/worldnews/ middleeast/syria/10582945/Al-Qaeda-training-British-and-European-jihadists-in -Syria-to-set-up-terror-cells-at-home.html.

20. Nihat Ozcan and Timur Goksel, trans., "Turkey Fires at Al-Qaeda in Syria – Al-Monitor: The Pulse of the Middle East," *Al-Monitor*, October 19, 2013, http://www .al-monitor.com/pulseen/security/2013/10/turkey-syria-alqaeda-isis.html.

21. Azmat Khan, "Syria Two Years Later: Bloody Civil War with no End in Sight – Syria Behind the Lines," *FRONTLINE*, March 15, 2013, http://www.pbs.org/wgbh/ pages/frontline/foreign-affairs-defense/syria-undercover/syria-two-years-later-bloody- civil-war-with-no-end-in-sight/.

22. Jason Rodrigues, "1982: Syria's President Hafez Al-Assad Crushes Rebellion in Hama," *Guardian*, August 1, 2011, sec. From the Guardian, http://www.theguardian.com/ theguardian/from-the-archive-blog/2011/aug/01/hama-syria-massacre-1982-archive.

23. David Arnold, "Syria's 1982 Hama Massacre Recalled: Lesson for Assad Today?," February 3, 2012, http://middleeastvoices.voanews.com/2012/02/syrias-1982-hama- massacre-recalled-lesson-for-assad-today/.

24. Neil MacFarquhar, "Hafez Al-Assad, Who Turned Syria into a Power in the Middle East, Dies at 69," *New York Times*, June 11, 2000, sec. Metro Section.

25. Khan, "Syria Two Years Later."

26. Azmat Khan, "The Troubled History of Hama, Syria – Syria Undercover," *FRONTLINE*, 2012, http://www.pbs.org/wgbh/pages/frontline/foreign-affairs-defense/ syria-undercover/the-troubled-history-of-hama-syria/.

27. Garry Blight, Sheila Pulham, and Paul Torpey, "Arab Spring: An Interactive Timeline of Middle East Protests," *Guardian*, January 5, 2012, sec. World news, http:// www.theguardian.com/world/interactive/2011/mar/22/middle-east-protest-interactive- timeline.

28. "MEMRI: Sheikh Al-Qaradhawi Reacts to the Murder of Four Americans in Al-Fallujah: 'How Could You Punish an Entire People Because Four Corpses Were Mutilated?,'" *MEMRITV – The Middle East Media Research Institute*, April 9, 2004, http:// www.memritv.org/clip/en/31.htm.

29. Martha Raddatz, "Inside the U.S.-Led Fallujah Airstrikes," *ABC News*, January 7, 2006, http://abcnews.go.com/WNT/story?id=160139.

30. Brisard, *Zarqawi, the New Face of Al Qaeda*.

31. Gerald Lira, "The Anger of a Great Nation: Operation Vigilant Resolve" (Marine Corps University, U.S. Marine Corps: Marine Corps University Press, May 4, 2009), http://www.dtic.mil/dtic/tr/fulltext/u2/a509044.pdf.

32. Ibid.

33. Ibid.

34. Unknown, *Falluja: The Resistance City (Falluja Almadinat Us Samidah)* (Unknown, 2005), http://archive.org/details/fallujaresistancecity.

35. Ibid.

36. Films for the Humanities & Sciences (Firm), Films Media Group, and NPO/ Netherlands Public Broadcast, *The Grand War of Civilizations* (New York: Films Media Group, 2012).

37. Lira, "The Anger of a Great Nation: Operation Vigilant Resolve."

38. Films for the Humanities & Sciences (Firm).

39. A. al-Zawahiri, "Letter from Al-Zawahiri to Al-Zarqawi," *Source Unknown*, 2005.

40. Jason Burke, *The 9/11 Wars* (London: Penguin, 2012).

41. Brisard, *Zarqawi, the New Face of Al Qaeda*.

42. Burke, *The 9/11 Wars*.

43. Colin Freeman, "Fallujah: The City That Has Never Stopped Rebelling," *Telegraph.co.uk*, 13:33, sec. World news, http://www.telegraph.co.uk/news/worldnews/ middleeast/iraq/10558161/Fallujah-the-city-that-has-never-stopped-rebelling.html.

44. Ibid.

45. Unknown, *Falluja*.

46. Yasir Ghazi and Tim Arango, "Qaeda-Aligned Militants Threaten Key Iraqi Cities," *New York Times*, January 2, 2014, http://www.nytimes.com/2014/01/03/world/ middleeast/Al-Qaeda-threatens-Iraqi-cities.html.

47. Ibid.

48. Freeman, "Fallujah."

49. Ibid.

50. Ghazi and Arango, "Qaeda-Aligned Militants Threaten Key Iraqi Cities."

51. Ibid.

52. Jane Arraf, "For Iraqis Fleeing Fallujah, It's 2004 Again – but Worse," *Christian Science Monitor*, March 1, 2014, http://www.csmonitor.com/World/Security-Watch/ 2014/0301/For-Iraqis-fleeing-Fallujah-it-s-2004-again-but-worse.

53. Ibid.

54. Freeman, "Fallujah."

55. Reuters, AFP, and Al-Akhbar, "Qaeda-Linked ISIS Claims Beirut Suicide Blast," *Al Akhbar English*, January 4, 2014, http://english.al-akhbar.com/content/qaeda-linked -isis-claims-beirut-suicide-blast.

56. Brisard, *Zarqawi, the New Face of Al Qaeda*.

57. Ibid.

58. Ibid.

59. Associated Press, "Girl's Death Is Turned Against Extremists: Egypt: Hundreds Attend Funeral of Child Killed by Bomb Meant for Premier. Cairo Seeks to Use Outrage in Drive on Terrorists," *Los Angeles Times*, November 27, 1993, http://articles .latimes.com/1993-11-27/news/mn-61430_1_public-outrage.

60. Ibid.

61. Brisard, *Zarqawi, the New Face of Al Qaeda*.

62. Raddatz, "Inside the U.S.-Led Fallujah Airstrikes."

63. Freeman, "Fallujah."

64. Raddatz, "Inside the U.S.-Led Fallujah Airstrikes."

65. Ibid.

66. Brisard, *Zarqawi, the New Face of Al Qaeda*.

67. Lira, "The Anger of a Great Nation: Operation Vigilant Resolve."

68. Ibid.

69. Ibid.

70. Ibid.

71. Brisard, *Zarqawi, the New Face of Al Qaeda*.

72. AP, "Assad Doubts Existence of Al-Qaeda," *USATODAY.COM*, May 25, 2003.

73. IHS Janes's Terrorism & Insurgency Centre, "Syria's Insurgent Landscape" (IHS Jane's Terrorism & Insurgency Centre, September 13, 2013), https://janes.ihs.com/ExternalItems/Janes/ReferenceFiles/JTIC-Syria-insurgent-landscape.pdf.

74. Al Jazeera, " 'Nearly 500' Killed in Syria Rebel Infighting," *Al Jazeera*, January 11, 2014, http://live.aljazeera.com/Event/Syria_Live_Blog.

75. Martin Chulov, "Syrian Opposition Turns on Al-Qaida-Affiliated ISIS Jihadists near Aleppo," *Guardian*, January 3, 2014, http://www.theguardian.com/world/2014/jan/03/syrian-opposition-attack-alqaida-affiliate-isis.

76. Ruth Sherlock, "Starving Syrians Told: 'Give up the Rebels, and You Will Have Food,' " *Telegraph.co.uk*, February 1, 2014, sec. World news, http://www.telegraph.co.uk/news/worldnews/middleeast/syria/10611738/Starving-Syrians-told-Give-up-the-rebels-and-you-will-have-food.html.

77. Ghazi and Arango, "Qaeda-Aligned Militants Threaten Key Iraqi Cities."

78. Ibid.

79. Ibid.

80. Ibid.

81. Associated Press, "ISIL Says It Faces War with Nusra in Syria," March 8, 2014, http://www.aljazeera.com/news/middleeast/2014/03/isil-says-it-faces-war-with-nusra-syria-20143719484991740.html.

82. Ibid.

83. Mushreq Abbas and Sammi-Joe Abboud, trans., "Al-Qaeda Militants Raid Iraq's Abu Ghraib, Taji Prisons: The Pulse of the Middle East," *Al-Monitor*, July 25, 2013, http://www.al-monitor.com/pulseen/originals/2013/07/iraq-al-qaeda-prison-raid-abu-ghraib.html.

84. Ibid.

85. Tim Palmer, "Life under ISIS: The Islamic State in Iraq and Syria," *ABC News*, March 8, 2014, http://www.abc.net.au/news/2014-03-08/life-under-isis-the-islamic-state-in-iraq-and-syria/5307788.

86. Ibid.

CHAPTER 9

1. Thomas Joscelyn, "AQIM Rejects Islamic State's Caliphate, Reaffirms Allegiance to Zawahiri," *The LongWar Journal*, July 14, 2014, http://www.longwarjournal.org/archives/2014/07/aqim_rejects_islamic.php.

2. Ibid.

3. Walid Ramzi, "ISIS Caliphate Splits AQIM," *Magharebia*, July 18, 2014, http://magharebia.com/en_GB/articles/awi/features/2014/07/18/feature-01.

4. Ibid.

5. Ibid.

6. "Boko Haram Quick Facts" (American Foreign Policy Council, 2013), http://almanac.afpc.org/sites/almanac.afpc.org/files/Boko%20Haram%20August%202014_0.pdf.

7. May Ying We;sj, "Making Sense of Mali's Armed Groups," News, *Al Jazeera*, (January 17, 2013).

8. *Orphans of the Sahara -Episode 1 - Return*, Orphans of the Sahara, 2014, https://www.youtube.com/watch?v=UKY3scPIMd8&feature=youtube_gdata_player.

9. Wesj, "Making Sense of Mali's Armed Groups."

10. http://ngm.nationalgeographic.com/2011/09/sahara-tuareg/tuareg-map.

11. Thomas Fessy, "Gaddafi's Influence in Mali's Coup," News, *BBC News*, (March 22, 2012), http://www.bbc.com/news/world-africa-17481114.

12. Ibid.

13. Hugh SchofieldBBC News and Paris, "France Confirms Mali Military Intervention," *BBC News*, January 11, 2013, http://www.bbc.com/news/world-africa-20991719.

14. "Library of Congress Country Studies Algeria FLN" (Library of Congress, December 1993), http://lcweb2.loc.gov/cgi-bin/query/r?frd/cstdy:@field(DOCID+dz0037).

15. "Library of Congress Country Studies Algeria FLN."

16. Ibid.

17. Stephen Harmon, "From GSPC to AQIM: The Evolution of an Algerian Islamist Terrorist Group into an Al-Qa'ida Affiliate and Its Implications for the Sahara-Sahel Region," *Association of Concerned Africa Scholars Analysis and Action on Policies Impacting Africa*, June 2010, http://concernedafricascholars.org/bulletin/issue85/harmon/.

18. Ibid.

19. Ibid.

20. "Global Terrorism & Insurgency Attacks Rapidly Increase in Five Years, According to IHS Jane's Terrorism and Insurgency Centre," *Business Wire*, February 13, 2014, http://search.proquest.com/docview/1497411598.

21. Harmon, "From GSPC to AQIM."

22. Ibid.

23. Ibid.

24. Ibid.

25. Ibid.

26. Ibid.

27. Ibid.

28. Ibid.

29. Ibid.

30. Ibid.

31. "Global Terrorism & Insurgency Attacks Rapidly Increase in Five Years, According to IHS Jane's Terrorism and Insurgency Centre."

32. Ibid.

33. Harmon, "From GSPC to AQIM."

34. Ibid.

35. Ibid.

36. Dr Michael S. Toney, *Organizational Behavior Profile: Al Qaeda in the Islamic Maghreb*, n.d.

37. J. Peter Pham, "The Dangerous 'Pragmatism' of Al-Qaeda in the Islamic Maghreb," *Journal of the Middle East & Africa* 2, no. 1 (January 2011): 15–29, doi:10.1080/21520844.2011.567445.

38. Ibid.

39. Ibid.

40. Ibid.

41. Camille Tawil, *The Al Qaeda Organization in the Islamic Maghreb: Expansion in the Sahel and Challenges from Within Jihadist Circles* (New York: The Jamestown

Foundation, April 2010), file:///Users/shieldanalysis/Downloads/Jamestown%
20Foundation-Tawil_Al%20Qaeda%20in%20the%20Islamic%20Maghreb-Expansion%
20in%20the%20Sahel%20and%20Challenges%20from%20Within%20Jihadist%
20Circles-2010%20(1).pdf.

42. Ibid.

43. Toney, *Organizational Behavior Profile*.

44. Ibid.

45. Tawil, *The Al Qaeda Organization in the Islamic Maghreb*.

46. Ibid.

47. Toney, *Organizational Behavior Profile*.

48. Tawil, *The Al Qaeda Organization in the Islamic Maghreb*.

49. Ibid.

50. Senan Murray and Adam Nossiter, "Suicide Bomber Attacks U.N. Building in Nigeria," *New York Times*, August 26, 2011, sec. World/Africa, http://www.nytimes.com/2011/08/27/world/africa/27nigeria.html.

51. "Al-Qaeda in the Islamic Maghreb (AQIM)," *Janes Terrorism and Insurgency Centre*, October 22, 2014, https://janes-ihs-com.mutex.gmu.edu/CustomPages/Janes/DisplayPage.aspx?DocType=Reference&ItemId=+++1320774&Pubabbrev=JWIT.

52. Robin Simcox, "Boko Haram and Defining the 'Al-Qaeda Network,'" *Al Jazeera*, June 6, 2014, http://www.aljazeera.com/indepth/opinion/2014/06/boko-haram-al-qaeda-201463115816142554.html.

53. "Niger's Foreign Minister Claims Boko Haram Receives Explosives Training from Al-Qaeda Group," *Jane's Country Risk Daily Report* 19, no. 19 (January 25, 2012), http://search.proquest.com.mutex.gmu.edu/docview/917829567.

54. Simcox, "Boko Haram and Defining the 'Al-Qaeda Network.'"

55. David Kimble, "Operational Aftermath: Measuring the Threat of Terrorism Through Attack Efficiency," *Seaching for Balance in the Middle East and Africa* (presented at the Association for the Study of the Middle East and Africa, Washington, D.C, 2014).

56. "Al-Qaeda in the Islamic Maghreb (AQIM)."

57. Yahia Zoubir, "The Sahara-Sahel Quagmire: Regional and International Ramifications," *Mediterranean Politics* 17, no. 3 (2510 2012): 452–58, doi:10.1080/13629395.2012.725307.

58. Ibid.

59. Ibid.

60. Cedric Jourde, "Sifting Through the Layers of Insecurity in the Sahel: The Case of Mauritania," *Africa Center for Strategic Studies*, September 6, 2011, http://africacenter.org/2011/09/sifting-through-the-layers-of-insecurity-in-the-sahel-the-case-of-mauritania/.

61. Ibid.

62. Zoubir, "The Sahara-Sahel Quagmire."

63. Jourde, "Sifting Through the Layers of Insecurity in the Sahel."

64. Ibid.

65. Ibid.

66. Ibid.

67. Afua Hirsch, "Mali's Conflict and a 'War over Skin Colour,'" *Guardian*, July 6, 2012, http://www.theguardian.com/commentisfree/2012/jul/06/mali-war-over-skin-colour.

68. AFP, "Ahram Online – New Qaeda Spin-off Threatens West Africa," December 22, 2011, http://english.ahram.org.eg/NewsContentPrint/2/0/29968/World/0/New-Qaeda-spinoff-threatens-West-Africa.aspx.

69. Ibid.

70. "Al-Qaeda in the Islamic Maghreb (AQIM)."

71. Ibid.

72. Ibid.

73. Ibid.

74. Ibid.

75. Audrey Kurth Cronin, *How Terrorism Ends: Understanding the Decline and Demise of Terrorist Campaigns* (Princeton, NJ: Princeton University Press, 2009), http://site.ebrary.com/lib/alltitles/docDetail.action?docID=10386040.

76. Adam Nossiter, "Islamist Group with Possible Qaeda Links Upends Nigeria," *New York Times*, August 17, 2011, sec. World/Africa, http://www.nytimes.com/2011/08/18/world/africa/18nigeria.html.

77. "Al-Qaeda in the Islamic Maghreb (AQIM)."

78. Ibid.

79. Ibid.

80. Ibid.

81. Ibid.

82. Ibid.

83. Zoubir, "The Sahara-Sahel Quagmire."

84. "Al-Qaeda in the Islamic Maghreb (AQIM)."

85. Ricardo René Larémont, "Al Qaeda in the Islamic Maghreb: Terrorism and Counterterrorism in the Sahel," *African Security* 4, no. 4 (2011): 242–68, doi:10.1080/19392206.2011.628630.

86. Ibid.

87. Ibid.

88. "Al-Qaeda in the Islamic Maghreb (AQIM)."

89. Larémont, "Al Qaeda in the Islamic Maghreb."

90. Ibid.

91. Ibid.

92. Ibid.

93. Peter Gwin, "The Sahara's Tuareg – Pictures, More from National Geographic Magazine," *National Geographic Magazine*, September 2011, http://ngm.nationalgeographic.com/2011/09/sahara-tuareg/gwin-text.

94. Denise Baken and Ioannis Mantzikos, "The Cyber Terrorism Shadow Networks in Africa: AQIM and Boko Haram," *African Renaissance* 9, no. 1 (June 2012).

95. Ibid.

CHAPTER 10

1. *Former Leader in Egyptian Islamic Jihad: Al-Qaeda Died with Bin Laden; Ayman Al-Zawahiri Is All Talk*, 2013, http://www.youtube.com/watch?v=P_JrQcxz9DE&feature=youtube_gdata_player.

2. Ibid.

3. Jarret Brachman, "Al Qaeda's Dissident," *Foreign Policy*, November 29, 2009, http://www.foreignpolicy.com/articles/2009/11/29/al_qaedas_dissident.

4. Ibid.

5. Camille Tawil, "Dr. Fadl: Bin Laden and Al-Zawahiri Should Face an Islamic Trial," *Magharebia*, February 24, 2010, http://magharebia.com/en_GB/articles/awi/features/2010/02/24/feature-01.

6. Omar Ashour, "De-Radicalization of Jihad? The Impact of Egyptian Islamist Revisionists on Al-Qaeda," *Perspectives on Terrorism* 2, no. 5 (November 19, 2010), http://www.terrorismanalysts.com/pt/index.php/pot/article/view/36.

7. Haifa Zangana, "Here Is a List of the Real Forces behind the Violence in Iraq," *Al Jazeera*, January 18, 2014, http://www.aljazeera.com/indepth/opinion/2014/01/here-list-real-forces-behind-violence-iraq-201411613100570815.html.

8. D. Baken, "An Analysis of the Potential Direct or Indirect Influence Exerted by an Al Qaeda Social Network Actor on Future Biological Weapon Mission Planning," 2007, http://digilib.gmu.edu:8080/xmlui/handle/1920/2881. Used with permission of author.

9. Ibid.

10. *Ottoman Empire – The War Machine (Documentary)*, 2013, http://www.youtube.com/watch?v=ikEsO9cGigo&feature=youtube_gdata_player.

11. "McMahon-Husain Correspondence – Report of Arab-UK Committee – UK Documentation Cmd. 5974 (excerpts)/Non-UN Document (16 March 1939)," June 18, 2008.

12. David Fromkin, *A Peace to End All Peace: The Fall of the Ottoman Empire and the Creation of the Modern Middle East* (New York: Henry Holt and Company, 2009).

13. Ibid.

14. Ibid.

15. Ibid.

16. Ana María Salinas de Frías, Katja Samuel, and Nigel White, *Counter-Terrorism: International Law and Practice* (Oxford University Press, 2012).

17. Thomas Hegghammer, *The Future of Anti-Western Jihadism Prepared Testimony for the Hearing on Global Al-Qaeda: Affiliates, Objectives, and Future Challenges* (Washington, D.C.: 2013), http://docs.house.gov/meetings/FA/FA18/20130718/101155/HHRG-113-FA18-Wstate-HegghammerT-20130718.pdf.

18. Balasubramaniyan Viswanathan, "An Al Qaeda-Indian Mujahideen Alliance Spells Trouble for Pakistan," *Geopolitical Analysis & Forecasting*, June 10, 2014, http://www.geopoliticalmonitor.com/an-al-qaeda-indian-mujahideen-alliance-spells-trouble-for-pakistan-4937/.

19. Syed Saleem Shahzad, *Inside Al-Qaeda and the Taliban: Beyond Bin Laden and 9/11* (New York: Pluto Press, 2011).

20. Thomas Michael McDonnell, *The United States, International Law, and the Struggle against Terrorism* (London; New York: Routledge, 2010).

21. Ibid.

22. Lawrence Wright, *The Looming Tower: Al-Qaeda and the Road to 9/11*, 1st ed. (New York: Knopf, 2006).

23. Lawrence Wright, "The Rebellion Within," *New Yorker*, June 2, 2008, http://www.newyorker.com/reporting/2008/06/02/080602fa_fact_wright.

24. Jason Burke, "Al-Qaida's Membership Declining and Leadership Damaged, but Threat Remains," *Guardian*, August 5, 2013, sec. World news, http://www.theguardian.com/world/2013/aug/05/al-qaida-anniversary-attacks-reduced.

25. Alix Spiegel, "So You Think You're Smarter Than a CIA Agent," *NPR.org*, April 2, 2014, http://www.npr.org/blogs/parallels/2014/04/02/297839429/-so-you-think-youre -smarter-than-a-cia-agent.

26. Khalil Al-Anani, "Saye Imam and the Jihadists," Middle East Political Islam Analysis, *Islamists Today*, November 27, 2008, http://islamists2day-e.blogspot.com /2008/11/sayed-imam-and-jihadists.html.

27. Ibid.

28. Ibid.

29. "Al-Qaeda Criticizes Treatment of Elderly in Japan and China," *Taipei Times*, December 18, 2011, http://www.taipeitimes.com/News/world/archives/2011/12/18/ 2003521049.

30. Ibid.

31. Ibid.

32. Ibid.

33. Seth G. Jones and Martin C. Libicki, "Stop the 'War' on Terror: Calling It a 'War' Is a Boon to Terrorist Recruiters | RAND," 20088-08-06, http://www.rand.org/comme ntary/2008/08/06/CSM.html.

34. "Amriki Auto-Biography Book," *Wandanka*, December 9, 2011, http:// wadanka.com/Somali-News/6746.html.

35. Ibid.

36. Thomas Hegghammer, "The Rise of Muslim Foreign Fighters: Islam and the Globalization of Jihad," *International Security* 35, no. 3 (December 1, 2010): 53–94, doi:10.2307/40981252.

37. CBC.CA News 2, "Ahmed Said Khadr," *CBC.Ca Interactives*, May 20, 2014, www.cbc.ca/news2/interactives/khadr/slides.html.

38. Michelle Shephard, *Guantanamo's Child: The Untold Story of Omar Khadr*, 1 ed. (Mississauga, Ont.: Wiley, 2008).

39. AAP, "Sabirhan Hasanoff, the Aussie Accountant Who Turned to Terror," *Sydney Morning Herald*, October 1, 2013, http://www.smh.com.au/world/sabirhan -hasanoff-the-aussie-accountant-who-turned-to-terror-20131001-2upqd.html.

40. Mike Gribble and Tory Shepherd, "Adelaide-Raised Sabirhan Hasanoff Jailed in the US for 18 Years for Supporting Al-Qaeda," *NewsComAu*, October 1, 2013, http:// www.news.com.au/world/adelaideraised-sabirhan-hasanoff-jailed-in-the-us-for-18 -years-for-supporting-alqaeda/story-fndir2ev-1226731092191.

41. Michael Scheuer, "Central Asia in Al Qaeda's Vision of Anti-American Jihad 1979-2006.pdf," *China and Eurasia Forum Quarterly* 4, no. 2 (2006): 5–10.

42. Matthew Levitt, "Zawahiri Aims at Israel: Behind Al Qaeda's Pivot to the Levant," *The Washington Institute for Near East Policy*, February 3, 2014, http://www .washingtoninstitute.org/policy-analysis/view/zawahiri-aims-at-israel-behind-al -qaedas-pivot-to-the-levant.

43. Andrew Bringuel, *Interview with Andrew Bringuel, Supervisory Special Agent— FBI*, GarageBand Project taping, 2012.

44. Ibid.

45. Ibid.

46. Ibid.

47. Ibid.

48. Ibid.

49. Ibid.

50. Ibid.

51. Ibid.

52. Ibid.

53. Sabahi staff, "Al-Amriki Blasts Al-Shabaab Leader in Final Communications to the World," *Sabahionline.com*, September 20, 2013, http://sabahionline.com/en_GB/articles/hoa/articles/features/2013/09/20/feature-01.

54. Harun Maruf, *Interview with Omar Hammami by Harun Maruf*, audio tape, 2013, http://www.voasomali.com/audio/audio/324662.html.

55. Aaron Y. Zelin, "Al-Katāi'b Media Presents a New Video Message from Ⱨarakat Al-Shabāb Al-Mujāhidīn: 'The Woolwich Attack: It's an Eye for an Eye,'" *JIHADOLOGY*, October 15, 2013, http://jihadology.net/2013/10/15/al-kataib-media-presents-a-new-video-message-from-%e1%b8%a5arakat-al-shabab-al-mujahidin-the-woolwich-attack-its-an-eye-for-an-eye/.

56. Thomas E. Ricks, "FoW (13): You Think Innovation Means Better Drones? Faster Jets? Wrong. We've Been Out-Innovated for the Last 13 Years," *Foreign Policy Blogs*, March 4, 2014, http://ricks.foreignpolicy.com/posts/2014/03/04/fow_13_you_think_innovation_means_better_drones_faster_jets_wrong_weve_been_out_inn.

57. Julia Harte, "In Cradle of Civilization, Shrinking Rivers Endanger Unique Marsh Arab Culture," *News Watch*, March 9, 2014, http://newswatch.nationalgeographic.com/2013/04/24/in-cradle-of-civilization-shrinking-rivers-endanger-unique-marsh-arab-culture/.

58. Rohan Gunaratna, *Inside Al Qaeda: Global Network of Terror* (New York, NY: Columbia University Press, 2002).

59. Ibid.

60. APS, "Al-Qaeda's Spreading Terror Threatens Europe, While the US Is Losing Respect," *Industry: Email Alert RSS Feed*, April 23, 2007.

61. Reuven Paz, "Programmed Terrorists? Analysis of the Letter of Instructions Found in the September 11th Attack," n.d.

62. Kim Craigin, "Early History of Al Qai'da," *The Historical Journal* 51, no. 4 (December 2008): 1047–67.

63. Shahzad, *Inside Al-Qaeda and the Taliban*.

64. Fawaz A. Gerges, *Journey of the Jihadist: Inside Muslim Militancy*, 1st ed. (Orlando, FL: Harcourt, 2006).

65. Jane Corbin, *Al-Qaeda: In Search of the Terror Network That Threatens the World* (New York: Nation Books, 2003).

66. Gerges, *Journey of the Jihadist.*

67. Corbin, *Al-Qaeda.*

68. John Hooper and Nick Hopkins, "Al-Qaida Cell in UK 'Planned Attack,'" *Guardian*, October 26, 2001, http://www.guardian.co.uk/uk/2001/oct/26/afghanistan.world1.

69. "Abu Nidal Organization (ANO), Aka Fatah Revolutionary Council, the Arab Revolutionary Brigades, or the Revolutionary Organization of Socialist Muslims," *Council on Foreign Relations*, http://www.cfr.org/israel/abu-nidal-organization-ano-aka-fatah-revolutionary-council-arab-revolutionary-brigades-revolutionary-organization-socialist-muslims/p9153.

70. Patricia Hurtado, "Ex-Terrorist Violated Release Terms, Judge Rules," October 28, 2010, http://www.lacp.org/2010-Articles-Main/102910-Ex-TerroristViolatedRelease Terms.htm.

71. Shahzad, *Inside Al-Qaeda and the Taliban*.

72. Abdel Bari Atwan, *The Secret History of Al Qaeda* (London: Saqi Books, 2012).

73. *Syria Will Not Allow Another Sykes-Picot*, 2013, http://www.youtube.com/watch?v=k9mSRs9te4E&feature=youtube_gdata_player.

74. *Inside Story – Al-Qaeda and Al-Shabab: Double the Trouble?*, 2012, http://www.youtube.com/watch?v=mXFw6Ed0xC0&feature=youtube_gdata_player.

Index

About the Authors

DENISE N. BAKEN retired as a Colonel with more than 27 combined years in the Army Reserve and National Guard. During her career, her assignments ranged from Plans, Programs, Analysis, and Evaluation to Chief of Staff for the Special Advisor to the Deputy Secretary of Defense on Chemical and Biological Defense. After retiring, she obtained a PhD in Biodefense from George Mason University. Since then her research has focused on terrorism as a business industry, highlighting the more formal business perspective terrorism has taken since al Qaeda entered. Most recently she has examined the continually changing tools used by this now growth industry to ensure that growth continues. Dr. Baken has published and presented on topics that include: *Framing the Biothreat Using the Business Concept of Return on Investment, An Examination of the Return on Investment Islamic Economics Provides the Terrorism Industry, The Cyber Terrorism Shadow Networks in Africa: AQIM and Boko Haram*, and *Cyberspace Improvised Explosive Device and the Failed State Catapult: The Strategic Symbiotic Relationship Failed State Status Offers Nation-State Cyberwarfare Arsenals.*

IOANNIS MANTZIKOS is a doctoral candidate at the University of the Free State in South Africa. He had postgraduate research at King's College London and holds a Masters Degree from the School of Oriental and African Studies (SOAS), University of London. He is a commentator and analyst for leading Greek and international news outlets. He has served as Research Analyst for Wikistrat and Consultancy African Intelligence, as Associate Editor for *E-International Relations* and the *Freedom Observatory*, and as columnist for the *News Chronicle*, a Nigerian daily.